the *Macintosh*™ *Bible*

thousands of basic and advanced tips, tricks and shortcuts

Dale Coleman & Arthur Naiman

with major contributions by
Eric Alderman, Dennis Klatzkin & Steve Michel

Goldstein
& Blair

Box 7635
Berkeley, California 94707

Book design—Arthur Naiman
Cover photography—Guy Orcutt
Type composition and electronic pasteup—Dale Coleman, Arthur Naiman
Proofreading and physical pasteup—Nancy Krompotich, Gloria Zarifa
Index—Dale Coleman
Printing consultants—Lou Tomafsky, Allen Glazer
Design consultant—Edith Allgood
Margin icons—Esther Travis, Miles Computing (Mac the Knife), Arthur Naiman
Illustrations on pages facing part titles—Gerry Clement, Esther Travis, Mei-Ying Dell'Aquila
(See Appendix C for addresses.)

Notes for this book were compiled with Filemaker 1.0, and the book itself was written in MacWrite 4.5 and Word 1.05, on Macs with SuperMac 1-meg upgrades and DataFrame 20 hard disks. Spelling was checked with Spelling Champion and MacSpell+. We used FModem, MicroPhone and 1200-baud PopCom modems to communicate between the machines. The book was typeset on a LaserWriter in Adobe's ITC Benguiat, 11 on 13, with running heads in 14-point ITC Zapf Chancery Medium Italic from Adobe and page numbers in 12-point Benguiat bold. The same typefaces were used on the cover. Pages were laid out electronically using Ready,Set,Go! 3.0. Some graphics were prepared in FullPaint 1.0 and MacDraw 1.9. Because of the slowness of PostScript scaling, margin icons were pasted in by hand. Color separations were made by Production Resources of Menlo Park, California, in collaboration with Color Response of Charlotte, North Carolina. The book was printed and bound—on the tightest possible schedule—by DD Associates of Santa Clara, California.

The Macintosh Bible is distributed to bookstores and book wholesalers by Publishers Group West, Box 8843, Emeryville CA 94662, 800/982-8319 (in California, 415/658-3453). For information on sales to other outlets and direct sales to individuals, contact Goldstein & Blair, Box 7635, Berkeley CA 94707, 415/524-4000.

Library of Congress Cataloging-in-Publication Data

```
Coleman, Dale, 1951–
    The Macintosh bible.

    Includes index.
    1. Macintosh (Computer)--Programming.  I. Naiman,
Arthur.  II. Title.
QA76.8.M3C64  1986        005.265           86-33498
ISBN 0-940235-00-5
```

Printed in the United States of America.   Printing # 1 2 3 4 5 6 7 8 9

To H.M. Coleman and Betty Coleman
for a lifetime of love and support

—Dale

To Roger Horwitz (1941–1986)

—Arthur

Contents

Trademark notice

Because a major purpose of this book is to describe and comment on various hardware and software products, many such products are identified by their tradenames. In most—if not all—cases, these designations are claimed as legally protected trademarks by the companies that make the products. It is not our intent to use any of these names generically, and the reader is cautioned to investigate a claimed trademark before using it for any purpose except to refer to the product to which it is attached.

In particular: Macintosh is a trademark of McIntosh Laboratory, Inc., licensed to Apple Computer, Inc., which uses it with express permission of its owner. The Macintosh Bible is a trademark of Goldstein & Blair, which is not affiliated with Apple Computer, Inc. or with McIntosh Laboratory, Inc.

Disclaimer

Preface

Most computer books are out-of-date a few months after they're published. But not *The Macintosh Bible*. To keep the information in it current, we include two free updates in the price of the book. And they're not chintzy little flyers, either, but substantial booklets of at least 40 pages. To get them, all you have to do is send your name and address to: Goldstein & Blair, Box 7635, Berkeley CA 94707.

Even without the updates, this book has been needed for a long time. (In fact, we wrote it because we wanted it and it didn't exist.) *The Macintosh Bible* is a collection of thousands of basic and advanced tips, tricks and shortcuts that help you get the maximum power out of your Mac. The tips are logically organized and fully indexed, so it's easy to find what you're looking for.

This is a reference book and isn't meant to be read from beginning to end. Instead, use the table of contents and the index to dip into wherever you want. (But do read the section below titled *How to use this book* first.)

If you want to contribute tips to future editions of the book, contact us on the Macintosh Bible bulletin board; the number is 415/554-0421 (data transmissions only). Or write us at the address above. Contributors aren't paid, but do get mentioned in the book—unless they don't want to be.

If you want to try out some of the best shareware and public-domain programs mentioned in the book, as well as a few templates of our own devising, order our disk (see the last page in the book for details).

Acknowledgments

It's hard for us to imagine having written this book without the brilliant and unfailing help provided by Eric Alderman, Dennis Klatzkin, Steve Michel and Gloria Zarifa. Certainly the book wouldn't have been as good, and certainly writing it would have been a much more onerous task.

Tom Bennett, Brad Bunnin, Allen Glazer, Paul Hoffman, Don and Roxie Lum McCunn, Carol Pladsen and Steve Rosenthal offered advice whose wisdom was only surpassed by the generosity with which it was given.

Much useful information was obtained from *MacUser*, *Macworld*, *MACazine* and the BMUG newsletters.

We also want to thank the following people for favors too various to specify, but which were greatly appreciated in every case: Nancy Krompotich, Ira Rosenberg, Peter Lewis, Andy Hertzfeld, Dan Farber, Guy Orcutt, Lou Tomafsky, Ed Kelly, Michael Castleman, Art Kleiner, Ron Lichty, Larry Press, Matt Foley, Paul Towner, Edith Allgood, Esther Travis, Jerry Clement, Rita Gibian, Martha Steffen, Randy Fleming, Charlie Winton, Bill Hurst, Bonnie Beren, Cherlyn Oto, David Jouris, Ed Rosenthal, Marty Schiffenbauer, John Boeschen, Malcolm Margolin, Ruth Gendler, David Goldman, Esther Wanning, Eric Angress, Carole Alden, Kal Rabinowitz, Gar Smith, Tony Bove, Cheryl Rhodes, Vic Fisher and Cheryl Nichols.

Finally, Arthur would like to thank his ophthamolgist, Rod Cohen.

Notes on contributors

Contact information (for those who want it listed) is in Appendix C.

Eric Alderman is coauthor of *Advanced WordPerfect: Features and Techniques*, a word processing columnist, and director of Whole Earth Access Computer Training.

Chris Belec is a microcomputer consultant specializing in WordPerfect training and Paradox database development.

Brad Bunnin is an attorney who restricts his practice to literary law. He is the principal author of *Author Law* (Nolo Press).

Dale Coleman, a microcomputer consultant, spent four years as the manager of a Computerland store and worked with Computerland's Software Review Committee.

Paul Hoffman, a writer and microcomputer consultant, is the author of the best-selling *Microsoft Word Made Easy—Macintosh Edition* and other books.

Dennis Klatzkin is an independent Macintosh consultant specializing in word processing and computerized graphic design using PageMaker and MacDraw.

Steve Michel is an independent microcomputer consultant specializing in Macintosh databases and networking.

Arthur Naiman has written eight books about personal computers, including *MacBook* and the best-selling *Introduction to WordStar*.

Tom Swain is an engineer in the biology and medicine division of the Lawrence Berkeley Laboratory, University of California, Berkeley.

How to use this book

The Macintosh Bible is made up of entries (whose titles look like this: ⁂ *entry title*). Each entry contains at least one tip, and often dozens. With rare exceptions, entries are meant to stand on their own—although we have, of course, grouped them into subject areas and have also put them into logical order wherever possible.

Entries range from very basic to fairly advanced, and we've tried to put the basic ones toward the start of each section and the more advanced ones toward the end (except when basic and advanced tips are on the same topic, in which case we usually put them next to each other).

If you want to read everything we have to say about a particular subject—tips on handling text in MacPaint, say—look in the table of contents at the start of the book. If your focus of interest is narrower—how to correct an icon name you've accidentally changed, say—use the very complete index at the back of the book. (In addition, some entries are cross-referenced to other, related ones.)

All the entries were written by Dale and Arthur in collaboration, except for those with a name—usually that of a contributor—in parentheses after the title. (If the name is Dale or Arthur's, it means we couldn't agree on that particular entry, or that it reflects the experience of just one or the other of us.)

The word COMMAND indicates, of course, the Mac's distinctive pretzel-like symbol: ⌘. (We would have liked to use the symbol itself throughout the book, but that would have involved using one more font and we kept running into the LaserWriter's font limitations as it was.)

Prices, when shown, are just to give you a general idea of what things cost, in early 1987, at list. Prices change rapidly and discounts are almost always available, so don't rely on them too heavily. Since this book is written for people with IQs in three figures, all prices are rounded ("Oh, it's only $995? What a relief! I thought I was going to have spend at least a thousand dollars.").

We use eight margin icons to draw your attention to items of particular interest. They are:

All our tips are hot, but these are *particularly* hot.

If you're new to the Mac, it might make sense for you to check out all of these first.

Isn't that a beautiful icon? We got it from the Mac the Knife clip art disk.

We're critical enough when that's what's called for, so we like to also give credit where credit is due.

These two icons are a subtle plug for left-handers.

We use this to indicate particularly good values for the money, regardless of what they cost.

Nobody can predict the future, but we try.

This icon is for stuff that's probably not useful but sure is interesting. Look for it when you need a break. (These last two icons are the work of the brilliant Mac artist Esther Travis.)

The Macintosh Bible is divided into five main parts.

Part I tells you how to get the most out of systems software (like the Finder, the System, the MiniFinder and Switcher), utilities (like Font/DA Mover), fonts, desk accessories (like Control Panel and Scrapbook), programming languages and the like.

Part II tells you how to get the most out of applications: word processing programs, spreadsheets, databases, painting and drawing software, digitizers, communications and networking programs, and desktop publishing software.

Part III tells you how to get the most out of hardware: the ImageWriter, the LaserWriter and other components both large and small.

Part IV tells you how to get the most out of your purchasing dollar by giving you our opinions—based on many user years of (sometimes tortured) experience—on the best buys in Mac hardware and software.

Finally, there are three Appendixes.

Appendix A is a brief glossary of Macintosh terms, mostly those that we deemed too basic to define in the text of the book.

Appendix B tells you where to find more high-quality information about the Mac and good, inexpensive software to run on it. It covers other books, magazines, user groups and bulletin boards.

Appendix C is a list of all the products, companies, Mac consultants and artists mentioned in the book, as well as all the contributors to it (except those who didn't want to be listed).

Street Scene. Copyright © 1984 by Gerald Clement.

Part I—

Maximizing systems software and utilities

Chapter 1

Windows, files & other basics

Tips about windows

🍎 opening windows temporarily

If you're using HFS (the Hierarchical File System—see the glossary in Appendix A if you don't know what that is), you probably have some files that are buried several folders deep. When you exit from one of these files after working on it, there's a long wait as the Finder recreates the cluttered Desktop you left, with all the windows still opened that you opened to get down to the file. (This can particularly be a problem on a hard disk.)

very
hot
tip

There's a way to avoid this delay. Hold down the OPTION key while working your way down through all of those folders on the way to the file. Then when you exit from the program, the Finder will forget that they were ever open and return you to the Desktop much more quickly.

In other words, if you hold down the OPTION key when you open a window, it won't stay open after you leave the Desktop to run an application. When you come back to the Desktop, the window will be closed. You can use this technique for as many windows as you want, and for disk windows as well as folder windows. (For other variations on this theme, see the next two entries.)

♦ *speedy return to the Desktop*

Even if you didn't hold down the OPTION key while opening windows (as per the previous entry), you can tell the Mac to close them from within an application. Just hold down the OPTION key when you choose Quit from the File menu; you'll be returned to an empty Desktop, with no open windows, in much less time than it would otherwise take.

♦ *closing all the windows on the Desktop*

The 128K ROMs provide a quick way to close all the windows open on the Desktop. Just hold down the OPTION key when you close a window and every other window on the Desktop will close too. (For other variations on this theme, see the two previous entries.)

shortcut

♦ *moving inactive windows*

It can be annoying to always have to select a window before moving it. To move a window that's not active (not selected), just hold down the COMMAND key while dragging it.

♦ *moving icons into windows Viewed by Name, Kind, etc.*

Be careful when you move a file to a window that's displayed in any mode other than by Icon, especially if a number of names on the list are for folders rather than for files. It's very easy to select one of those folders by accident, and then the file you moved will be hidden away inside of it, rather than out in the larger window where you meant to put it. You can have quite a time trying to find it, opening one folder after another.

The best way to avoid this problem is to drag the icons you want to copy to the part of the window just below the title bar (the rectangular space where the words *Name, Size, Kind* and *Last Modified* appear). Since no icons can appear there,

there's no danger of the icons you're dragging disappearing into a folder.

● *aligning dragged icons*

To save housekeeping time when you drag a group of icons, hold down the COMMAND key while dragging. The icons will align along an invisible grid. (It's the same grid they align along when you hold down the OPTION key while choosing Clean Up; for more details, see the entry below about Clean Up.)

● *using Clean Up to rearrange icons*

There are two ways to have the Mac automatically organize a window in which the icons are strewn messily about. If the icons are more or less where you want them, choose Clean Up from the Special menu. The icons will move to the nearest available location along an invisible grid.

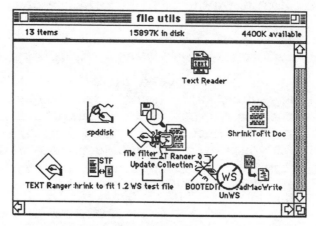

Messy window before Clean Up

If the icons are totally disorganized, you can do a more thoroughgoing rearrangement by holding down the OPTION key

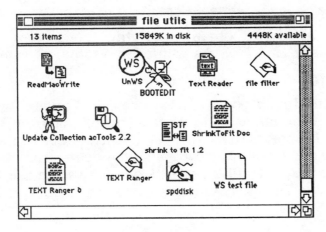

Same window after Clean Up

when you choose Clean Up. The icons will then be moved from wherever they are and placed in neat horizontal rows, beginning in the upper left corner of the window.

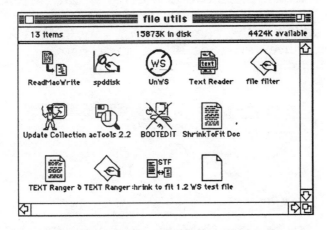

Same window after OPTION Clean Up

For an even better way to organize your icons (although one that requires more of your personal attention), see the entry on "Naimanizing" below.

✦ organizing icons alphabetically

Here's a way to organize all the icons in a window alphabetically, and it works with every version of Finder from 4.1 on.

Open the folder you want to organize. Choose 'by Name' from the View menu. Now choose Select All from the Edit menu (or hit COMMAND-A). Drag all the icons out of the folder and onto the Desktop. Now select 'by Icon' from the View menu and drag the still-selected icons back from the Desktop to the folder. Finally, hold down OPTION and choose Clean Up from the Special menu.

Your files and folders will now be arranged alphabetically, from left to right.

✦ tucking icons into each other (Naimanizing)

On most icons, the name is wider than the picture, giving them the shape of stovepipe hats (with the name as the brim). In addition, the names usually vary in length, so that some icons have very wide brims, some narrower ones, and some no brim at all.

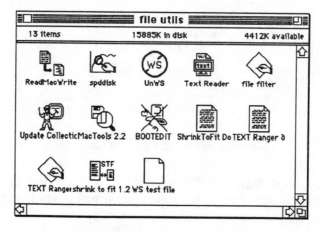

Icons with some overlapping names

If you simply ignore this fact when you line icons up (as the Clean Up command does), the names will either interfere with each other, or you'll be forced to put icons farther apart than you'd like.

Here's a simple way to neatly organize your icons so that none of the names overlap, and so that you can get the maximum number of icons possible on the screen. First, choose Clean Up from the Special menu (if your icons are really scrambled all over the window, hold down the OPTION key while choosing Clean Up). This will organize your icons in neat rows along the invisible grid. They will also be aligned in neat columns, and that's the key to this trick.

Use the selection rectangle to select the second column of icons. Now move the column down just enough so that its icon names don't overlap with the icon names in the first column. Repeat this procedure with all the other pairs of columns. Now your window will look something like this:

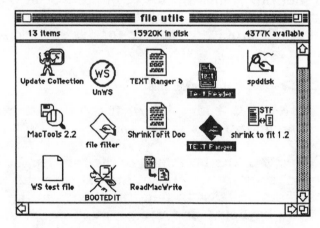

Icons arranged so names don't overlap

If you want to fit as many icons as possible into the window, you can also move the columns closer together, and switch icons around to accommodate unusual shapes. This tightest possible packing looks something like this:

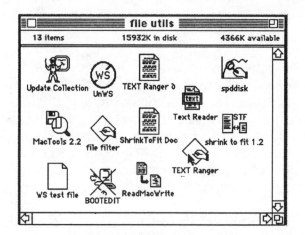

The same icons Naimanized

**gossip/
trivia**

This technique of tucking the name of an icon under the names of its neighbors is known as *Naimanizing* (NAY-mun-eye-zing), but the origins of this term are lost in the mists of history. (Some authorities suggest that it's a play on the word "name," but that wouldn't account for the spelling.)

⬥ *fast scrolling in list boxes*

Scrolling through a long list of files in a list box can be tedious. Here are two shortcuts:

To go directly to the beginning of the list, use the tilde (~) key; to go directly to the end of the list, use the BACKSPACE key. Those keys are easy to find (the tilde is in the upper left corner of the keyboard and BACKSPACE is in the upper right) and their position makes it easy to remember what they do (the tilde, at the start of the line, takes you to the start of the list and the BACKSPACE key, at the end of the line, takes you to the end of the list).

Tips about files

⚫ two kinds of files

There are two basic kinds of files: *documents*, which contain data you've created, and *programs*, which you use to create documents and to run the system. Because application programs are far and away the most commonly used kind of programs, we often write "documents and applications" instead of the more technically correct "documents and programs." In any case, both phrases are equivalent to the word "files."

⚫ easy way to tell if a file is locked

Just select the icon and put the pointer over its name. If the pointer changes to an I-beam, the file isn't locked; if it stays an arrow, the file is locked.

⚫ easy way to put away files

If you have an file icon out on the Desktop that you want to put away, you don't have to drag it back to its original folder (which can be quite a task if it's nested several folders deep). Just select the icon, then choose Put Away from the File menu. The file will scurry back to wherever it was you got it from.

very
hot
tip

⚫ printing multiple documents

You can only do this from the Desktop. All you have to do is select the documents you want to print (either by shift-clicking or using the selection rectangle) and then choose Print from the File menu. The documents will be printed one after the other, in the order in which you selected them.

This technique will work only if the application that created the documents is on an active disk. For example, if you insert a MacPaint data disk in the external drive but MacPaint itself is not on a disk in any of the drives, the files will not print.

✎ *Mac Plus keyboard shortcuts*

shortcut

These shortcuts require a Mac Plus running HFS and the standard Mac Plus keyboard (with the built-in numeric keypad).

up arrow moves you up through a list of folders

down arrow moves you down through a list of folders

OPTION *up arrow* moves you up through a hierarchy of folders

OPTION *down arrow* moves you down through a hierarchy of folders

TAB *(in MiniFinder)* is the same as hitting the Drive button

✎ *colons in file names*

You can use just about any symbol you want in the name of a Mac file, except for the colon (:). The Mac uses colons as 'file separators', so if it finds one in the name of a file, it assumes that the part of the name in front of the colon is the name of the volume or folder containing the file. If there's no such volume or folder, it beeps at you and gives you a message that reads, "Bad character in name, or can't find that disk."

✎ *correcting mistaken icon names*

Sometimes when you're renaming a file or folder, you realize that you were better off before you starting changing realize that you were better off before you starting changing the name. Even more often, you accidentally hit a key while an icon is selected and rename it "z" or "/" or something.

If either of these things happens, all you have to do is hold down the BACKSPACE until all the characters in the new name have been deleted, then hit RETURN. Voila! The original name is back.

⚫ *comparing files with Get Info*

The File menu's Get Info option (or COMMAND-I) tells you many things about a file, including its size, creation date, type and the amount of space it uses on the disk. Another thing it's very useful for is comparing files quickly.

You may want to compare files for a variety of reasons—for example, to determine which copy of a document is the most recent. You can open several Get Info windows on screen at one time, and you can move them all around. But you can't shrink them, which is too bad, because they're kind of large.

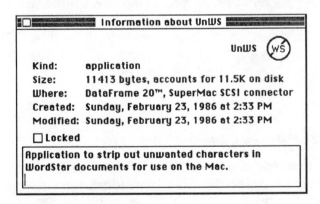

A Get Info window showing an unlocked application

⚫ *locking documents with Get Info*

To lock a file, simply click on the box marked Locked in the Get Info window. When a document is locked, you can only save it to disk if you use Save As to give the document another name, and you can't throw it in the Trash.

To unLock a document, simply Get Info again and click on the Locked box. The X in the box will disappear and you'll be able to modify the document and save it under its own name. You can Lock and unLock documents as often as you like.

⚫ *protecting templates*

A template is a document with a special format that you use repeatedly—for example, one containing your letterhead, so you don't have to recreate the letterhead every time you want to write a letter.

Because of the way templates are used, they run a special risk of being overwritten. You can avoid this risk by Locking them (see the last entry for details on how to do that). This will prevent you from saving a modified template under the original name, and will force you into the correct habit— always Saving As as soon as you open the template.

If you you need to change the template itself, it's easy enough to unLock it. But don't forget to Lock the document again when you've finished making changes to it.

⚫ *finding the size of folders*

One annoying feature of HFS is that when you're Viewing by Size, Kind or Date, the size of folders isn't listed (unless the folder's window is open). One solution is to select a folder, then choose Get Info from the File menu (or, easier, hit COMMAND-I). The Get Info window will tell you the size of the folder. This figure, in K, is the sum of the size all the files and folders contained in the folder.

♦ *using (and cancelling) Set Startup*

You can use the Set Startup command (on the Finder's Special menu) to cause any application on the disk to automatically launch when you boot from that disk. All you have to do is select the application by clicking on it, then choose Set Startup.

This is a handy feature, but the time may come when you want to turn it off. The way to do that is quite elegant—you simply make the Finder the startup application. The procedure is the same as for an application: Click on the Finder icon to highlight it, then choose Set Startup.

Miscellaneous basic tips

♦ *preserving the contents of the Clipboard*

The contents of the Clipboard are lost if you use Cut (COMMAND-X) to delete text, but if you use BACKSPACE, the Clipboard remains unchanged.

important warning

If you accidentally Cut when you didn't want to flush the Clipboard, choose Undo immediately (or hit COMMAND-Z). The contents of the Clipboard will be restored, along with the text in your document.

♦ *flushing the Clipboard to free up memory*

If you run low on memory while using any application that supports the Clipboard (and all good applications do), you may be able to free up some memory by clearing out the Clipboard's contents. You do that by Copying a single character to the Clipboard, then doing it again.

very hot tip

The reason that you have to do it twice is that the first time you Copy to the Clipboard, its previous contents remain in memory, in an area called the Undo Buffer. This is so you can undo the last Copy, in case you didn't actually want to flush the buffer. When you Copy the single character to the Clipboard the second time, the first letter you Copied is placed in the Undo Buffer, so that between them they only take up two bytes of memory.

⚫ *cancelling requests with COMMAND-period*

Sometimes you may accidentally drag an icon to the wrong window, or double-click on an application icon—thereby launching it—when you only meant to move it.

very hot tip

To abort what you've done, trying using COMMAND-period. But you've got to be quick. COMMAND-period will only abort the launching of an application if you strike the keys during the brief moment when the application's name is displayed on the title bar. After that, it has no effect. You have a similarly short amount of time to abort the copying of a file.

⚫ *... after a command name*

When the name of a command on a menu is followed by ..., choosing it brings up a dialog box. When a command name isn't followed by ..., choosing it makes the command execute immediately.

⚫ *shift-clicking* (Steve Michel)

One way to select a number of different objects is with the *selection rectangle* (if you don't know what that is, see the glossary). Shift-clicking is another essential technique. Normally when you click on something to select it, the thing you selected last is automatically deselected. But if you hold the SHIFT key down, previously selected items stay selected.

You can see how useful this would be. Let's say you're working with the Font/DA Mover and want to copy fifteen fonts into the System file. Instead of having to select one, click on the Copy button, select another, hit the Copy button, and so on, you just select all fifteen by shift-clicking on each one, hit the Copy button once, and go do something else while the copying takes place.

Shift-clicking is also useful in object-oriented graphics programs like MacDraw, MacDraft, Mac 3D and Filevision, and on the Desktop to select several icons for copying, moving, deleting, or putting into a folder. (There's another way to select multiple objects in these contexts—you draw a box around them with the *selection rectangle*. If objects you don't want fall into the rectangle, just shift-click on them and they'll be deselected.)

Shift-clicking can also be used to select large portions of continuous material like text. Let's say you want to select the whole of a MacWrite document. You'd click in front of the first character in the document, then use the scroll bar to move to the end of the document, position the I-beam after the last character, hold the SHIFT key down, and click again. This causes everything between the two clicks—the whole document, in this case—to be selected.

(This same technique works in Microsoft Word, but with Word it's sometimes easier to use the "selection bar." See our tips on Word in chapter 6 for more details on this and other Word tricks.)

Shift-clicking works in a similar manner in spreadsheets: If you click in one cell, then shift-click in another, a rectangle of cells will be selected, with those two cells in the corners.

After you've selected a large hunk of text, you can use shift-clicking to deselect some of it (in other words, make your selection smaller without having to do it all over again), or to extend the selection. Position the I-beam at either the beginning or end of the selected text, hold down the SHIFT key, click, and drag in the appropriate direction.

About the only drawback to this technique is that you can just use it at one end or the other of a given selection. So, for example, if you've dragged at the end of a selection and then go to the beginning to drag there, the Mac will treat your click as the beginning of a new selection (even though you're holding down the SHIFT key) and you'll have to start over from scratch.

You can deselect objects in a similar manner: If you shift-click on an object that's already selected, it deselects. In fact, you can toggle an object between selection and deselection by shift-clicking on it repeatedly.

🍎 *Option Trash*

very
hot
tip

Holding down the OPTION key when dragging a file to the Trash has two effects: It lets you throw away locked files (so they don't bounce back from the Trash) and if you're throwing away an application, you won't be asked to confirm the decision.

🍎 *flushing the Trash*

Files placed in the Trash are not actually deleted from the disk until you do one of the following things:

- empty the Trash.

- launch an application.

- drag the disk's icon to the trash.

- copy a file to the disk.

- Shut Down the system.

If you haven't done any of those things, you can open the Trash and retrieve whatever you put in it.

❡ *losing files retrieved from the Trash*

There's a bug in Finder 5.1, 5.2, and 5.3 that can cause you to lose a file you put in the Trash and then retrieved when you realized you made a mistake and needed to keep it. If you return it to the disk window, folder and/or volume it came from, you won't have any problem. But if you put it in a different disk window, folder and/or volume, the file will be permanently lost.

The best way to ensure that files retrieved from the Trash are put back where they came from is to open the Trash, select the files, and then choose Put Away from the File menu. Anytime Put Away is not dimmed, you can use it to return any selected file to its original folder.

important
warning

❡ *recovering from some crashes and system hangs*

Every Mac user experiences the dreaded bomb message from time to time. Most users have also experienced a *system hang* (that's when the Mac simply decides to ignore the mouse and the keyboard). In either case, your options are limited. You can click on the restart button (if you have a bomb message), push the reset button on the programmer's switch (if you have it installed) or turn the Mac's power switch off and on.

But if you do any of those things, all the information you hadn't saved to disk is lost forever. If you're using a hard disk, you'll also have to wait from one to five minutes while the hard disk checks to make sure everything is all right before putting you back on the Desktop.

So we always try the following technique first. It only works if you have the 128K ROMs and the programmer's switch installed, and even then it fails most of the time (often giving you a bomb message from a system hang, for example). But you have nothing to lose, because if it doesn't work, you're no worse off than when you started. Here's what to do:

very
hot
tip

Behind the reset button on the programmer's switch is another button labeled INTERRUPT. When you hit it, a large rectangular box with a > in the upper left corner appears on the screen. (If it doesn't, just give up and push the reset button. If your system wasn't hung, it will be now.) This box is the command area for the internal debugger that comes with the 128K ROMs. It's used primarily by Mac software developers, but this is an instance when regular users like us can use it too.

Type in **g 40f6d8** or **sm fa700 a9f4**
                          pc fa700
                          g

If you use the second group of commands—which seem to work slightly more often than the first but are also more trouble to type—you'll get a bunch of numbers on the screen each time you hit RETURN to end a line. But the > will be there with room after it for your commands, so just ignore in the numbers and type in the next line.

Whichever one you use, be sure to type them in exactly as shown here, with spaces and line breaks where indicated. The characters you type will show up as caps, but we've written them lowercase because that's how you should type them; you gain nothing by holding down the SHIFT key. All the 0's are zeros, not capital O's.

As we said above, we don't guarantee that either of those commands will work; in fact, most of the time they probably won't. We can't even promise you that they won't damage your files, although we've never experienced anything like that and we use this technique ourselves all the time. We think you have nothing to lose by trying it, but feel free to be conservative and just restart the system.

🍎 *turning off alert beeps*

There are two ways to turn off the beep the Mac makes when it wants your attention. One way is to open the Control Panel and set the volume level to zero. Now, instead of beeping at you, the menu bar will flash silently to get your attention. (A few programs will override the Control Panel volume setting. These include MusicWorks and the game Go.)

Another way to silence the alert beeps is to plug a mini jack (like the one used for headphones on a Walkman) into the music socket on the back of the Mac. You can get a mini jack for about $2 at Radio Shack and similar places.

🍎 *software that's incompatible with the 128K ROMs*

When you update to the 128K ROMs and begin to use HFS, be aware that early versions of the programs listed below are incompatible. Be sure to get updated versions from the publishers.

ConcertWare+
ClickOn Worksheet
Dollars and Sense
Hayden:Speller
MockWrite
MusicWorks 1.0
Red Ryder (versions older than 9.2)
Sargon III
SideKick
Note-pad+
Smartcom II
ThinkTank 1.1
TurboCharger

If you use Excel, be sure to put all linked documents in the same folder so that reference sheets are located and updated automatically. Otherwise Excel will ask for each one.

⌘ *correct System and Finder for 128K Macs*

Apple advises users of machines with just 128K of RAM to stick with System 2.0 and Finder 4.1 rather than upgrade to System version 3.2 and Finder version 5.3 (or later), which are designed for systems with the 128K ROMs only.

⌘ *obscure bug in Finder 5.1 and 5.2*

Finder versions 5.1 and 5.2 both feature an obscure but fatal bug. If you try to duplicate a file that has been dragged to the Trash (why anyone would do this, we don't know), the system will crash. This bug was fixed with the release of Finder 5.3.

Chapter 2

Disks

Basic disk tips

one disk, one system

You can avoid a lot of problems by always remembering this simple rule: *Never put more that one system on a disk.* If you have two or more system files on a disk, you're almost guaranteed crashes, bombs and data loss. (This can happen on floppies, but it's much more likely on hard disks, and much more of a problem there.)

important
warning

While most people wouldn't consciously add a second system file, it's pretty easy to do accidentally, especially on a hard disk (as we can tell you from personal experience). It usually happens when you're putting new software on the disk. It seems so natural just to select all the files on the distribution disk and drag them over. Unfortunately, most distribution disks contain a system folder.

So get in the habit of always following this procedure: Select all the icons on the distribution disk, then deselect its system folder (by clicking on it while holding down the SHIFT key). Then—and only then—drag the remaining selected icons over to the hard disk.

backing up disks

There are two ways to backup disks (assuming, of course, they're not copy-protected). One is to select all the files on the source disk (using COMMAND-A is the fastest way) and drag them as a group to the backup disk. The second way is to drag the icon of the source disk onto the icon of the backup disk.

The second method erases anything that was previously on the backup disk—so if you only want files copied into the blank spaces on the backup disk, use the first method. When you use the second method, the Desktop of the backup disk ends up looking exactly the same as the source disk's, with all the icons in the same places. Any invisible (but unprotected) files on the source disk get copied too.

✎ changing the Startup disk

Because the Mac looks for desk accessories (including the Scrapbook) on the Startup disk, you may need to change Startup disks from time to time. (For example, you may have one set of desk accessories installed in the System file on your word processing disk and another on your MacPaint disk.)

**very
hot
tip**

You can change the Startup disk simply by choosing Shut Down from the Special menu and inserting the disk you want to be the new Startup disk into the internal drive. But there's an easier way to do it. Just double-click on the Finder icon of the disk you want to be the new Startup disk while holding down the OPTION and COMMAND keys.

This will also work with a hard disk as well as a floppy, as long as the hard disk is self-booting, i.e. doesn't require any particular startup procedure, like inserting a special floppy disk. (Hard disks that connect to one of the serial ports on the back of the Mac always need a floppy to start.)

✎ preventing Startup disk changes

Launching an application that resides on a disk other than the Startup disk makes the application disk the Startup disk (assuming, of course, that that disk contains a System file and a Finder). To prevent this from happening, drag the Finder on the application disk out of the System Folder.

This only works if you're using HFS. If you're still using MFS, the only way to avoid the switch is to rename the Finder on the disk containing the application and remove any MiniFinders that may be installed on that disk.

⚫ making the Finder into an application

Now that you know how to change the Startup disk (by holding down OPTION and COMMAND while double-clicking on the Finder icon), here's how to launch the Finder the same way you launch applications like MacWrite or Excel. (This is particularly convenient if you often need to change the Startup disk.)

Use a system utility like ResEdit to change the Finder's file type from FNDR to APPL. Once you've done that, you can launch the Finder with a simple mouse click. (See the section on system utilities in the advanced tips part of this chapter for details on how to use ResEdit and similar programs.)

Floppy disk tips

⚫ recovering data from trashed disks

If a disk bombs when inserted, you still may be able to recover the information it contains. Hold down the COMMAND and OPTION keys while inserting the disk and keep them held down. A message will appear asking if you want to rebuild the Desktop. Click on the YES button. If the recovery was successful, the Desktop will appear after a minute or two (how long it takes depends on how many files are on the disk).

very
hot
tip

If you're using a version of the Finder earlier than 5.0, all icon positions, folder titles, window sizes and positions will be lost, but all the actual data in your files will be preserved.

very
hot
tip

If the above technique doesn't work, you still may be able to save some or all of the documents. Insert a disk that contains the application that created the documents you want to save, launch the application and choose Open from the application's File menu. Then eject the application disk and insert the problem disk.

In most cases, the Mac will accept the problem disk and present you with a list box containing the documents you want to save. Load them into memory and save them to another disk. If the documents on the problem disk were created by more than one application, just repeat the process for each application.

If you're using a two-drive system, click on the Disk button and insert the problem disk in the external drive. If you're using a one-drive system, click on the Eject button, then insert the problem disk. The disk should load and the documents should be readable.

This won't work with every disk that goes bad, but it's worth a try. If no technique you use to recover the lost data works, try letting the disk rest for two weeks and repeat the above procedure. If *that* doesn't work, remember the entire episode the next time you think you just don't have time to make backups of your documents.

⚜ *recycling trashed disks*

If you can't—or don't need to—recover the data from a trashed disk, here's a way to at least try to recycle it, so you can use it for new data. (If you *do* need to recover the data, see the last entry.)

If you're still using the 64K ROMs, try this: Eject any disk that may be in the drive and very carefully stick your little finger into the drive slot near the right side. You should feel a small button that responds to gentle pressure. Push it a few times until the "This disk is unreadable" message appears on your screen, then insert the trashed disk. Click on OK when the dialog box asks if you want to initialize the disk.

*very
hot
tip*

If you're using the 128K ROMs, you can keep your pinky on the keyboard and accomplish the same thing much more elegantly. Hold down the OPTION, COMMAND and TAB keys while inserting the trashed disk. You'll get the standard dialog box asking you if you want to initialize the disk Single-Sided or Double-Sided. The trashed disk should now initialize with no further problems. Click on whichever one you prefer.

If these methods don't work, your disk is *really* trashed and you should recycle it as a high-tech coaster.

¢ *how many backups to make* (Arthur)

Floppy disks cost a couple of dollars each—less than that if you get them at a discount. Even a 400K one will hold at least 20 hours work. So if you value your time at more than 10¢ an hour, the lesson is simple: you should *always* have enough disks around to make multiple copies of your work.

*important
warning*

When I used to have a floppy disk system, I made three copies, each on a separate disk, of every piece of work I did (so that when I was working on a document, I actually had four copies, three on disk and one in memory). Tony Pietsch got me into that habit years ago, when he described the following scenario: "Let's say you only have two copies of something and your disk drive screws up. You insert the first disk and see garbage on the screen. Naturally you assume there's something wrong with that disk, but you're not worried, because you have a second disk with the same document on it. So you insert the second disk and the drive zaps that too. At *that* point you realize the problem is with the drive, not the disk, but it's too late—unless you have a third copy."

✿ *ejecting disks*

There are several ways to eject disks. The most straightforward method is to drag the disk's icon to the Trash. This will work with any disk except the Startup disk, which will simply bounce back to its original position.

You can also choose Eject from the Finder's File menu, or hit the Eject button in Save As... or Open... dialog box. Or you can use the following keyboard commands; they'll eject *any* disk, including the Startup disk, regardless of whether you're on the Desktop or in an application.

COMMAND-E ejects the selected disk(s).
COMMAND-SHIFT-1 ejects the disk in the internal drive.
COMMAND-SHIFT-2 ejects the disk in the external drive.

When you use these keyboard commands from the Finder (or choose Eject from the File menu), a dimmed version of the disk's icon—and of any of its windows that happened to be open—remains on the Desktop. When you throw a disk's icon in the trash (or eject a disk from within an application), all trace of it disappears from the Desktop.

If you try to close the dimmed window of an ejected disk, you'll be asked to reinsert the disk, so if you're not going to be using the disk again, drag the dimmed disk icon to the Trash. The Finder will remove any of that disk's windows that happen to be open (if you insert the disk again, it will remember which windows were open and put them back where they were).

important
warning

✿ *ejecting disks before turning off the Mac*

Never turn off your Mac without first ejecting any disks that are in either drive. The correct procedure is to close any application that may be running, then choose Shut Down from the Special menu. Failing to heed this warning is an excellent way to lose data.

⚫ *freeing up disk space*

If you find you're running out of space for documents on a disk that has both the Finder and an application on it, here's a way to save over 40K. (This tip assumes you're using a one-drive system. If you're using a two-drive system, you shouldn't be storing documents on the same disk as the application.)

very
hot
tip

Start the system with a different disk. Eject it and insert the crowded disk. Click once on the application's icon to select it, then choose Set Startup from the Special Menu. Now drag the Finder icon to the Trash and select Empty Trash from the Special menu. (That's right, delete the Finder.) From this point on, whenever you start your Mac with this disk, you'll find yourself in the application instead of on the Desktop.

There is one hitch with this method: when you quit the application, there's no Finder to go back to. If you're using a Mac with the 64K ROMs, you'll get a bomb message; if you're using a Mac with the 128K ROMs, the drive will whir for a moment and then the application will launch again.

If you want to continue working with a different application, push the reset button on the programmer's switch (or the Restart button on the bomb message) and then hold down the mouse button. The Mac will restart and eject your disk, so you can insert another one. This technique is not particularly elegant, but it works.

If you've finished working, go to the Open... or Save As... window, eject the disk, and then just turn the Mac off.

If you have the MiniFinder on the disk, you can use that as a substitute for the Finder, thus avoiding some of the procedures just mentioned. (For more information on the MiniFinder, see chapter 5.)

✎ *protecting confidential data*

If you keep confidential data on disk, be aware that deleting the file does not actually remove the data. It's still there, and the clever hacker can recover your secrets using any one of several utility programs. Writing another file to the disk will probably remove the old file, but a much safer way is to reformat the disk. (By the way, this fact of disk life is just as true for 5-1/4" disks.)

✎ *floppy disks and magnets*

important warning

The information on disks is stored magnetically, and magnets placed near disks can hopelessly scramble that information. So keep magnets as far away as possible from disks (and disk drives). And remember that most of the magnets you're going to run across are going to be in small appliances and other devices—telephones, for example—not lying around loose on your desk.

For example, the original Imagewriter cover has a magnet underneath the left side. Put your disks here at your own risk. The ImageWriter II cover has a much smaller magnet on the right side, but since the surface is slanted at an angle, disks will probably slide off if you try to put them there.

✎ *airport X-ray machines* (Dale)

Since 1977, I've been shlepping disks in my carry-on luggage. I've run them through the security X-ray machines at airports in Nashville, Cleveland, New York, Washington DC, San Francisco, Honolulu, Auckland, Melbourne, Sydney, Dahran and Frankfurt, and I've never lost so much as a bit. I recently heard a Mac enthusiast describe his trip to Australia and New Zealand, disks in tow. His experience is the same as mine.

In spite of all that, airport security can be dangerous to disks. The problem isn't the X-rays, but the powerful magnetic motors in the X-ray machines. So if you want to play it completely safe, have your disks hand-checked.

⚫ *using an 800K external drive with the 64K ROMs*

If you're adding an 800K external drive to an old machine but aren't upgrading to the 128K ROMs, you must include these new files in your system folder: System 3.2 (or later), Finder 5.3 (or later), and Hard Disk 20 (HD20). Without these files, the 64K ROMs can't recognize a drive larger than 400K.

These files are available free at Apple dealers, so ask for them when you buy an 800K external disk.

⚫ *400K HFS disks*

If you format a disk to be single-sided (400K), it will be set up with MFS rather than HFS. This is true even if you format it on an 800K drive connected to a Mac that uses the 128K ROMs, and regardless of whether you're initializing a disk that's never been used before or are erasing and reinitializing a used one.

But there's a way to get HFS on a 400K disk—just hold down the OPTION key when you click on the One-Sided button and continue to hold it down until the initialization is complete.

To tell if a disk is HFS or MFS, open its window and check to see if there's for an extra dot at the far left side of the horizontal lines in the window's title bar. If the dot's there, it's an HFS disk.

☀ *alleged miracle cures of bad disks*

Some users report that disks that have gone bad sometimes mysteriously heal themselves. They say that if the Finder suddenly decides that it can't read a previously good disk and asks if you want to initialize it, you should put the disk on the shelf for a couple of days, or even a couple weeks. They claim that after this period of recuperation, the Finder is often able to read the disk.

We have our doubts about this method, but we suppose it's worth a try, if you can afford to wait that long to recover the data.

☀ *cleaning label gum from disks*

Looking for the best way to remove the gummy residue that's left when you remove the label from a disk? Try dabbing on a little rubber cement thinner with a Q-tip. Just be careful to avoid the openings in the disk cover.

Hard disk tips

☀ *care and feeding of hard disks*

important
warning

Hard disks are remarkably tough, but cruel and unusual punishment can damage them. The most important rule is not to move a hard disk when it's turned on. And when you move it, pick it up—never scoot it across the desk surface.

Another thing to avoid is rapid temperature changes. Don't carry a hard disk around in your trunk all day in the dead of winter, bring it inside and start it up; give it a couple of hours to warm up to room temperature.

✦ converting a hard disk to HFS

If you're one of the pioneers who purchased a hard disk before the advent of HFS and haven't updated your system, the best way to do it is to first think about all the different kinds of files you have, and then organize them into logical categories that reflect the way you use them (see the next entries for some ideas on how to do this).

Next, copy each category of files to a different floppy disk (or set of disks), and make *at least* one backup of each floppy. Then reformat the disk to HFS and set up folders corresponding to each of the sets of floppy disks. Then just copy the files from the floppies into the corresponding folders. (Or you can just drag the floppy's icon to the hard disk. The Finder will create a folder on the hard disk with the same name as the floppy and will copy all the floppy's files into it.)

Converting a hard disk to HFS is a big job that will require a lot of time and thought, but the advantages of HFS fully justify the investment of your time. A byproduct of the process is that you'll have a complete, organized backup on floppy disks of all of your files.

✦ copying invisible files to hard disks

Some applications use invisible files—that is, files that aren't displayed on the Desktop—as a form of copy protection. When you copy such an application to the hard disk, the invisible files don't get copied (because they don't get selected) and the application doesn't run. Fortunately, versions of the Finder from 5.3 on provide a simple solution to this problem.

All you have to do is drag the icon for the floppy disk which contains the application onto the icon for the hard disk. The Finder will automatically create a folder on the hard disk with the same name as the floppy disk. (If there's already a folder with the same name on the hard disk, you'll get a dialog box asking you for a new name.) All the files on the floppy—including the invisible ones—will be copied into the folder on the hard disk.

important
warning

When using this technique, don't forget the first rule of hard disk management: *One hard disk, one system.* If the floppy you copied from contained a system folder, be sure to throw it in the Trash immediately.

● *starting and restarting hard disks*

very good
feature

The best hard disk to have is a self-starting SCSI. They're faster than disks that connect to the serial port, and all you have to do to start from them is turn them on and then turn on the Mac (if both are connected to a surge suppressor or a power strip, it's fine to turn them on simultaneously).

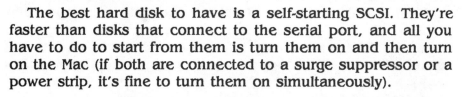

important
warning

When the smiling-face-inside-the-Mac icon appears, it means that the Mac has discovered the disk and is talking to it. *Never* turn off a Mac or a hard disk when the smiling face is on the screen. Don't even hit the reset button on the programmer's switch, because it will take much longer for the disk to restart. Wait until the Desktop appears, then choose Shut Down from the Special menu. If your disk is self-starting, see the next entry.

● *Shutting Down self-starting disks*

Most SCSI hard disks self-start; that is, you don't have to insert a floppy or anything—you just turn on the Mac and the drive and they start right up. When you choose Shut Down (from the Desktop's Special menu) on a system with such a disk, the screen blacks out, the Mac bongs, and then it immediately begins restarting from the hard disk. This could go on forever, if you didn't intervene.

The solution is simple (although seldom documented). As soon as you hear the bong, turn off the Mac, then the hard disk. Be sure you do this before the smiling-face-inside-the-Mac appears. If both the Mac and the disk are connected to the same power strip, it's fine to turn them off simultaneously—as long as you beat the smiling face. (If you don't, wait until the Desktop appears and Shut Down again.)

🍎 *organizing a hard disk*

There are two basic ways to organize folders—by application (MacWrite, MacPaint, databases, etc.) and by category (personal letters, business letters, budgets, etc.). Category folders may contain documents created by several different applications, and application folders may contain documents that belong in several different categories. Don't be afraid to use both kinds of folders on the same Desktop (even though you'll sometimes forget whether a given document is filed away under its category or under the kind of application that created it).

The guiding principle here is to set things up so they minimize effort and confusion. Obviously things should be organized, but don't lay down a rigid organizational scheme and then be afraid to break out of it. For example, if you use a particular program frequently, it's fine to put its icon by itself out in the disk window (also known as the "root directory"), even if all the related programs and documents are in a folder. (By the same token, if you use one particular document most of the time you use a given application, put its icon—rather than the application's icon—somewhere easy to get to, regardless of where related programs and documents are kept.)

In general, we prefer to View files by Date within folders (except if all the files are applications, in which case Viewing by Name is more convenient). This puts the last document worked on at the top of the list, and gives you nice, small icons that don't take up a lot of room.

One last general rule: *It's your Desktop. You can do whatever you want with it.* There's no right or wrong way to organize things, and you can name your folders whatever you want. (Arthur has one called "dealing with psychopaths"— which, unfortunately, is chock full of stuff.) Give your folders whatever names will help you remember what's in them, and where to find whatever you're looking for. And change them as often as you want—a good Desktop is constantly evolving.

Below are some snapshots of Dale's and Arthur's actual Desktops. They aren't intended to show you the "right" way to organize things, but merely to demonstrate that different approaches are possible and valid.

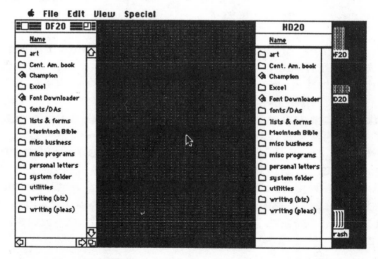

Arthur has two hard disks—a DataFrame 20 and an Apple HD20 for backup (he also periodically backs up important files on floppy disks).

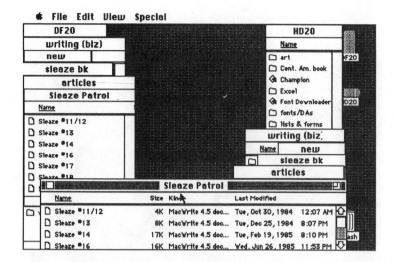

Arthur's Desktop with several windows open. Careful positioning and "staircasing" of nested windows allows a large amount of data to be displayed.

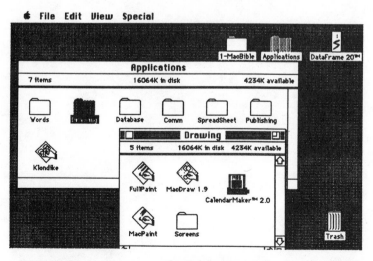

Dale prefers to group applications together in folders by type. He also likes to view applications by Icon rather than by Name.

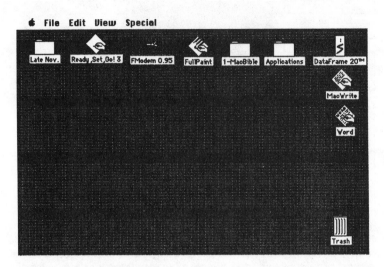

When Dale was doing the layout for this book, he kept frequently used applications out on the Desktop so they'd always be immediately available.

Chapter 3

Fonts

Font basics

♠ what is a font?

In regular typesetting, a font is a particular typeface in a particular size and a particular style (bold, italic, etc.) On the Mac, however, 'font' has come to mean a typeface in every size and every style (what a regular typesetter calls 'a type family').

For example, Geneva comes supplied in six sizes and, on the ImageWriter, it can be transformed into sixteen different *type styles* (bold, italic, etc—see the entry below on font styles for details). A regular typesetter would call that 96 different fonts; to a Mac user, it's all one font—Geneva.

With the introduction of the LaserWriter, which much more closely approximates regular typesetting, there's a move on to bring the two terminologies closer together. In the glossary in the LaserWriter manual, for example, the definition for 'font' is followed by one for 'font family'—"a font in various sizes and styles."

But we think Mac users have gotten too used to their own meaning of the word to be pushed back into line with the old terminology. When they change the size or style of a piece of type, they don't think of it as changing the *font*. So, throughout this book, we use 'font' in the classic Mac sense: a typeface in every size and style.

✦ font styles

very good feature

On the Imagewriter, every font can be made **bold,** *italic,* outline, shadow and any combination thereof: bold italic, bold outline, bold shadow, italic outline, italic shadow, outline shadow, bold italic outline, bold italic shadow, bold outline shadow, italic outline shadow, bold italic outline shadow and, of course, plain—which comes to sixteen possible combinations.

Some of these combinations may seem foolish to you, but it's not just a case of meaningless overkill—quite often one variation will have just the look you want, and no other variation will be quite right. And you'll find that in another font, that particular variation will look terrible and a different one will be just right. (For an easy way to see them all, see the entry on font templates below.)

Type styles (except for some on the LaserWriter) are derived algorithmically—that is, by the application of a rule like 'increase the width 10%' (to create boldface) or 'slant right 15°' (to create italics).

On the LaserWriter, you don't get all sixteen variations; how many you do get depends on the font. For more details, see the entry on font styles in the 'fonts on the LaserWriter' section of chapter 11.

✦ the two kinds of Mac fonts

Every Mac comes equipped with *ImageWriter fonts*—so called because they're designed for printing on dot-matrix printers like the ImageWriter. They're also what's used on the Mac's screen; Geneva and Chicago are two well-known examples.

Because they're made up of dots, like MacPaint images, ImageWriter fonts are also known as *bit-mapped fonts*. (A third name for them is *Macintosh fonts*—a hopelessly confusing term if there ever was one.)

There are 72 dots per inch in the pictures of the characters that make up an ImageWriter font—or, to say it a different way, ImageWriter fonts have a resolution of 72 dpi. (Actually, in a normal ImageWriter text printout, there are 80 dots per inch across and 72 down; to get 72 x 72, you have to ask for Tall Adjusted.)

ImageWriter fonts will print out on the LaserWriter and, with Smoothing on, they look pretty good. But *laser fonts* (so called because they're designed for printing on laser printers) look better. The characters in laser fonts aren't made up of dots—they're composed of instructions in a *page-description* programming language called PostScript, which was specifically designed to handle text and graphics and their placement on a page. For this reason, they're also known as *PostScript fonts*.

Because PostScript fonts are formed of outlines which are then filled in, they're also sometimes called *outline fonts*. (Technically, not all PostScript fonts are outline fonts. For example, when you send an ImageWriter font to the LaserWriter, a special, bit-mapped PostScript version of it is created. But when people speak of a PostScript font, they're virtually always referring to an outline font.)

When you send a laser font to a laser printer or typesetting machine, the printer reads the PostScript instructions and then draws the characters in as much detail—as high a resolution—as it's capable of. On the LaserWriter, that's 300 dpi, which amounts to 90,000 dots per square inch (300 across by 300 down), or about 16 to 17 times the resolution of an ImageWriter printout (which is 5760 dpsi in a regular Tall printout, and 5184 dpsi in a Tall Adjusted printout).

But 90,000 dpsi is nothing compared to what regular typesetting machines can do. For more information on them, see the entry about relative resolutions in the 'Basic LaserWriter tips' section of chapter 11.

Since the Mac's screen isn't a PostScript device, it can't display laser fonts directly. So each comes with a 72-dpi, bit-mapped *screen font* that's used to represent it on the screen. (Like any bit-mapped font, screen fonts will print out on the ImageWriter, but they won't look a whole lot like the actual laser font does when printed on the LaserWriter—both because of the lower resolution and because the person who designed the font knew it was only going to be used as an approximation, and therefore probably didn't spend a lot of time fine-tuning it.)

For tips on using fonts on the LaserWriter, see chapter 11.

❖ *font sizes*

gossip/
trivia

The sizes of Mac fonts are measured in *points*, which are 72nds of an inch. (Actually, to be more precise, a point is .0138" and 72 of them only make .9936", but since the difference between a point and a 72nd of inch is less than .0001", the distinction is pointless...so to speak.)

ImageWriter fonts come supplied in various sizes and, in general, they should be used in those sizes only, because *scaling* them—shrinking or enlarging them from one size to another—looks really dreadful. (At least on the ImageWriter it does; scaling PostScript versions of ImageWriter fonts and printing them on the LaserWriter produces much better results.)

You can tell what sizes of ImageWriter fonts (and *screen fonts*) are installed in the System file you're using by looking on the font size menu (which is usually part of another menu); the installed sizes are listed in outline type.

Laser fonts scale beautifully, since they're composed of instructions, not bit maps, and are designed to print at any size you say. But remember that the smaller the type size, the more the resolution of the device you're using matters. (At any given resolution, it's obviously easier to form a nice-looking 72-point character than a 6-point one, because you have more dots to work with.)

The standard type sizes that almost every application gives you are 9-, 10-, 12-, 14-, 18- and 24-point; other standard sizes—available in some applications—are 36-, 48-, 60- and 72-point. Microsoft Word lets you generate type of any size from 4-point to 127-point (whole numbers only), but the results will occasionally look a little funny (for more details, see the entry titled 'Word on the LaserWriter' in chapter 11).

very good feature

Point sizes aren't consistent and vary dramatically from font to font. For example, the type you're reading is 11-point (sitting on 13-point lines). The headers (the text at the top of the page, above the solid line) are in 14-point type, but they're smaller than the 12-point page numbers; in fact, they hardly look bigger than this 11-point type. (There's a longer discussion on relative font sizes toward the end of the next entry.)

⁂ *a template for viewing fonts*

Most font publishers don't give you full printouts of their fonts, so in order to evaluate which fonts you want to use, it makes sense to make up a template like the one below. (We use it in chapter 14 to display the fonts we recommend.) Once you've set it up—which might take half an hour—all you have to do is select the entire template and then change the font in order to get a printout of every character a given font can produce, as well as samples of the sixteen possible type styles in that font.

very good feature

It doesn't matter which font you choose to make the original template, since you're going to be changing it when you use the template anyway. We've picked the one this book is set in, because the LaserWriter has a lot of trouble handling several fonts in one document (for details, see chapter 11).

font: ITC Benguiat (BEN-gat)   **from: Adobe**

9 point: 1234567890 abcdefghijklmnopqrstuvwxyz
ABCDEFGHIJKLMNOPQRSTUVWXYZ

10 point: 1234567890 abcdefghijklmnopqrstuvwxyz
ABCDEFGHIJKLMNOPQRSTUVWXYZ

12 point: 1234567890 abcdefghijklmnopqrstuvwxyz
ABCDEFGHIJKLMNOPQRSTUVWXYZ

14 point: 1234567890 abcdefghijklmnopqrstuvw
ABCDEFGHIJKLMNOPQRSTUVWXYZ

18 point: 1234567890
abcdefghijklmnopqrstuvwxyz
ABCDEFGHIJKLMNOPQRSTUVWXYZ

24 point: 1234567890
abcdefghijklmnopqrstuvwx
ABCDEFGHIJKLMNOPQRST

unshifted symbols: ` - = [ ] \ ; ' , . /

shifted symbols: ~ ! @ # $ % ^ & * ( ) _ + { } | : " < > ?

option keys:

` ¡ ™ £ ¢ ∞ § ¶ • ª º – ≠
œ ∑ ´ ® † ¥ ¨ ^ ø π " ' «
å ß ∂ ƒ © ˙ ∆ ˚ ¬ … æ
Ω ≈ ç √ ∫ ~ µ ≤ ≥ +

shift-option keys:

Ÿ / ¤ ‹ › fi fl ‡ ° · , — ±
Œ „ ‰ Â Ê Á Ë È Ø Π " ' »
Å Í Î Ï Ì Ó Ô Ò Ú Æ
Û Ù Ç ◊ ı ˆ ˜ ¯ ˘ ¿

This is bold. *This is italic.* This is outline.
This is shadow. ***This is bold italic.***
This is bold outline. This is bold shadow.
This is italic outline. This is italic shadow.

This is outline shadow.

This is bold italic outline.

This is bold italic shadow.

This is bold outline shadow.

This is italic outline shadow.

This is bold italic outline shadow.

You'll note that the outline shadow variations look just the same as the shadow variations. This is a peculiarity of the LaserWriter and is discussed further in chapter 11. (At least one laser font has only three style variations—plain, outline and shadow.) ImageWriter fonts printed on the ImageWriter always have all sixteen variations—but *not* when they're printed on the LaserWriter.

Here are some pointers on how to set this template up for yourself. (You might as well begin by just copying ours, then customize it for your own use any way you want. Or, if you don't want to go to the trouble, send for our disk, which includes this template and a lot of other useful stuff; see the last page of the book for more information.)

The shifted and unshifted symbols are shown in the order in which they appear on the keyboard, from left to right and top to bottom. Because the characters produced by the option key (with and without the shift key) don't appear on the keyboard, we've set it up so that each row under the 'option keys' and 'shift-option keys' headings represents a row of keys. This makes it easy to find the symbol on the keyboard.

Although all fifteen type styles are shown at the bottom of the template (plain text is omitted because most of the rest of the template is in it), it makes sense to give yourself a bit more of a look at the three most useful ones: bold, italic and bold italic. So we've put the title (font and publisher) in bold italic, the type sizes in italic, and the subheads below the type sizes ('unshifted symbols', 'shifted symbols', etc.) in bold. We've also underlined those subheads and the type sizes, so we can see how underlining looks with the font.

Because the 8-1/2 x 11 page you'll use to print out the template is wider than this 4-3/4" text block, you should combine some of the lines we separated above. Otherwise the template will be too long to fit on the page.

Each time you select the template and change it to a different font, you may have to readjust line breaks and even lop a few letters off some of the larger alphabets to get the whole template onto a single page. That's because fonts of the same official point size vary quite a bit in actual size, both in height and width. For example, compare these five fonts, all technically 24-point:

Calligraphy

Times

Benguiat

𝖵𝖨𝖭𝖤𝖲

DREAM.

With a font like Dream (from Casady), you'll have to do more than lop off a few letters of the alphabet to make it fit. (On the other hand, it doesn't have any lowercase letters, numbers of symbols.) With an ImageWriter font, you'll only want the supplied sizes anyway, so that will save some room. And you certainly don't need to see Dream in bold italic outline shadow (but how can we resist?):

Like Benguiat in the sample template above, most laser fonts have special characters for every possible slot. ImageWriter fonts almost never do. When an ImageWriter font doesn't have a given special character, it will produce the 'missing character box': □   (its appearance varies with the font, but it always looks pretty much like that). But it will only do that on the ImageWriter; the LaserWriter won't print the missing character box (we had to paste that one in from the ImageWriter).

When using the template for an ImageWriter font, it makes sense to only show the sizes it's actually supplied in, because scaled sizes of ImageWriter fonts generally look wretched. (The one exception to this rule is when a scaled size is exactly half of a supplied size.)

You might want to underline the supplied sizes, so you know which are which. (In the template above, all the sizes are underlined, because laser fonts are—in effect—supplied in all sizes.)

Special characters

✦ *the standard special characters*

There are some pretty bizarre characters on the Mac's—or just about any computer's—keyboard. For example, there's the backslash (\ ), the vertical bar (|), the greater than and lesser than signs (<   >) and so on. But when people talk about special characters on the Mac, they mean ones that aren't shown on the keyboard at all. To get one of these special characters, you hold down the OPTION key while hitting another key (or keys).

Let's say you want to type: "Hein, salopard! Parlez-vous français?" To get the special character ç in "français," you hold down OPTION while hitting c. To get certain other special characters, you have to hold down the SHIFT key as well. For example, if you hit OPTION-SHIFT c, you get an uppercase Ç instead of a lowercase one. (In this case, the two characters are related, but sometimes the OPTION and OPTION-SHIFT characters have nothing to do with each other.)

very good
feature

Some fonts have idiosyncratic special characters of their own, but there's a set of standard special characters that virtually all fonts share. No ImageWriter font contains all of them—Geneva and Chicago seem to have the most—but most laser fonts have the full set. (You can see it—arranged by keyboard rows—in the font template for Benguiat in the previous entry, under the headings 'option keys' and 'shift-option keys'.)

In the following entries, we've listed these standard special characters by category. Since more people use ImageWriters than LaserWriters, we've restricted the list to the characters you'll find in Geneva or Chicago (the other ones are pretty self-explanatory anyway).

We show the special character first, followed by the regular character used to generate it in outline type. We don't bother putting OPTION in front of each of the regular keyboard characters, and we also don't use the SHIFT symbol—since it's simpler just to show you the capital letter instead. So when you see Å followed by 𝔸, it means that to get Å, you need to hit OPTION-SHIFT a.

Sometimes we have to clarify which regular keyboard character we're indicating—for example, when there might be a confusion between the capital letter O and the numeral 0 (or, for that matter, between a small o and a capital O, since standing alone, they can be hard to tell apart). For maximum legibility, we've set both regular and special characters in larger type.

Unless you're a whole lot more knowledgable than we were, you won't know what half these characters are, so we provide the name—and, when appropriate, the common foreign name—for most of them.

Some special characters do double duty; for example, the square root sign doubles nicely as a check mark. When a character serves more than one function, we list it under each category where it can be used.

⚫ *accent marks for foreign languages*

Two foreign accent marks—the tilde (~) and the accent grave (`)—are regular characters on the Mac's keyboard, marked right on the key. But it's not clear what you're supposed to use them for, since if you just press those keys, the characters always appear on a space of their own, not above another character.

The accent marks listed below—which include a different tilde and a different accent grave—work the way they should: when you hit OPTION + the regular character indicated, nothing shows up on the screen; then, when you type the next character, the appropriate accent mark appears above it.

These accent marks won't appear over just any letter you type—it has to be one the Mac thinks makes sense. If you try to put an accent over a different letter, the accent appears by itself on one space and the letter on the next—like this: ´A.

In the table on the next page, we've listed the letters that work with each accent in curly brackets after it. If you want to produce an accent over a blank space, you can always do that simply by hitting the appropriate key, then the space bar.

´ acute accent; accent aigu {á é í ó ú É}　ℰ

` grave accent; accent grave {à è ì ò ù}

(In other words, if you just hit the ` key by itself, you get ` on a space of its own; if you use OPTION, ` appears above the next letter you type.)

^ circumflex; circonflexe {â ê î ô û}　î

•• diaresis; umlaut {ä ë ï ö ü Ä Ö Ü}　U

~ tilde {ã ñ õ Ñ}　m

 foreign letters, letter combinations and abbreviations

å	a	Å	A
æ	' (apostrophe)	Æ	" (regular quote mark)
ç	C	Ç	C
ø	O (small o)	Ø	O (capital O)
œ	q	Œ	Q
ª	g	º	O (zero)

ß　s

❡ foreign punctuation marks

¿ (begins questions in Spanish)

¡ (begins exclamations in Spanish)

« (European open quote mark)

» (European close quote mark)　｜ (vertical bar)

These last two symbols are called **guillemets** (GEE-MAY).

❡ monetary symbols

£ (pound sign)　　　　　¥ (yen sign)

¢ (cent sign)

❡ legal symbols

§ (section mark)　　　　¶ (paragraph mark)

TM (trademark)　　　　　® (registered mark)

© (copyright symbol)

❡ well-known mathematical and scientific symbols

— (minus sign)　⁃ (hyphen)　÷ (division sign)

Ø (to distinguish zeros from capital Os)　Ⓞ (capital O)

√ (square root)　Ⅴ (small v)　∞ (infinity sign)

π (lowercase pi)　　　° (degrees)　＊ (asterisk)

⌘ *not so well known mathematical and scientific symbols*

Since some of the symbols below can represent about a dozen different things, depending on the field of study, we simply give you their Greek names and/or what they most commonly stand for.

≠ (not equal to) ≡   ≈ (more or less equal to) $\mathbb{X}$ (small x)

≤ (less than or equal to) ≪   ≥ (greater than or equal to) ≫

« (much less than) \   » (much greater than) ∣ (vertical bar)

± (plus or minus) ✢   Å (Angstroms) $\mathbb{A}$

∂ (lowercase delta; differential, variation) $\mathbb{d}$

Δ (capital delta; increment) $\mathbb{j}$ μ (lowercase mu; micro-) $\mathbb{m}$

Ω (capital omega; ohms) $\mathbb{Z}$ (small z) f (function, f-stop) $\mathbb{f}$

Σ (capital sigma; sum) $\mathbb{W}$ (small w)   ∫ (integral) $\mathbb{b}$

∏ (capital pi; product) $\mathbb{P}$ ¬ (logical not) $\mathbb{l}$ (small l)

⌘ *typographic and graphic symbols*

" (double open quote) ⟦   " (double close quote) {

' (single open quote) ⟧   ' (single close quote) }

— (dash) _ (underline—i. e., OPTION-SHIFT hyphen)

√ (check mark) $\mathbb{V}$ (small v)   ◊ (diamond) $\mathbb{V}$ (capital V)

† (dagger) $\mathbb{t}$ • (bullet, for lists) $\otimes$

••• (ellipsis points, to indicate something left out) $\overset{\circ}{\mathbb{D}}$

Finally, there's the missing character box ☐ . This is produced by ⓗ or ⓚ in all ImageWriter fonts, or by any other OPTION or SHIFT-OPTION key that has no special character assigned to it in the particular font you're using. London, for example, has only three special characters, so almost any OPTION or SHIFT-OPTION key you hit in it produces the box.

You can't get this character in laser fonts, for several reasons: many laser fonts have special characters assigned to all the OPTION and SHIFT-OPTION keys; some laser fonts use a different missing character symbol; and even if the missing character box shows up on the screen, the LaserWriter won't print it (in fact, we had to paste that one in from the ImageWriter).

⧀ *pictorial characters*

One of the best features of the Macintosh is the availability of *pictorial characters*—little images you can place in a document with nothing more than a keystroke or two. The two most famous pictorial fonts are Cairo and Mobile (formerly know as Taliesin), ImageWriter fonts published by Apple.

very good
feature

Century Fonts publishes five pictorial laser fonts, including laser versions of Cairo and Mobile. Fluent Fonts offers some useful pictorial fonts for the ImageWriter, including one that contains architectural symbols and drawings (like a little toilet and an overhead shot of a person walking), and a whimsical one called Images. (See the fonts section of chapter 14 for more details on some of them.)

The best way to arrange a pictorial font for reference is by categories. The next entry gives you an example of that, using Cairo.

◉ *Cairo by categories*

When Cairo is the selected font, all you have to do to generate the picture shown is hit the key indicated below it.

animals

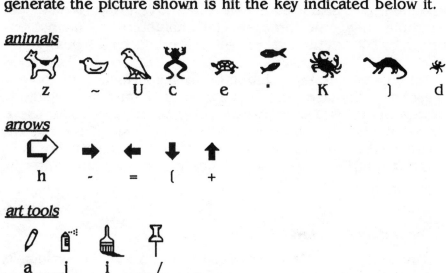

| z | ~ | U | c | e | ' | K |] | d |

arrows

| h | - | = | (| + |

art tools

| a | j | i | / |

buildings

| E | Q | R | T | W | % |

celestial objects

| @ | 7 | 8 | g |

electrical symbols

| q | r | s | 0 |

everyday objects—bigger than a breadbox

| ; | D | 3 | _ | (| t |

everyday objects—smaller than a breadbox

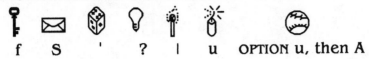

f	S	'	?	I	u	OPTION u, then A

food and drink

`	!	5	\	4	6

fruits

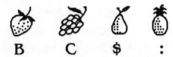

B	C	$	:

miscellaneous

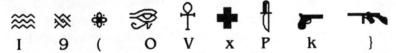

I	9	(	O	V	x	P	k	}

musical symbols

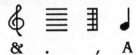

&	.	,	A

parts of the body

o	n	m	2	p	M	N

plants & parts of plants

L	1	^	X	Y	Z	)	#	w	*

things you wear

| b | < | v | > | y |

transportation

| H | F | G | J | l | OPTION A |

■ non-Roman alphabets

very good feature

Another exciting aspect of fonts on the Mac is the ability to generate foreign—that is, non-Roman—alphabets, especially since you can mix them in freely with regular text. (Roman alphabets—like the ones used for English, French and Spanish—have more or less the same characters as Latin does. Non-Roman alphabets—like the ones used for Greek, Russian, Hebrew, Japanese and Chinese—have different characters.)

There's a wide variety of both laser and ImageWriter non-Roman fonts available—everything from common ones like Greek, Hebrew, Katakana (Japanese phonetic characters) and Cyrillic (Russian, etc.) right down to totally obscure ones like Linear B (an early form of Greek writing dating from around 1500 BC).

This last was designed by Gary Palmer, who teaches anthropology at the University of Nevada in Las Vegas and also helps run the Center for Computer Applications in the Humanities there. Here's a short sample of it:

$$\text{ᛞᛟᛥᛝᛤᚷᛟᚨ}$$

Pretty hot, huh?

One last note about non-Roman alphabets: remember that generating the characters may be only half the battle. For example, unless a Hebrew font comes with a word processor that lets you write from right to left, you'll have to type out the Hebrew text backwards (from left to right).

Key Caps

It's often hard to remember which key combination to hit to produce the special character you need, or even whether the font you're using has that character. That's what the desk accessory called Key Caps is for. When you select Key Caps from the menu, it displays the following:

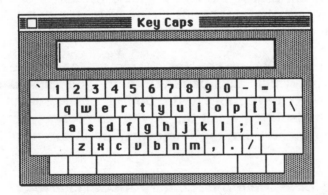

When you choose Key Caps, it puts a new menu—titled Key Caps—at the right end of the menu bar. You select the font you're interested in from that menu (let's do Benguiat, since that's the font you're reading right now) and the Key Caps display switches over to it (see illustration at top of next page).

(The original Key Caps didn't have the font menu, and only displayed characters in the Chicago font, which made it pretty useless.)

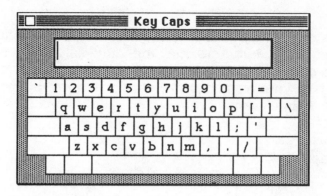

If you hold down the OPTION key, Key Caps displays the special characters you can generate by holding down OPTION and pressing another key, and likewise when you hold down the SHIFT as well as the OPTION key. (Unfortunately, *we* can't show you what that looks like because to take a snapshot of the screen, you have to hold down COMMAND-SHIFT 3; if you hold down OPTION at the same time, it doesn't work.)

If you use a lot of special characters and have trouble remembering which keys generate them, you can resize your text window to leave room at the bottom of the screen for Key Caps to be displayed at all times. But it's probably easier just to print out a chart like the one described in the next entry.

🍎 *a chart for locating the standard special characters*

If you use the standard special characters a lot, you'll want a chart on the wall that tells you where to find them on the keyboard. One way to do that is to photocopy the special character entries above; that will give you a list of them by categories.

If you want them arranged by where they are on the keyboard, create the MacDraw chart shown on the opposite page—or send for our disk, which includes the chart and a lot of other useful stuff (see the last page of the book for more information).

Chicago

The quick brown fox jumped over the lazy dogs.

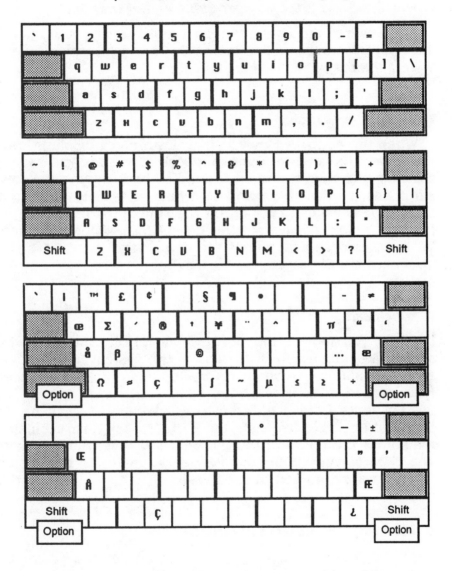

Font/DA Mover tips

🍎 don't use any F/DA Mover version earlier than 3.0

**important
warning**

There were some *very* serious problems with versions of the Font/DA Mover earlier than 3.0. They can screw up your system file but good, so *don't* use them.

🍎 OPTION at launch

shortcut

When the Font/DA Mover opens, it normally displays fonts. If you want to install or remove a desk accessory, you have to click on that button and sit around while it dumps the fonts and loads the desk accessories. A faster way is to hold down the OPTION key when clicking on the Font/DA Mover icon, and keeping it held down until the F/DA Mover window appears. That makes desk accessories the default and the F/DA comes up with them displayed.

🍎 quick exit

shortcut

When you launch the Font/DA Mover, it can take what seems like minutes for it to read in the System file. This can be a real annoyance when it's not opening the file you want (you wanted desk accessories instead of fonts, say, or the System fonts from a different disk). Well, just click on the Quit button. Even thought the F/DA Mover hasn't finished reading in the file, and the list box is blank, Quit will work. The F/DA Mover will immediately stop reading in the System file and will return you to the Desktop.

🍎 attaching fonts & DAs to applications

**very
hot
tip**

Although the Font/DA Mover normally installs fonts and desk accessories in the System file and makes them available to all applications, you can avoid clutter in your system file (and save disk space) by attaching fonts to specific applications. To do that, hold down the OPTION key when clicking on the Font/DA Mover's Open button. You'll then be free to choose the application you want to attach the fonts to.

You can also attach desk accessories to applications (which is particularly useful with DAs that only work with one or two specific applications). To do that, hold down the OPTION key while clicking on the OPEN button to place desk accessories in the program's resource file, instead of the System file.

very
hot
tip

This technique will help you get around the nasty limit of only sixteen desk accessories in the system file, and you won't have to listen to the Font/DA Mover beep at you when you try to choose a desk accessory after you've reached the limit.

⬤ *ejecting disks from within F/DA Mover*

There are two ways to eject disks from within the Font/DA Mover. The most obvious is to click on the eject button (it's in the dialog box that appears when you click on the Open button). But you can also eject a disk from the F/DA Mover's main window by holding down OPTION key while clicking on the Close button. This second method will save you some time if you need to use F/DA Mover to work on several disks.

⬤ *getting file information from within F/DA*

You can see how much memory a desk accessory uses from within the Font/DA Mover. Just hold down the OPTION key while clicking on the desk accessory. The Font/DA Mover will then display the size of the Desk Accessory's data and resource forks, and will also tell you if the Desk Accessory has a PICT resource.

❖ *Font/DA Mover OPTION command summary*

<u>OPTION</u>	<u>effect</u>
at launch	opens DAs instead of fonts.
+ click on Open	opens applications
+ click on Close	closes the open file & ejects the disk
+ when quitting	exits F/DA Mover, ejects both disks
when selecting DA in list box	shows data and resource forks

Chapter 4

Desk accessories

ᒃ *the power of desk accessories*

You open most programs by clicking on their icons on the Desktop. But you open the programs called *desk accessories* by choosing their names under the ᒃ Menu. The advantage of that is that DAs can be used from within an application (since no matter what application you're in—with a few rare exceptions—the ᒃ symbol will be in the upper left corner of the screen and the menu under it will contain all the items it does on the Desktop.)

very good
feature

So, for example, you can open up Apple's Calculator desk accessory in the middle of a MacWrite session and use it to add up a column of figures. As a matter of fact, you can Copy the column directly into the calculator and then Paste the result into your document. Other DAs allow you to take notes, dial the phone, open MacPaint documents, name and delete files, create new folders, check spelling and play games; there's even one that will nag you about your work habits. All in all, the power that DAs can give you is astounding.

Unfortunately, there are some tradeoffs. Officially you're limited to sixteen DAs installed in any system file (in other words, at any one time), but there are a couple of ways around that problem. You can attach additional DAs to specific applications, so that they only show up when you're running that program (for information on how to do this, see the Font/DA Mover section of chapter 3). And there are two programs that let you have more than sixteen DAs at a time; they're both discussed in the desk accessories section of chapter 14.

But there's no way around the space that DAs—particularly big, powerful ones—take up on disk. Even just ten DAs can add significantly to the size of your system file. If you're lucky enough to be using a hard disk, this is nothing to worry about. But if you're using floppy disks, you'll have to weigh the advantages offered by a particular DA against how much space it will cost you on your system disk(s).

Control Panel tips

✪ recommended Control Panel settings

When you first see the Control Panel (accessed via the ✪ menu), you may think it gives you more choices than you want. But in time you'll be glad to have them.

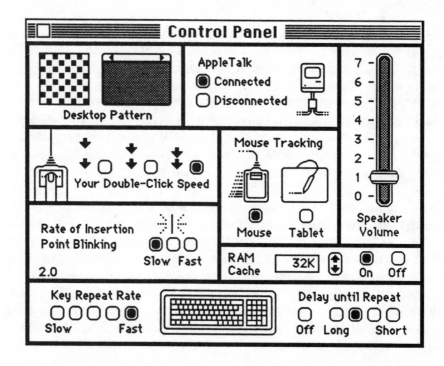

Here's a brief discussion of what each control does, and our recommendations on how to set them:

In the upper left corner is the control that lets you change the background of the Desktop. The rectangle on the right shows what the pattern is currently, and the two small arrows at the top cycle you through the other available patterns. The box on the left shows an enlargement of the "tile" that makes up the pattern (the pattern is created by repeating the tile over and over again). You can modify the tile of any pattern by the normal Mac method of clicking on dots to turn them on and off.

The pattern shown above is the default, a medium gray you should probably stick with, because it's quite pleasant for daily use. If you use a floppy-based system (and therefore have a variety of system files), you may find it convenient to use a different Desktop pattern to identify the different systems.

The control to the right of Desktop pattern, AppleTalk, is simple. You just check 'Connected' if your Mac is connected to an AppleTalk network (even one that simply goes to a LaserWriter), and check 'Disconnected' if it isn't.

At the top right is the Speaker Volume, which controls how loud the Mac's beeps (and any other sounds it makes) will be. There are 8 settings, 0 through 7, with 7 being the loudest. If you don't want to hear any beeps at all, slide the control to 0; instead of making sounds, the Mac will flash the menu bar when it wants your attention (except when starting or restarting—the Mac always bongs then).

very good
feature

When you change the Speaker Volume setting, the Mac gives you a sample of what the new beep sounds like, making it easy to find the volume level you want. We recommended starting with 1, then trying to 2 if you want it louder. After you've been using the Mac for a while and have a good feel for how it works, you may want to try 0.

The Double-Click Speed control tells the Mac how long it should wait after one click to see if you're going to double-click. With the long interval set (the one on the right), the Mac will treat clicks that are fairly far apart as double-clicks; with the short interval set (on the left), you'll have to double-click pretty fast or the Mac will think you're giving two separate clicks, rather than double-clicking.

We recommend either the short interval or the medium one (in the middle); if you use the long interval, you'll always be accidentally double-clicking on things and opening them when you only want to select them.

The Mouse Tracking control only concerns you if you're using a digitizing tablet (for precision drawing). Otherwise leave this set to Mouse.

very good
feature

As you might imagine, Rate of Insertion Point Blinking controls how fast the insertion point blinks. This is a totally subjective matter, so set it wherever you like (but do try Slow at some time and see if you don't find it more relaxing).

The number in the lower left corner of the Rate of Insertion Point Blinking box is the version number of the Control Panel. By the time you read this, the new Control Panel should be out; it doesn't look anything like this, but most of our comments will still apply. (For free updates on this and other matters, be sure to send in your name and address; details are inside the front and back covers.)

RAM Cache (pronounced the same as "cash") is one of the more powerful Control Panel options. A RAM cache is a portion of memory that has been set aside to store information that's recently been read in from the disk. If the Mac needs the information again, it gets it from the RAM cache, rather than from the disk. This works transparently—after you've set the RAM cache, the Mac does all the work for you. Since memory access is much faster than disk access, RAM caching can significantly speed up performance.

The larger the RAM cache, the more information can be held in it, and the longer it will be before new information read in from the disk flushes it out. On the other hand, the larger the RAM cache, the less RAM you have left for other purposes.

The best setting for the RAM cache depends on how much memory you have and what software you generally use. Steve Michel keeps 128K of RAM caching on his Mac Plus since he needs a lot of available memory for large databases. Dale finds that a setting of 512K on his 1-meg Mac yields greatly improved performance and still leaves enough memory to do word processing. If you use a 512K Mac, experiment with settings between 64K and 128K. (Also see the entry below titled "changing RAM caching.")

The final two options on the Control Panel relate to the keyboard. Delay until Repeat controls how long it takes before a key you're holding down begins to automatically repeat, and Key Repeat Rate controls how fast the key repeats after it begins repeating. We recommend that you set Key Repeat Rate at either of the two fastest speeds and Delay until Repeat at either of the two middle choices.

All of these Control Panel settings, plus the system time and date, are kept in a portion of memory called *parameter RAM* (except for the Desktop pattern, which is stored on disk). Because parameter RAM is powered by the Mac's battery, these settings aren't lost when you turn the Mac off. And because these settings are held in memory, not on disk, they stay the same regardless of what disk you're using (until you change them).

◉ *changing RAM caching*

Any change you make to the RAM cache (available on the Control Panel on the Mac Plus, the Enhanced 512K or any machine with the 128K ROMs) doesn't take effect until you restart the Mac, either by choosing Shut Down from the

Special menu or by turning the machine off and then on again. This is true both for turning RAM caching on or off, and for changing the size of the RAM cache.

♠ *how to get features missing from the Control Panel*

The Control Panel shown above (in the entry titled 'recommended Control Panel settings') has a couple of nice additions from the earlier version, such as RAM caching and AppleTalk, but two useful features found on the previous control panel are no longer available.

On the previous Control Panel, you could set the Mac's date and time, but this Control Panel doesn't let you—you have to use the Alarm Clock desk accessory to do it. This is annoying since it takes up an additional DA slot for an accessory you might not otherwise use. (For a couple of ways around the fifteen-DA limit, see the descriptions of Quick & Dirty DA Installer+ and of the desk accessory called Other... in chapter 14.)

The previous Control Panel also let you set the number of times a menu item blinks when it is selected, and also let you turn the blinking off. To do that with this Control Panel, you really have to jump through hoops. One approach, if you're technical, is to dip into the ToolBox and change SetMenuFlash.

If you're not technical, you can boot up your Mac with a disk that contains earlier versions of the System and Finder, use the previous Control Panel to set menu flashing, then reboot with the current System and Finder. (You can also use this technique to set the system date and time if you decide that you need to use the Alarm Clock's slot for different desk accessory.)

bargain

But the easiest solution is use the excellent public-domain program called PARMS (short for "parameters"). It lets you set any option that can be set with the Control Panel. PARMS is available from the Boston Computer Society (see Appendix C for the address).

Miscellaneous desk accessory tips

🍎 *programs that black out the screen* (Dennis Klatzkin)

There are several utilities—both in the form of desk accessories and FKeys—that automatically black out the screen if you don't strike a key or click the mouse for a period of time. This keeps your screen from developing a phosphor burn (for more details, see 'protecting the phosphor on your screen' in chapter 12).

very good
feature

When your machine has been inactive for the determined period of time, these utilities suspend all activity except watching for a keystroke or mouse click (some also bounce a dot of light around the screen so you'll know the Mac is on). But watch out for ones that don't also watch the modem port for activity. If you're using a modem to send or receive a long file when the utility blanks the screen, the connection will be lost, and you'll have to initiate the file transfer all over again.

important
warning

AutoBlack is one screen-saving desk accessory that doesn't ignore the modem port. (For the technically inclined, AutoBlack uses the 'alternate' screen in a different part of memory, and paints the alternate screen black.)

🍎 *FKeys*

Few people realize that the Mac has an equivalent to the function keys on an IBM PC or clone. They're called FKeys (EF-kees), which is short for "function keys," and you get them by holding down COMMAND, SHIFT and one of the ten number keys (1-0) that run across the top of the keyboard (the ones on the numeric keypad don't work).

Like desk accessories, FKeys are available from within applications. Five are programmed into the Mac:

COMMAND-SHIFT 1—ejects the disk in the internal drive.

COMMAND-SHIFT 2—ejects the disk in the external drive.

COMMAND-SHIFT 3—takes a snapshot of the screen and saves it as a MacPaint document on disk.

COMMAND-SHIFT 4—prints out whatever's in the active window on the Imagewriter (but not on the LaserWriter or on an ImageWriter connected on AppleTalk).

If you hold down the CAPS LOCK key along with COMMAND-SHIFT 4, you get a printout of the entire screen, instead of just the active window.

That leaves COMMAND-SHIFT 5 through COMMAND-SHIFT 0 available for commands you choose yourself (apparently CAPS LOCK-COMMAND-SHIFT 4 is the only instance in which you can add to the standard COMMAND-SHIFT-number combination).

bargain

To install an FKey, you need a program like Dreams of the Phoenix's FKey Installer, which is included in their Quick & Dirty Utilities, volume 2, and is also available free of charge on many bulletin boards with their blessings. (We highly recommend Dreams of the Phoenix's products. See chapter 14 for more info about their Q&D Utilities.)

Many ready-made shareware and public-domain FKeys are available on bulletin boards and electronic information services like CompuServe and GEnie. (See Appendix B for information about these services.) They do things like send commands to the printer, customize the keyboard, and automatically blank the screen when you're not using the Mac (so you don't exhaust the phosphor). Dale uses and likes the FKey version of Q&D's desk accessory SetFile, which allows you to change file attributes and also provides the same information you get with Get Info.

⚫ *SideKick on floppy-disk systems*

Because SideKick is a large program, it works best on a hard disk system. But there are several strategies that allow you to use it successfully on a system with floppy drives, even if they're both 400K. Here's how to do it:

If you use SideKick more than half the time you use your Mac, create a disk with the System, the Finder, the printer drivers, and SideKick and its data files on it. Then create disks that contain various applications and their data files, but no System or Finder.

If you use SideKick infrequently, it makes more sense to set up a disk with the system software and your utilities on it, and put SideKick and its data files on a separate disk. SideKick will prompt you to insert that disk as needed.

⚫ *text attributes are preserved in the Scrapbook*

When you Copy or Cut text into the Scrapbook, it looks like it's been converted to 12-point Geneva plain text, but in reality, none of the text formatting characteristics are lost. You get them back when the text is pasted into any application that can handle them.

very good
feature

⚫ *Scrapbook index*

If your Scrapbook is crammed full of stuff, you can reduce the time you spend scrolling through it by creating an index for it in your word processor, and printing it out. Then you can use the scroll bar at the bottom of the Scrapbook to move directly to the page you want.

⚫ *Copying to and from the Calculator*

Few people realize that you can Copy and Paste to and from the Calculator with the same standard techniques used with other Macintosh applications. If you're dealing with a

very good
feature

complex calculation within a word processor or some other application that doesn't do math, Copy the calculation into the Calculator and Paste the result to your document.

Chapter 5

Miscellaneous system software and utilities

Switcher tips

⚫ minimum memory allotments

For maximum efficiency, use at least as much memory as is listed below when setting up Switcher partitions:

very
hot
tip

program	minimum recommended memory allotment
Chart	192K
Excel	304K-512K
File	288K
Finder	128K
MacWrite	144K
MacDraw	128K
MacPaint	128K
MacPaint/ClickArt Effects	190K
Multiplan	128K–160K
PageMaker	256K
Paint Cutter	244K
Red Ryder	128K
Word	160K

♦ converting the Clipboard

Switcher offers you a choice of two methods for dealing with the Clipboard when switching from one partition to another. If you choose 'Always convert Clipboard', anything you copy to the Clipboard in one partition will be available in all the other partitions. If you choose 'Don't always convert Clipboard', each partition will maintain its own Clipboard.

Selecting 'Always convert Clipboard' takes up extra memory unnecessarily and slows down switching dramatically. 'Don't always convert Clipboard' is the almost always the better choice, because you can still· convert the Clipboard on a case-by-case basis whenever necessary (by holding down the OPTION key when switching).

One time you should use 'Always convert Clipboard' is when the reason you're running Switcher is to transfer many separate chunks of data between applications. In that case, it's silly to always have to hold down the OPTION key.

♦ using the same program in two partitions

important
warning

Most programs, while running, use one or more temporary files that are deleted when the program is terminated. If you put the same program in two or more different partitions of the Switcher, the program will get confused and not know which temp files belong to which partition.

There's a rather simple solution to this limitation, however. Most programs keep their temporary files on the disk from which they are launched. Therefore, if you want to run two copies of MacWrite, for example, use a copy of MacWrite on a disk in another drive for the second partition. (The disk with the second copy does not need a System and Finder.) This works with both hard disks and floppy disks.

❖ *putting the Finder in a partition*

When using Switcher it's very convenient to have the Finder loaded in a partition (if you have enough memory). This makes it possible to copy and delete files without having to quit all the applications you might have loaded. But be sure to load the Finder in the first partition. Otherwise you run a high risk of crashing.

important warning

❖ *quitting the Finder partition*

If you're running Switcher 4.9 or later and want to quit the Finder partition, look at the last item under Special menu. You'll find Quit where Shut Down would be if you weren't running Switcher. Choosing Quit in this case works just like choosing Quit from the File menu of an application: it frees up that partition and makes the memory it formally used available for launching another application.

❖ *running applications from the Finder partition*

If you're running a Finder partition, resist the temptation to run an application from there. The application will probably run, assuming there's enough memory allotted to the partition. But quitting an application started from the Finder partition will probably produce a bomb message—within minutes, if not within seconds.

important warning

MiniFinder tips

❖ *the MiniFinder*

The main purpose of the MiniFinder is to let you move from application to application without returning to the Desktop. This can save a lot of time, particularly if you're using a hard disk. To get to the MiniFinder, simply choose it under the Special menu on the Desktop.

Sometimes, however, you may need to return to the Desktop to move icons around, delete files, create new folders, etc. To do that, you just click on the Finder button in the MiniFinder. There's also a nice shortcut you can use instead. When quitting an application, hold down the OPTION key; the MiniFinder will be bypassed and you'll return directly to the Finder.

♠ one hard disk, many MiniFinders

very
hot
tip

You can create separate MiniFinders for different groups of applications on a hard disk. First, use the Use MiniFinder command on the Special menu to choose the applications you want to be grouped in an individual MiniFinder. Then rename that MiniFinder file. (For example, you could create a MiniFinder containing MacWrite, Word, PageMaker and ThinkTank and call it "Word Processing.")

You can now install the MiniFinder named Word Processing into your main MiniFinder. When you click on the Word Processing button there, you'll find yourself in the Word Processing MiniFinder—with just four buttons: MacWrite, Word, PageMaker and ThinkTank—rather than in an application (as you usually are when you click on a button in the MiniFinder).

You can nest one MiniFinder within another for as many levels as you want. This sort of hierarchical structure can be very useful on a hard disk. Another solution to the same problem is to use one of the desk accessories that allow you to go directly from one application to another, such as SkipFinder (see Chapter 14 for details).

If you often proceed directly from one particular program to another, or work with a small set of programs, it makes more sense to install them in one MiniFinder file. But be aware that you can't select files from different folders to create a MiniFinder; they all have to be in the same folder.

❖ *quitting the MiniFinder with Finder 4.3 and earlier*

If you're using the OPTION key when quitting an application to bypass the MiniFinder and go directly to the Desktop, be careful to avoid also holding down the COMMAND key. If you hold down OPTION and COMMAND while quitting an application, Finder 4.3 (or earlier) will automatically rebuild the Desktop file and rename all your folders "Unnamed #__ ."

Fortunately, this problem has been fixed in Finder 5.3. This newer version of the Finder displays a dialog box that asks you if you're sure you want to rebuild the Desktop. And even if you tell it to, your folder names will be retained.

very good feature

Programming tips

❖ *out of memory message in Mac Pascal*

Macintosh Pascal programs sometimes give you an "out of memory" error. To get around it, try hiding all the windows (with the Hide All command) and then only use the windows as needed by the program. Open program windows consume up to 20% of the available memory on a 512K Mac.

❖ *Version 2.1 of Microsoft BASIC vs. version 2.0*

Version 2.1 of Microsoft BASIC is quite a bit faster than version 2.0. In a test conducted by BYTE magazine, version 2.0 took 113 seconds to run the Sieve of Eratosthenes (a famous benchmark), while version 2.1 only took 58 seconds.

❖ *speeding up printouts in Microsoft BASIC 2.0*

Microsoft BASIC 2.0 is very slow when printing listings on the ImageWriter using the Print option from the File menu. Here are some commands that will speed things up:

LPRINT CHR$(27)+"C":LPRINT DATE$,TIME$:LPRINT:LLIST

Put them in the Note Pad, then Paste them into the BASIC Command window. (The printout will have date and time annotations, but not boldfaced keywords).

undocumented commands in Microsoft BASIC 2.0

Microsoft BASIC offers a variety of undocumented keyboard shortcuts for common commands. These commands do not appear on the screen until you press RETURN. For example, if you press OPTION-L, the letter L will appear on your screen, but if you then hit RETURN, the letter L changes to AND, which is the command OPTION-L stands for.

It makes more sense to type out some of the simple commands rather than try to memorize all the keyboard shortcuts, but some of the more commonly used shortcuts for commands such as 'PRINT' or 'STRING$' can be quite useful.

Note that these keyboard shortcuts are case sensitive (that is, it makes a difference whether you type in a lowercase or a capital letter). That's particularly important to remember if you usually enter your BASIC programs all in caps.

important
warning

this statement produced by:	this key sequence:	this statement produced by:	this key sequence:
AND	OPTION-L	ASC	OPTION-A
ATN	OPTION-C	CVS	OPTION-a
DATA	OPTION-c	EQU	OPTION-X
IMP	OPTION-B	LOC	OPTION-*
LOF	OPTION-4	LOG	OPTION-3
LSET	OPTION-6	MID$	OPTION-8
MKD$	OPTION-7	MKI$	OPTION-s
MKS$	OPTION-r	MOD	OPTION-N
NEXT	OPTION-g	NOT	OPTION-Y
ON	OPTION-2	OPEN	OPTION-e

OR	OPTION-:	PRINT	OPTION-u
PUT	OPTION-=	READ	OPTION-'
REM	OPTION-O	RETU	OPTION-5
RIGHT$	OPTION-+	RND	OPTION-,
RSET	OPTION-.	SGN	OPTION-y
SIN	OPTION-m	SPAC	OPTION-d
SQR	OPTION-w	STATIC	OPTION-W
STRING$	OPTION-p	STR$	OPTION-P
TAN	OPTION-b	THEN	OPTION-T
TO	OPTION-R	USING	OPTION-E
VAL	OPTION-0	XOR	OPTION-Z
WEND	OPTION-z	WHILE	OPTION-'
WRITE	OPTION-o		

◆ *printing with Microsoft BASIC versions 1.00 and 1.01*

Microsoft BASIC 1.00 and 1.01 do not require the ImageWriter driver to print, so you can safely delete it to free up disk space.

Advanced tips

◆ *determining System version with ResEdit*

ResEdit, Apple's resource editor, can be used to find out what version of the System you're running. To do that, start ResEdit and double-click on the System file. Scroll through the resource file to the STR resource, and double-click on it to open it. When the STR resource is opened, scroll until you see the STR with ID=0. Double click on ID=0 and you'll see the version number and creation date of the System.

Be careful not to change any values. Even when you're just looking, it's always smarter to use a copy of the System file rather than the original.

⬢ *meanings of 'file descriptor flags'*

The Macintosh file directory keeps a description of each file, which includes a set of file flags (or "bits"). These can be turned on or off with several programs, including Fedit ($30) and a desk accessory called SetFile ($10—see Appendix C for addresses).

Here's an alphabetized list of the flags, with their meanings:

Bozo—This file is copy-protected. (This is an obsolete method of copy protection, ignored by Finder versions 5.0 and later.)

Bundle—The Finder won't display this file's icon unless it's set ON.

Busy—This file is open (currently being used).

Changed—This file has been changed since the very first time it was saved. (As you can imagine, most files have this flag set ON.)

Inited—(Pronounced 'in-IT-ed'.) This file's icon has been given a specific location on the Desktop. (If you create a document from within an application, it won't be inited until you quit the application and return to the Desktop.

Invisible—The Finder won't display this file's icon.

Locked—The Finder can't delete, rename, or replace this file. (This is the only flag that can be changed without a special utility like Fedit or SetFile.)

Protected—The Finder can't move or duplicate this file.

System—This is a system file.

🍎 *clearing memory with the programmer's switch*

The programmer's switch is handy to restart your system, but you should be aware that it doesn't completely clear all of memory or start the self-diagnostic routines. You'll have to turn off the system with the power switch if you need to start with a completely reset system.

Morning Light. Copyright © 1984 by Gerald Clement.

Part II—

Maximizing application programs

Chapter 6

Word processing

General word processing tips
(Unless otherwise indicated, all tips in this section refer to version 4.5 of MacWrite and version 1.05 of Word.)

⬥ estimating the number of words in a document

To get the most accurate word count of a MacWrite or Word document, use one of the many spelling checkers that give you this information. But if you don't need to be absolutely precise, you can just divide the number of characters by six.

Some people divide by five, but it's hard to figure how they arrive at that number, since anywhere this side of 3rd grade, there are more than five characters in an average word. We're sure of that because for many years Arthur used a word processing program that gave him both word and character counts; he divided one into the other countless times—in order to decide this very issue—and always came up with a number very close to six. Since he doesn't use a lot of fancy, sesquipedalian words (except for that one), most normal writing should average about the same.

(Maybe they came up with five-characters-per-word by not counting spaces. That might explain it.)

Since Word displays the number of characters in a document in the lower left corner of the screen immediately after you save, all you have to do is divide that figure by six. There's also desk accessory called *wc* (for "word count") that very quickly counts the number of words and lines in Word documents; it's described in chapter 14.)

MacWrite doesn't count words or characters—although you can of course get a character count by exiting to the Desktop and using the Get Info command. But from within MacWrite you can get the number of K (kilobytes) in the document you're working on (it's in the About MacWrite... window on the menu, and that's enough for a quick and dirty word count estimate. Here's how you figure it:

There are 1024 characters in a K (except when someone is trying to sell you a disk drive) and 1024 divided by 6 equals 170.67—for you, 170. So to get the number of words in a document, you can just multiply the number of K by 170.

Here's a table with some convenient (but approximate) conversions:

1K = 170 words	30K = 5000 words
3K = 500 words	50K = 8500 words
6K = 1000 words	60K = 10,000 words
10K = 1700 words	75K = 12,500 words
15K = 2500 words	100K = 17,000 words

To make your estimate more accurate, you should subtract some figure for the "overhead" of your word processing program. For example, if you open a new (empty) MacWrite document and immediately save it, you'll find that it contains 1148 bytes (although there are no words in it). As you add rulers and other formatting instructions, the amount of overhead increases.

A good rule of thumb is to subtract 2K for overhead in MacWrite documents of less than 40K, and 5% in documents larger than that. But you should up those figures if you change the font, type style, type size, margins and other formatting parameters a lot.

Finally, be aware that graphics will inflate the figures for both the number of K and the number of characters in a document, thus throwing your calculations off.

● selecting large amounts of text

When you want to select a large amount of text, your first impulse may be to start at the beginning and drag until you reach the end, waiting patiently while MacWrite scrolls through your document. To speed things up, try the shift-click method:

Click the pointer at the beginning of the text you want to select, then use the scroll bar to move to the end of the selection, hold down the SHIFT key, and click the pointer where you want the selection to end. All the text between the two clicks will be selected.

This technique also works if you start at the end of the selection and shift-click at the beginning. (Shift-clicking is a general Mac tip that works with many applications. For more details, see the tip on it in the 'Miscellaneous basic tips' section of chapter 1.) Word offers a number of other ways to select large amounts of text. See the entry on selecting text in the Word section below.

● finding your place in a document

very
hot
tip

When you open a MacWrite document, it displays the screen you were looking at when you last saved it. That isn't always where the insertion point is, or where you were last working. To get to that place, hit the ENTER key. (You can also get there by hitting any key that generates a character, but then you have to delete the character when you get there; ENTER leaves no mark.) This same technique is also useful when you're looking through a document and have lost track of where you were working.

But—if you had some part of the document selected when you last saved, it will be deleted (technically, it will be replaced with the ENTER character, which is invisible). You can still recover the deleted text with Undo (COMMAND-Z)—assuming you realize what happened before the next mouse click or keystroke.

For this and other reasons, it's a good idea—except in certain special situations—to *never leave part of a MacWrite document selected when you close it.* For that matter, it's a good idea never to leave text selected in a document any longer than you have to, even while you're working on it. You might go off somewhere else and forget about it, and then accidentally delete it.

You don't run this danger in Word, because it ignores selected text when saving (that is, if text is selected before you save, it won't be afterwards). But you can't use ENTER to find your place in a Word document that you've saved, because Word always places the insertion point at the beginning of the document after saving.

🍎 *text markers*

Neither MacWrite nor Microsoft Word has a specific function that lets you mark places in a document so you can return to them later. But it's easy enough to do that simply by inserting unique characters (like '&&1', '&&2', and so on, or any other combination of characters that wouldn't appear in normal text). Then you just use the Find command to move to these points in your document quickly. This technique will work with any word processing program available for the Macintosh.

🍎 *deleting text without flushing the Clipboard*

If you're keeping a picture or important text in the Clipboard for later use, it's important not to unintentionally flush the Clipboard's contents by using Cut from the Edit menu (or the keyboard shortcut COMMAND-X). To avoid this, delete the text by hitting the BACKSPACE key rather than COMMAND-X. (You can still change your mind and restore what you deleted by choosing Undo Typing from the Edit menu or by using the keyboard shortcut COMMAND-Z.)

**important
warning**

❂ *aligning columns*

When setting up a table (or anything else with columns in it) in MacWrite or Word, always use tabs—never spaces—to align the columns. If you use spaces, the columns will almost never print out straight. (But see the next entry for an even better way to deal with multiple columns.)

❂ *multiple columns*

MacWrite won't automatically format text in more than one column, and while Word will, it won't show the columns on the screen. Thus in both programs it's very difficult to create tables. One solution is to use a spreadsheet program like Multiplan or Excel to create the table, then Paste the information into a word processing document. The tabs you've set in your word processing program will determine where the spreadsheet columns will appear.

❂ File Edit Search Character Paragraph Document Workshee

═ClickOn™ Worksheet #1═

	A	B	C ⁻	D	E	F	G	H	I
1									
2		1st	2nd	3rd	4th				
3	Alderman	4.3	3.9	3.8	5.6				
4	Coleman	4.1	3.7	3.6	5.5				
5	Michel	4.2	4.1	4.1	5.3				
6	Naiman	4.3	3.7	3.7	5.0				
7									
8	Total	16.9	15.4	15.2	21.4				
9									

The ClickOn Worksheet desk accessory

bargain

If you create tables frequently, you really should get ClickOn WorkSheet (originally published by T/Maker, but purchased by Borland in late 1986). It's a small but full-featured spreadsheet in the form of a desk accessory, so you don't have to keep exiting your word processing program every time you want to make a table. It's so easy to Cut and Paste back and forth between ClickOn Worksheet and your word processing document that it's just about as good as having a multiple-column feature built right into the word processor.

▤□▭▭▭▭▭▭▭ Annual Report to the President ▭▭▭▭▭▭▭▭

The following table shows quarterly sales (in thousands of dollars) by the top sales people for each quarter in 1986:

	1st	2nd	3rd	4th
Alderman	4.3	3.9	3.8	5.6
Coleman	4.1	3.7	3.6	5.5
Michel	4.2	4.1	4.1	5.3
Naiman	4.3	3.7	3.7	5.0
Total	16.9	15.4	15.2	21.4

Table from ClickOn Worksheet pasted into a word processing document

🍎 *mixing words and pictures*

Neither MacWrite or Word will let you put text on the same line as a graphic you've pasted in, with two exceptions. One is that in the header and footer of a MacWrite document, you can place the special icons for page number, date and time on top of graphics and they'll print out there. The second is that you can assemble images that include text in a graphics program and then Paste them into the word processor.

New word processing programs just coming out as this book is being written do let you put text of all sorts next to graphics anywhere in a document. For example, the word processing module of Microsoft Works lets you place text on either side of your picture—although it does lack many other power features. (For more information on the next generation of word processors, be sure to send away for the free updates to this book. Look inside the cover for details.)

⚫ distorted graphics

You may notice some distortion when you paste MacPaint pictures, especially ones that contain circles, into word processing programs. This is because word processors typically squeeze the image of the page to make it narrower, in order to make text look better when printed out on the ImageWriter.

To correct this distortion, choose Tall Adjusted in the Page Setup window. Your text will now print out wider on the ImageWriter than usual, but graphics will look just the way they do when you print them directly from MacPaint.

⚫ editing italicized text

Because italicized text (as displayed on the Mac's screen) bends over so far, it's sometimes difficult to tell just where a given character falls. If you try to select it, you often get one of its neighbors.

very
hot
tip

The more you work with italicized text, the better your eye gets, and the less this problem bothers you, but it's often easier just to change the text to plain, do your editing, and then change it back to italic again.

Another useful technique is double-clicking to select words. You may not be able to figure out exactly where they begin, but the Mac can do it for you.

⚫ spacing after italics

On the ImageWriter (and the Mac's screen), italics bend so far over that they crowd, or even run into, the plain-text characters that follow them. This is particularly a problem when the last italic character and/or the first plain character is a lowercase b, d, f, h, k or l or a capital letter. (On the LaserWriter, things are easier. Laser fonts are designed so that the italic characters don't crowd the following plain text.)

Putting two spaces after the italics gives you too much room. The solution is to use Option Space, which produces a space that's larger than a regular one but smaller than two (you get it, of course, by holding down the OPTION key while hitting the space bar). See the next entry for more details.

⁣ *Option Space*

This character, generated by holding down the OPTION key while hitting the space bar, has two unique features. The first is that it's always a *hard space*—which means that if it falls at the end of a line, it won't break; instead, it will drag the word before and after it down to the next line. This is useful when you want to keep phrases like WW II and J. B. S. Haldane all on the same line, but can make for a very uneven right margin (or, if your text is justified, for lines with very loose spacing).

very good
feature

The second feature is that, in some fonts, Option Space is wider than a regular space (but narrower than two). This is also useful for keeping italic characters from leaning into the plain text that follows them (see the previous entry).

The easiest way to see if a font makes the Option Space wider is to type a character (let's say you use X), hit the space bar five times, type another X, hit RETURN, type X, hold down the OPTION key and hit the space bar five times, and type a final X. If Option Space is wider than regular spaces, the second X on the second line will be to the right of the one on the first line; if Option Space is the same width as the regular spaces, the Xs will line up.

very good
feature

The wider Option Space only occurs in proportionally spaced fonts (which is what most Mac fonts are); in monospaced fonts like Monaco, hard spaces are always the same width as regular spaces.

This combining of two features into Option Space is far from ideal. When you want a hard space, you normally don't

things
to come

want a wide space, and when you want a wide space, you normally don't want a hard space. Eliminating the wider space only solves half the problem. Hopefully some savvy font designer will soon start providing hard spaces and wide spaces as separate characters (Option Space and Command Space, say).

♦ em dashes, en dashes and hyphens

An *em dash* is the technical name for what people normally just call a dash—there's one right there. (It gets its name from the fact that it was originally the same width as a capital M). An *en dash* is half the length of an em dash and is used to indicate ranges of numbers (1926–66) or as a minus sign. (It gets its name from the fact that it was originally the same width as a lowercase n.) Hyphens are shorter than either. Here's a comparison of the three:

em dash   —
en dash   –
hyphen   -

very good
feature

On the Mac, you get an em dash by holding down the OPTION and SHIFT keys while hitting the hyphen key, and you get an en dash by holding down the OPTION key and hitting the hyphen key.

♦ nonproportional printing

On rare occasions you may want to produce a Mac document that doesn't have proportional spacing. Just format the entire document in Monaco (or any other monospaced font). The result will look a lot like a traditional typewritten page.

♦ MacWrite to Word and vice-versa

MacWrite 4.5 can only accept Word documents that have been saved as 'text only', but Word can convert formatted

MacWrite documents and preserve the formatting (pictures, graphs, everything).

To bring a MacWrite document into Word, just enter Word and open the document. To bring a Word document into MacWrite, you have to first save it as 'text only' (from within Word), then quit Word, enter MacWrite, close the Untitled document that appears, and open the document you want to convert. In both cases you'll get a dialog box telling you that the document is being converted and will open as Untitled.

⚜ *recovering trashed MacWrite documents*

If you have a MacWrite document MacWrite itself can't read, try reading it with Word (enter Word, go to the Open list box, open the document and click OK when Word tells you it's converting it). Word is somewhat more sophisticated in this area than MacWrite and will sometimes succeed where MacWrite failed.

⚜ *MacWrite and Word have different margin defaults*

One problem with converting documents from MacWrite to Word is that Word's default left margin is 0 while MacWrite's ruler comes preset with an eighth-inch indent. To reset the indent to zero once you've got the document in Word, select the entire document, choose Formats on the Paragraph menu, and enter a zero in the Left Indent box.

⚜ *importing word processing documents to the Mac*

If you need to import a word processing document from another type of computer to the Mac, the first step takes place on the foreign computer. Regardless of the word processing program being used, save the document as a text file. Some word processing programs call text files "ASCII" (which, in case you're interested, stands for "American standard code for information interchange" and is pronounced 'ASK-ee').

If you neglect this step, you almost certainly won't be able to use the document after it gets to the Mac, because most word processing programs embed formatting codes in the text that appear as gibberish on the Mac's screen.

bargain

Unfortunately, WordStar won't allow you save a document as a text file (although it will let you create text-only documents from scratch). If you need to import WordStar documents, you'll be happy to hear there's a public domain utility called UnWS that strips out the unwanted embedded format commands from the WordStar document. (It was written by Paul Hoffman, who also contributed several tips to this book.)

⚫ *excess carriage returns in imported documents*

Sometimes when you transfer a document created on another computer into a word processing program on the Mac, you'll find carriage returns at the end of each line. Since MacWrite, Word and most other Mac word processors only use carriage returns to mark the end of paragraphs, having them at the end of every line which will make the text look ragged and strange, you'll need to remove all the excess ones.

very good feature

If you're using MacWrite, you'll have to go through the document and remove each carriage return manually, but Word's Change command can search for carriage returns and thus will do the job automatically. See the entry on this same subject in the Word section below for details on how to do that.

⚫ *custom letterhead*

There are no particular tricks for creating a letterhead—although creating a nice one requires a great deal of skill and taste. But here's a trick on how to deal with one once it's been created:

Assuming you have access to the Mac and its printer on a regular basis, don't waste your time printing out blank sheets of letterhead that you'll then have to feed one by one into the printer when you want to use them. Instead, create a dummy letterhead document with your letterhead at the top and a few words in the font you use for letters below it. Here's a sample, using Fluent Fonts' Monterey and Monterey Medium, from Casady:

Jack Twiller
512 Pet-de-Loup Boulevard
Halitosis ND 58353
701/ 555-1941

Month 00, 1987

Dear

Save this document as 'letterhead' or some similar name. Then every time you want to write a letter, open it and immediately Save As under whatever name is appropriate for the letter you're going write.

Then select 'Month 00' and change it (unless the date actually happens to be Month 00), then place the insertion point after 'Dear' and begin writing. When you print out the letter, the letterhead will print out at the top.

You can (and probably should) have more than one letterhead for use with different sorts of letters (business, personal, etc.)

If you have a specialized signature, you can either make it the last item in your dummy letterhead document or drop it in from the Scrapbook. Here's one Arthur uses:

Of course there's no need for *you* to feel limited to something as stodgy as this.

(The gorilla was drawn by master Mac artist Mei-Ying Dell'Aquilla and is available on the ClickArt Personal Graphics disk from T/Maker.)

Basic MacWrite tips
(Unless otherwise indicated, all the tips in this section refer to version 4.5.)

✸ maximum screen width

Because it doesn't have horizontal scrolling, MacWrite only lets you to see 6-1/8 inches of text on the screen—if you want the scroll bar to stay its full width—or 6-1/4 inches if you don't mind a thin scroll bar.

To display the maximum width possible, first move the MacWrite window as far as you can into the upper left corner of the screen (it doesn't come up in that position). Then use the size box to stretch the window as far right and down as possible (either leaving the scroll bar full width or squeezing it down, as you wish). If the ruler isn't showing, choose Show Rulers on the Format menu. Then move the little black triangles that mark the margins to 1" on the left and to either one or two marks past 7" on the right.

You can still see all your text if the scroll bar cuts the right margin marker in half. But if the marker is any more hidden than that, the last letters on some lines will be cut off.

❤ *maximum print width*

Although MacWrite only allows you to display documents on the screen up to 6-1/8 or 6-1/4 inches wide (without a lot of incredibly inconvenient window-moving), you can print documents up to 7" wide on the ImageWriter. You should only expand the margins to 7" when you're about to print, because it's very hard to edit with lines of text that are wider than the screen.

To do expand the margins, drag the MacWrite window way off to the left, then use the size box to stretch it as far to the right as it will go—which will be to 8-1/4". (If the ruler isn't showing, choose Show Rulers on the Format menu.) Then move the right margin marker as far right as it will go—which will be to 8". Since you can move the left margin marker to 1", this gives you a print width of 7".

❤ *minimum tab spacing*

Tabs in MacWrite can be no closer than 3/16" to each other or to a margin.

❤ *deleting words*

Double-clicking on a word in MacWrite highlights the word, but not the spaces on either side. If you BACKSPACE to delete the word, you'll have to BACKSPACE again to delete the remaining extra space.

The solution? Use Cut (COMMAND-X) instead of BACKSPACE. This deletes the space to the left of the word along with the word itself.

❡ *aligning text*

Text in MacWrite can be aligned four ways:

- flush left (the left margin is straight but the right isn't)
- flush right (the right margin is straight but the left isn't)
- justified (both margins are straight)
- centered.

There are two ways to change the alignment. If you're changing the alignment of a lot of text, insert a ruler and click on the appropriate text-alignment box in it. Then go to where you want the alignment to revert to what it was before, insert another ruler and click on the appropriate text-alignment box in it.

If you're changing the alignment of a small amount of text (from a single line to a few paragraphs), it's easier just to select the text and chose the appropriate alignment command from the Format menu. You can also use keyboard commands for each kind of alignment:

centered — COMMAND-M

flush left — COMMAND-N   *flush right* — COMMAND-R

justified — COMMAND-J

(The M in COMMAND-M stands for 'middle'—or at least it's useful to assume it does. COMMAND-N is the only one of the four commands that isn't mnemonic, and you can remember that—if your mind is as weird as Arthur's—by telling yourself that it stands for 'nonmnemonic'.)

Alignment of text is a paragraph function, which means that these commands change all the text from one carriage return to the next. So to change a whole paragraph (or a single line ending in a carriage return), you don't have to select it all before giving the alignment command—just click anywhere in it.

There is a down side to this. To make a small piece of text at the start of a line automatically align left and another small piece at the end of the same line automatically align right, you have to center or justify the line and then put a lot of spaces in the middle of it—which is what we did to create the middle line of the table above. (But also see the next entry.)

✎ *right-aligned tabs*

MacWrite has no built-in right-aligned tab feature, but you can simulate them when needed. All you have to do is insert a ruler, move the right margin 3/16" or more to the right of its present position, and add a decimal tab where the old right margin was. (This will only work for text that doesn't include periods.)

✎ *an easy way to change fonts, styles and sizes*

Say you're writing a document in 12-point Chicago plain with subheads in 18-point Oblique bold italic. Switching between the two can cost you a lot of keystrokes and trips to the menu bar. But there's an easier way to do it (it may sound a little confusing when you read about it, but just try it).

shortcut

Let's say you just finished typing a paragraph (in 12-point Chicago) and now you want to type a new subhead. Just go to another subhead somewhere nearby and select any character in it. Then Copy that character and Paste it where you want the new subhead to be, select it, and start to type. What you type will be in the font, size and style of the other subhead (18-point Oblique bold italic, or whatever).

When you're inserting text into some already-existing text (instead of adding it on to the end of a new file you're creating), you often don't have to do any Copying. Let's say you've finished typing the subhead and want to go back to your text font. If the text immediately after the subhead is in the text font, just select the first character in it and begin typing. The character you selected will be deleted, so be sure to retype it at the end of what you're inserting.

(The reason for selecting the first character is that the space in front of the text may be in a different font, style and/or size than the text itself. Often it will be the same and all you'll have to do is click in the space, but it's different enough of the time that you're better off always selecting the first letter as a matter of habit.)

This also works if the text immediately before the place where you want to make your insertion is in the font you want. In that case, you begin by retyping the character you selected, then go on to type your insertion.

font styles in headers and footers

You can have multiple fonts and font sizes in MacWrite headers and footers, but the automatic page number, date and time always print out in the format of the first character. For example, if you boldface the first word of your header, then use plain text for the following lines, the page number will be bold—regardless of the text surrounding it.

very hot tip

One elegant way around this problem is to precede the first character of the header or footer with a space and then simply format that space with the font, style and size you want the automatic features to print out in.

defects in MacWrite's search function

The Find... and Change... commands on MacWrite's Search menu are two of the most limited functions of the program.

They won't let you do "case-sensitive" searches (that is, they ignore whether letters are caps or lowercase), you can't search for carriage returns, and sometimes the item found isn't visible on the screen, even after you move the Search window around to get it out of the way.

very bad feature

❡ *Tempo macros in MacWrite*

Tempo is a desk accessory that lets you create "macro commands"—combination commands that include one or more smaller commands within them. This can be very useful in MacWrite, which doesn't even have a way to save or print from the keyboard.

very good feature

Commands you create with Tempo override built-in keyboard commands. To help you avoid doing that, here's an alphabetical list of MacWrite's commands (with mnemonics in parentheses and italics, where they exist and aren't obvious):

COMMAND +	effect	COMMAND +	effect
b	bold	p	plain text
c	Copy	s	shadow
h	superscript *(high)*	u	underline
i	italic	v	Paste
l	subscript *(low)*	x	Cut *(x out)*
o	outline	z	Undo

That leaves the following characters available: **a, d, e, f, g, j, k, m, n, q, r, t, w, y**. You can also use any number, any symbol or any capital letter (i.e., any COMMAND-SHIFT character except the numbers).

❡ *poor man's Glossaries in MacWrite*

MacWrite has nó provision for what Word calls "Glossaries" (pieces of text that can be quickly substituted for a short code you type in, a feature that's quite useful for entering repetitive phrases). One way around this lack in MacWrite works as follows:

Use two or three unique characters as abbreviations for the longer text. For example, you might type 'tmb' every time you want the phrase 'The Macintosh Bible' to appear. Then, when you've finished entering your text, just use the Change command on the Search menu to substitute 'The Macintosh Bible' for 'tmb' everywhere it appears in the document.

Many people find this technique of using abbreviations more convenient than permanently setting up Glossaries.

⚫ *footnotes in MacWrite*

MacWrite doesn't have a footnote feature, but you can create documents with endnotes with just a little extra effort. Use the Note Pad (or an improvement on it like Super Note Pad or MiniWriter) to store your footnotes as you write, then Paste them all at the end of your document. If you're really patient, you can even Paste them at the bottom of the appropriate pages, thus creating true footnotes, but this is a lot of work.

If you regularly create documents with footnotes, consider getting Microsoft Word, which has excellent footnoting capabilities.

⚫ *larger top and bottom margins*

The default settings for both the top and bottom margin in MacWrite is one inch. Increasing them will give your printed document a more professional appearance. To do that, just add lines below the text in the header and footer. If you don't want any text printed in the header and footer, just hit RETURN several times.

🍎 *underlining*

When you select some text and choose Underline from the Style menu (or hit COMMAND-U), everything, including spaces, is underlined. If you want to underline the words but not the spaces between them, you have to select each word (by clicking on it twice) and underline it individually.

🍎 *changing the ruler in large documents*

If you've ever changed the formatting of a ruler that controlled a large section of a MacWrite document, you know it can take forever for the document to reformat to the new ruler settings. (It even takes a while if there are no changes, since MacWrite still has to go through and check.) This can get to be pretty frustrating, particularly if you need to make several changes (both margins, the line indent marker and a couple of tabs, say), since you have to wait after each change.

There's an easy way around this—just insert a new ruler right below the one you want to change (either with the Insert Ruler command or by Cutting and Pasting the ruler you want), then change the old ruler. Since there's no text between the old ruler and the new ruler, you won't have to wait for reformatting. When you've got the old ruler the way you want it, delete the new one. The document will now reformat to the new settings, but you'll only have to sit through the process once.

very
hot
tip

🍎 *text formatting in headers and footers*

The text you have in the header and footer of a MacWrite document is not affected by any font, style or formatting changes you make to the text in the body of the document. You have to Open the header and footer (from the Format menu) to change their margins or any other formatting characteristic of them.

♦ *trouble printing*

Sometimes MacWrite won't obey your command to print a document. Usually you get a message that reads "MacWrite cannot print this document," but other times nothing happens. There are at least four reasons why MacWrite won't be able to print a document.

1. The text is too long. Try printing a few pages at a time.

2. The disk is so full that there's no room for the temporary print file MacWrite creates every time it prints a document. Print a few pages at a time, or delete unneeded files from the disk.

3. The wrong printer resource is selected. Check the Chooser desk accessory to make sure that you've selected the correct printer (ImageWriter, LaserWriter or whatever you're using) and that MacWrite knows which port (on the back of the machine) the printer is connected to.

4. The cables aren't properly connected, or the printer is either turned off or "off-line" (not paying attention to what the computer tells it). On the ImageWriter, the Select button toggles the printer between on-line and off-line.

♦ *title pages*

To create a MacWrite document with an unnumbered title page, choose Title Page from the Format menu. No header, footer, or page number information will appear on the first page.

If you want the page right after the title page (the second page of the document) to be numbered 1, choose Set Page # from the Format menu and set the number to 0 (zero). (There's one tiny drawback to doing this—you won't be able to print the title page all by itself unless you set the beginning page number back to 1.)

✎ *automatic collation on the LaserWriter*

One nice thing about MacWrite is that when it prints on the LaserWriter, it outputs the last page first. This saves you having to collate the pages the way you do with Word and many other programs. (Of course if you're printing more than one copy, you'll still have to do some collating, but at least the pages will be in the right order.)

very good feature

✎ *"Too many paragraphs for this document"*

Occasionally MacWrite may give you the above message. That's because it keeps track of carriage returns and rulers rather than words (most other word processors count words). This lets MacWrite scroll quickly, at least when compared to Microsoft Word.

Apple says that your document can have 500 paragraphs on a 128K Mac and 2000 on a 512K Mac, so you only need worry about a "too many paragraphs" message if you create very heavily formatted documents on a 128K machine. (But Arthur got the message on a 1-meg machine, because he was trying to put too many lines into headers and footers.)

There is a klugy way around this problem, but it won't work with justified text, and you have to indent the first line of every paragraph. Put the indentation arrow flush with the left margin arrow on the ruler, and set a tab for the indent you want. Then press the tab key instead of RETURN to end each paragraph. This will fool MacWrite into thinking that you have fewer paragraphs than you do.

✎ *centering text top to bottom*

Here's a simple way to center text between the top and bottom of the page in a MacWrite document:

very hot tip

1. Remove all blank lines from top of the page to the beginning of the text.

2. Go to the end of the text you want vertically centered and add RETURNs until you see the page-break marker.

3. Move the I-beam to the middle of the blank lines, select from there to the end of the page, and Cut the highlighted blank lines.

4. Move to the top of the page and Paste the blank lines you cut.

(This will only work if you've removed the headers and footers, or if they are of exactly the same length.)

🍎 *minimum free disk space required*

If your MacWrite data disk is close to full, you may get a message that reads, "The disk is too full to create a new document." MacWrite needs at least 11K of disk space available for the temporary files it sets up when creating a new document.

🍎 *current version*

The current version of MacWrite, as of December, 1986, is 4.5. If you have an earlier version, take your master disk to any authorized Apple Dealer and they'll give you version 4.5 for free.

🍎 *MacWrite on 128K Macs*

If you have a 128K Mac and deal with relatively short documents, you'll get much better performance using the memory-based version of MacWrite (2.2) than you will with the disk-based version (4.5).

But you do run the risk of running out of available RAM when you use 2.2 for longer documents on a 128K Mac. You can check how much memory remains available for your document by choosing About MacWrite from the menu.

MacWrite 2.2 on 1-meg Macs

If, for some unaccountable reason, you want to use the RAM-based version of MacWrite (2.2) on a 1-meg Mac, you'll find your maximum document size will be something like 337K.

gossip/
trivia

don't use MacWrite 3.95

MacWrite 3.95, an earlier version of MacWrite 4.5, was never officially released, and should not be used, since it's buggy. If you have version 3.95, take your master MacWrite disk to any authorized Apple Dealer, who will give you a copy of version 4.5 at no charge.

important
warning

Advanced MacWrite tips

(Unless otherwise indicated, all the tips in this section refer to version 4.5.)

leading control in MacWrite

Leading (pronounced LEHD-ing, not LEED-ing) is a typesetter's term that refers to the space between lines of text. MacWrite doesn't offer the automatic leading control that Microsoft Word does, but you can exert some limited control over leading by using the following technique:

To change the leading between two lines of text, select a blank space in the second line and change it to a different size. (You're limited to six sizes: 9-, 10-, 12-, 14-, 18- and 24-point.) That line will then adjust itself accordingly. When you're satisfied with the results, repeat the procedure for each successive line of text.

● *making the default window wider*

If you want MacWrite's window to cover the whole screen without having to stretch it each time you enter the program, you can permanently change its size with the system utility ResEdit. But remember the first rule of ResEdit: only modify a *copy*, not the original.

Here's how you do it: open MacWrite with ResEdit, open WIND, and change ID=301. New boundsRect should be 38, -58, 337, 550. If wanted, change the ID 302 (header) and 303 (footer) windows to 45, -58, 205, 550.

● *printer delay at end of printout*

Printing with MacWrite 4.5 on the ImageWriter can be pretty slow, and there's usually an extra delay when the printer gets to the end of your document—it pauses before advancing the paper to the bottom of the last page. The more blank space there is between the end of your document and the end of the last page, the longer the pause.

The solution is to click on the Cancel button (it shows on the screen while you're printing) when the last line of text on the last page has been printed. This makes the ImageWriter scroll the last page out immediately.

● *double-sided MacWrite printouts*

very
hot
tip

Both the LaserWriter and the ImageWriter II with a sheet feeder let you print out double-sided copies, but the method varies slightly because on the LaserWriter, MacWrite automatically collates the pages for you, printing the last page first. Here's how to do double-sided copies on both machines so that the correct pages will print back-to-back:

On the LaserWriter:

First print half as many copies of the document as you

need. Then arrange them so that the copies of page 2 are on the bottom, followed by the copies of page 1, followed by page 4, then page 3, page 6, page 5, and so on, continuing to count up by even numbers and subtracting 1 in between. If there are an odd number of pages in your document, set aside the copies of the last page and substitute blank pages for them in the pile.

Place the pile of arranged pages in the paper tray face up, with the top edge of the pages pointing towards the end of the tray that goes into the LaserWriter. Insert the tray and print the other half of the copies.

On the ImageWriter II with a sheet feeder:

First print half as many copies of the document as you need. Then arrange them so that the copies of page 2 are on the top, followed by the copies of page 1, followed by page 4, then page 3, page 6, page 5, and so on, continuing to count up by even numbers and subtracting 1 in between. If there are an odd number of pages in your document, set aside the copies of the last page and substitute blank pages for them in the pile.

Place the pile of arranged pages in the input tray so that you can see the printing, with the top edge of the pages facing down. Print the other half of the copies.

⚫ *inserting text without the mouse*

If you want to insert some text at a point that's only a few words back from where you're typing, you don't need to move your hand from the keyboard to the mouse and reposition the insertion point. Just backspace to where you want to insert, type in the new text, then hold down the COMMAND and BACKSPACE keys. MacWrite will retype the text you backspaced over.

MacWrite only stores 50 characters deleted with the BACKSPACE key, so if you backspace more than that, you'll lose some text. And, from a practical point of view, if you need to go back more than four or five words, it's probably quicker to use the mouse.

◉ deleting text with the ENTER key

A very fast way to delete text is to hold down the ENTER key while selecting it. The text is deleted as soon as you release the mouse button. (This is a little *too* fast for our taste, but if you have nerves of steel, you may want to give it a try.)

◉ easy address book

You can set up a useful and flexible computerized address book without having to buy a program specially designed for that purpose. Just use MacWrite—or any other word processing program—to create a document with one entry (name, address, phone number, etc.) per page.

You can format each entry any way you like for printing labels, and you have the Search command available for rapidly finding a specific entry.

◉ trouble Pasting large MacDraw pictures

You may run into trouble trying to Paste a large MacDraw picture into a MacWrite document when using some versions of MacWrite and MacDraw. If this happens, you'll get a message saying that the Clipboard is too large for the transfer, then the Paste command will fail.

You may be able to get around the problem with the following procedure: Open the MacDraw document that contains the picture you want to put into your MacWrite document. Copy the picture into the Clipboard. Quit MacDraw.

Now open a new (blank, untitled) MacWrite document (with the New command on the File menu). Paste the picture from the Clipboard into the new MacWrite document. Next Copy the picture from the new MacWrite document into the Clipboard. Now close the untitled MacWrite document. When the Mac asks you if you want to save the changes made to it, answer No.)

The final step is to open the MacWrite document into which you want to Paste the picture in the first place. Place the insertion point where you want the picture to go and Paste. MacWrite should accept the Paste command with no difficulty.

Basic Word tips
(Unless otherwise indicated, all the tips in this section refer to version 1.05.)

❤ *text selection shortcuts*

Word gives you several easy ways to select text:

shortcut

To select a word, just point to it and double-click. If you keep the mouse button held down on the second click, you can then drag in either direction to select text word by word.

To select the word to the left of the insertion point, press SHIFT-BACKSPACE. (This is great for correcting a word you just typed.)

To select a line of text, place the pointer in the selection bar (the space to the left of the document where the I-beam changes to a right-pointing arrow) and click once.

To select a sentence, hold down the COMMAND key while double-clicking anywhere in the sentence. If you hold down the mouse button on the second click, you can then drag in either direction to select text sentence by sentence.

To select an entire paragraph, place the pointer in the selection bar and double-click. Anywhere in the paragraph will do—it doesn't matter which line. If you hold down the mouse button on the second click, you can then drag in either direction to select text paragraph by paragraph.

To select the entire document, place the pointer in the selection bar, hold down the COMMAND key and click the mouse once.

⚫ *text deletion shortcuts*

To delete the word to the left of the insertion point, press OPTION-BACKSPACE.

shortcut

Double-clicking on a word selects not only the word but also the space to its right, thus saving you the trouble of having to delete the space separately.

⚫ *bypassing the Clipboard when moving text*

Moving text within a document usually means Cutting or Copying to the Clipboard, then Pasting the text in the new location. But this flushes the present contents of the Clipboard, and you may have stuff in there you don't want to disturb. Word has a way to let you do this.

Just select the stuff you want to move, put the pointer where you want to move it to, hold down the OPTION and SHIFT keys, and click. That's all there is to it. To Copy text rather than Cut it, follow the same procedure but only hold down the OPTION key.

very good feature

Since this method is faster than the standard Clipboard commands (Cut, Copy and Paste), you'll probably want to use it all the time, even when you don't have anything important in the Clipboard.

☀ *style change shortcuts*

It's tiresome always having to go to the Character menu to change the style of a piece of text, so Word also provides some keyboard shortcuts. They're particularly useful when you want to change the style of a single word or a short phrase within a line.

shortcut

To change the style of a piece of text, select it, hold down both the COMMAND and SHIFT keys and hit:

b for bold	**i** for italic
o for outline	**d** for shadow
u for underline	**k** for small caps
= for superscript	**-** (hyphen) for subscript

space bar for plain text

Note that the commands for bold, italic, underline and outline are mnemonic.

☀ *quickly matching style attributes*

You'll often want to format different parts of document with the same style attributes. To do that, select the text you want to format, hold down the OPTION and COMMAND keys, and click on some text that's already formatted in the style you want. The style attributes will be transferred to the selected text.

shortcut

Using two windows can really speed this technique up. Drag down the *window bar* (the small black bar at the top of the vertical scroll bar) to create two views on the same document, position some text that has the style attributes you want in the upper window, and bring the various pieces of text you want to transfer the style attributes to into the lower window.

♣ *using the Glossary to store character formats*

You can use Word's Glossary feature to store character formats as well as words, phrases, and pictures. This is particularly useful when for complicated formats like 18-point bold italic outline small caps. All you have to do is Copy a single character in the desired format into the Glossary window and give the Glossary a name that will help you remember what it is—'subheads', say, or 'captions'. (Don't worry that the character appears in the Glossary window as plain Chicago; the formats are intact.)

To use the format, just type in the name of the Glossary and press COMMAND-BACKSPACE to retrieve it. Then select the character (OPTION-BACKSPACE will select it automatically) and begin typing. The character will be replaced with the text you type, and it will all be formatted the way you want it.

♣ *copying paragraph formats*

You can quickly and easily format a paragraph by giving it the attributes of any other paragraph in the document. Just click anywhere within the paragraph you want to format, then point in the selection bar to the paragraph whose format you want to copy, hold down OPTION and COMMAND, and click.

♣ *pointer-movement shortcuts*

Word displays the list of pointer-movement commands when you type COMMAND-? and then click the mouse. But here's a chart of all of them, both the documented and undocumented ones.

Holding down COMMAND, OPTION and the following characters moves the pointer as indicated:

k left one letter	**l** right one letter
j left one word	**;** (semicolon)—right one word
o up one line	**,** (comma)—down one line
p up one screen	**.** (period)—down one screen

Holding down COMMAND, OPTION, the apostrophe key (') and the following characters moves the pointer as indicated:

k to start of line	**l** to end of line
j back one sentence	**;** (semicolon)—to start of next sentence
o to top of screen	**,** (comma)—to bottom of screen
p to top of document	**.** (period)—to bottom of document

Using the SHIFT key with any of the above commands will select all the text from the pointer's present position to its new position. (Since this involves holding down five keys—COMMAND, OPTION, SHIFT, apostrophe and the character—you may be better off simply using the mouse.)

The following commands move text on the screen without moving the pointer:

COMMAND-OPTION [(left bracket)—scrolls text up one line
COMMAND-OPTION / (slash)—scrolls text down one line

🍎 *dialog box shortcuts*

Microsoft Word and some of Microsoft's other Mac programs (such as Excel) let you respond to choices in a dialog box with the keyboard as well as with the mouse. The usual method is to press the first letter of one of the choices. For instance, in a yes/no dialog box, pressing 'y' or 'n' will suffice.

shortcut

shortcut

In dialog boxes that allow text entry, use the command key along with the letter to let the program know you're not entering text. For example, in the Save As dialog box you can press COMMAND-E for Eject.

In any dialog box, pressing COMMAND-1 is the equivalent of clicking on the first button, COMMAND-2 for the second button, and so on.

⬤ *new paragraph vs. new line*

Word can seem like a quirky program when you first start using it, particularly if you're used to MacWrite. One of Word's idiosyncrasies that can cause a great deal of confusion is the way Word handles formatting information.

Word makes a distinction between a new paragraph and a new line. Unlike other word processing programs, Word stores each paragraph's format in the carriage return (generated by hitting the RETURN key) at the end of each paragraph. You may need to start a new line in a document without starting a new paragraph (and therefore a new format). This is particularly useful when creating a table.

Rather than use the RETURN key at the end of each line, use SHIFT-RETURN. This will start a new line, but Word will not treat it as the beginning of a new paragraph and the formatting will stay the same. (This is also known as a soft carriage return; the regular one that ends paragraphs is called a hard carriage return.)

When you hit COMMAND-Y to cause Word to display hidden characters, Word uses ¶ to indicate new paragraphs (hard carriage returns) and · to indicate new lines (soft carriage returns). You can even Search for them. Just use ^P to represent the new paragraph symbol and ^N to represent the new line symbol in either the Find... or Change... dialog box.

❤ *soft hyphens*

Word doesn't have automatic hyphenation, so you have to do it manually. But first a little background:

There are two kinds of hyphens, hard and soft. Hard hyphens print no matter where they fall in the document, while soft hyphens only print (and show on the screen) when they fall at the end of a line. (You can think of a soft hyphen as a conditional hyphen, the condition being whether or not the word comes at the end of a line.)

To insert a soft hyphen, hold down the COMMAND key while hitting the hyphen key.

Most of the time you'll probably want to insert soft hyphens, since it's difficult to judge when a word will fall at the end of a line as your document goes through several revisions.

❤ *nonbreaking hyphens*

Normally Word breaks a word after a hyphen if it falls at the end of a line. If you want the whole word—hyphen and all—to move down to the next line, you need a nonbreaking hyphen. Although the Word manual (naturally) doesn't tell you so, you can generate a nonbreaking hyphen by pressing OPTION-hyphen.

❤ *preventing pointless saves*

Word has a nice feature that prevents you from wasting time with pointless saves. If you try to save a document that you haven't made any changes to since the last time you saved, Word simply ignores the command.

very good
feature

✎ nonstandard type sizes

very good
feature

Unlike MacWrite, which only lets you enter text in six standard sizes (9-, 10-, 12-, 14-, 18- and 24-point), Word lets you specify anything from 4-point to 127-point (in whole numbers). You specify the point size by choosing Formats... on the Character menu (or hitting COMMAND-D) and then simply typing it in.

✎ Word on a one-drive system

Although Word is designed to work on a 128K Mac, it isn't a good idea to try to use it on one unless you have two drives. The program and its help file are *big* and to squeeze them onto a 400K disk you'll have to strip your system file of all but the most basic fonts. Even if you do that, you won't have much room for documents. If you have an 800K drive (which means you must also have at least 512K of RAM), one drive is OK.

(For information on the various hardware options available on the Mac, see chapter 13.)

✎ current version of the ImageWriter driver

If you've been using Word for a long time and haven't updated your system file in a while, Word may tend to pause every few lines when printing on the ImageWriter, and it may stop before advancing to the top of the next page at the end of the printout.

These problems are corrected in versions of the ImageWriter driver released with Finder version 4.1 and later. (For Finder 5.3 and System 3.2, the driver version is 2.3.) When you update your system file you'll find that printing progresses much faster and more smoothly.

Advanced Word tips
{*Unless otherwise indicated, all the tips in this section refer to version 1.05.*}

🍎 *leading control*

Leading (pronounced LEHD-ing, not LEED-ing) is what typesetters call the space between lines of text, and Word gives you a lot of power to control it. To change the leading, go to the Paragraph Formats window (the keyboard shortcut is COMMAND-M) and type the leading you want into the Line Spacing box. Be sure to add the letters 'pt' after the number so Word knows you're telling it how many points to make the lines (you don't need to type in a space; '12pt' works as well as '12 pt').

So, for example, if you wanted to print out text 11/13 (11-point type on 13-point lines—one of the most common ways to set body copy), you'd first select the text, then go to the Character Formats window and type '11' in the Font Size box, then go to the Paragraph Formats window and type '13pt' in the Line Spacing box.

🍎 *scaling graphics*

There are two ways to scale graphic images you have Pasted into a Word document. The most obvious is to use the little square black "handles" that appear when you click on the image to select it. The advantage of this method is that you can change the proportions of the image in addition to resizing it. The disadvantage is that it's almost impossible *not* to change the proportions.

The other technique gets around this problem. After you've selected the image, press COMMAND-SHIFT-Y, then one of the number keys on the top row of the keyboard. They will change the image to ten different, preset sizes—1 being the smallest and 0 the largest. While this method obviously doesn't allow you as many sizes as dragging the size box, the image will retain its original proportions.

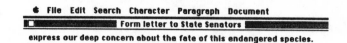

express our deep concern about the fate of this endangered species.

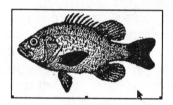

We're certain that you share our views regardless of the influence in the State Senate of the major environmental pollutors.

Word document with graphic selected, showing the handles at the bottom

very good feature

When you use the COMMAND-SHIFT-Y method, the number you type roughly corresponds to a percentage of the size of the original picture. For example, COMMAND-SHIFT-Y-9 reduces the picture to 90% of the original, COMMAND-SHIFT-Y-8 to 80%, and so on. COMMAND-SHIFT-Y-0 returns the picture to 100%.

✸ *paragraph formatting shortcuts*

shortcut

There are four paragraph formatting options that don't appear in the Format or Paragraph menus. You can accomplish the same results with the ruler or within the text window, but these keyboard shortcuts are much faster.

COMMAND-SHIFT-N — nest (i.e. indent left margin half an inch more than the paragraph above)

COMMAND-SHIFT-M — un-nest

COMMAND-SHIFT-F — indent first lines half an inch

COMMAND-SHIFT-T — indent all lines but the first (i.e. create a hanging indent, or outdent, on the first line of each paragraph)

⬤ *quick paragraph formatting*

Word keeps paragraph format settings (tabs, justification, line spacing, etc.) in the ¶ (paragraph) symbol at the end of each paragraph. To copy these settings, first make the ¶s and other format symbols visible by pressing COMMAND-Y. Then select the ¶ (by double-clicking on it), Copy it, and Paste it over the ¶ of any paragraph you want to change the settings of.

shortcut

An even slicker technique is to save the ¶ as a Glossary. Then you can insert it at the end of a paragraph and the paragraph will be formatted instantly. Just store the ¶ in the Glossary with a name that will help you remember what it is. Nothing will be displayed in the Glossary, but be assured that the format is stored.

When you want to use that format, type the Glossary name, and press COMMAND-BACKSPACE to retrieve the symbol. Position the pointer to the left of the paragraph marker and type the paragraph. (You can also retrieve the paragraph marker from the glossary to format any existing format.)

⬤ *quick division formatting*

Word keeps division format settings (page numbering, headers, footnotes, etc.) in the 'division terminator' symbol— the double dotted line at the end of each division. To copy these settings, first make the division terminators and other format symbols visible by pressing COMMAND-Y. Then select and Copy the division terminator, and Paste it over the division terminator of any division you want to change the settings of.

shortcut

As with paragraph formatting settings stored in the ¶s, you can save the division terminator (a double row of dots) as a Glossary entry. Then you can insert it at the end of a division and the division will be formatted instantly.

very
hot
tip

♠ *miscellaneous uses of the Glossary*

You can also use the Glossary to store running heads and frequently misspelled words. For example, if you frequently type 'teh' instead of 'the', simply make a Glossary entry 'the' with the name 'teh'. Then every time you type 'teh', all you have to do is hit COMMAND-BACKSPACE to correct the mistake.

♠ *printing multiple documents from within Word*

You can do this by using the print merge functions. Here's a step-by-step.

Create a new document and on the first line of it, type «include *name*», where *name* is the name of the first document to be printed. (The « character is generated by OPTION backslash (\ ) and the » character by SHIFT-OPTION backslash.) Create a similar line with the file name of each document you want to print, and separate each line with Word's page-break command: SHIFT-ENTER.

When you have a line for each of the documents you want to print, choose Print Merge from the File menu. In addition to letting you print multiple documents, this technique will also speed up the printing, because Word will only have to create one print file on disk, instead of a separate one for each individual document.

♠ *double-sided Word printouts*

very
hot
tip

Nowhere in the LaserWriter or Word documentation will you find instructions for printing on both sides of the paper so that the correct pages will print back-to-back. Here's how you do it:

First print half as many copies of the document as you need. Then arrange them so that the copies of page 2 are on the top, followed by the copies of page 1, followed by page 4, then page 3, page 6, page 5, and so on, continuing to count up by even numbers and subtracting 1 in between. If there are an odd number of pages in your document, set aside the copies of the last page and substitute blank pages for them in the pile.

Place the pile of arranged pages in the paper tray face up, with the top edge of the pages pointing towards the end of the tray that goes into the LaserWriter. Insert the tray and print the other half of the copies.

The same technique works on the ImageWriter II with a sheet feeder. The only difference is how you place the pile of arranged pages (printed on one side)—in the case of the sheet feeder, put them upside down, with the printed side facing you.

✦ *printing custom envelopes on the LaserWriter*

The LaserWriter is great for printing stationery. Letterhead is easy, but envelopes can be tricky—especially if you use Word to do them. That's because its commands for margins are so confusing. You can change them both on the Ruler and in the Page Setup window and the effect of one on the other is quite mysterious (and, needless to say, is not explained with perfect lucidity in Word's manual).

very
hot
tip

But these difficulties are more than made up for by Word's ability to produce type in any point size, not merely in the standard six to ·nine sizes most programs give you. This is particularly important if you like the way an envelope looks with your name and the return address printed across the end, instead of lengthways like the name and address of the person you're sending it to, because this format makes copyfitting even more critical.

To center the type across the end of a standard #10 business envelope (and to keep the top of the type from getting cut off by the LaserWriter's invisible image border), create a Word document with the following settings:

• *on the ruler:* a left margin of 4-7/16˚ and a right margin of 8-1/2˚;

• *in the Page Setup window:* a top margin of 0.4"; all other margins set to zero;

• *in the Paragraph menu:* center all text.

If text gets cut off on either side, reduce the size of the type on that line (one point at a time) until it fits.

For more about printing stationery on the LaserWriter, see the LaserWriter section of chapter 11.

⚫ *hyphenation via MS-DOS*

The Macintosh version of Word won't take a document and automatically insert hyphens where needed. There are add-on products to do this, but there's also a way to do it just using Word—assuming you have access to Word on an IBM PC or compatible.

Since the MS-DOS version of Word does do automatic hyphenation, just type in your text on the PC using the same margins as you want in the final Mac document, then transfer the file to the Mac. (Word on the Mac has a Convert utility that makes the transfer easy.) This solution isn't elegant, but it works.

⚫ *removing carriage returns from imported documents*

Sometimes when you transfer a document created on another computer into Word, you'll find carriage returns at the end of each line. (Use COMMAND-Y to see where all the carriage returns are; they show up as ¶s.) Since Word only uses carriage returns to mark the ends of paragraphs, you'll need to remove all the ones that fall elsewhere. Here's how to do that:

Select the entire document. Now choose Change from the Search menu, and change each occurrence of '^p^p' (Word uses '^p' to represent carriage returns) to some unique characters that don't appear anywhere in the document, such as '&&'. Click on the Change All button.

Next, choose Change again and change each occurrence of '^p' to a single space (just use the space bar). Click on the Change All button. Now choose Change for a third time and change each occurrence of '&&' (or whatever you're using) to '^p'. Again, click on the Change All button.

All the carriage returns in your document should now be at the ends of paragraphs. (COMMAND-Y will reveal if any unwanted ones remain.)

♦ *recovering from crashes*

You may be able to recover a Word document that you've lost in a system crash. After restarting the system, look on the Word disk for a document named MW0000 (or MW0001, MW0002, etc.). This is the name Word uses for the temporary file it creates when you're working with a document.

very
hot
tip

If you find such a document, there's at least a fifty-fifty chance you'll be able to recover the text you were working on—if you have a system utility (like Resedit, Fedit, or MacTools) that allows you to change the file type. Use the utility to open the document named MW0000 (or whatever) and change the type from WTMP to WDBM. Then exit to the Desktop and rename the document from MW0000 to 'lost text' or any name you like (as long as it doesn't begin with 'MW' followed by four numbers). With any luck, Word will then be able to read the file.

♦ *avoiding the "Session too long" message*

Since Word 1.05 was designed in the era of 128K Macs, it isn't as efficient in dealing with memory as more modern programs. So its performance suffers when you make a lot of global changes or Cuts and Pastes in a large document. You may even get the dreaded message: 'Session too long: low on memory. Save your document before continuing' just before the system hangs or crashes.

You can avoid this message and keep Word performing as well as it can simply by Saving frequently. But since Word is notoriously slow at Saving, particularly to floppies, try to Save when you need a short break from your work.

🍎 *converting long MacWrite documents to Word*

important warning

Word can open any MacWrite document and make it into a Word document, retaining most of the formatting. But if the MacWrite document is longer than fifteen pages or so, Word gets confused, gives you the 'Session too long...' message and asks you to save the document. For some reason, such a save can take up to *40 minutes!*

Fortunately, there's a way around this problem. Just break the MacWrite document into smaller documents of ten pages or less before converting it to Word. Once all the smaller documents are converted, just Paste them back together.

🍎 *Switcher warning*

important warning

If you're using Switcher with Microsoft Word and the Finder as partitions, be sure not to delete any documents from the Finder partition that are in use by Word. To be safe, quit Switcher before deleting anything from the Finder.

🍎 *creating blank lines on forms*

very hot tip

When designing forms, you usually want to create blanks where people can fill in the information you're requesting. The common way to do this is just to knock out a bunch of underlines (SHIFT-hyphens). But this method will seldom produce lines of the length you planned, especially on the LaserWriter. Here's a method for producing underlines of an exact length:

Set a plain left tab at the point where the line is to begin, and a right tab with a solid underscore leader at the point where the line is to end. Underscore leaders are chosen in the bottom center of the Tabs dialog box (COMMAND-T). This will fill the space between the tabs with an underline, and the tabs will keep the line length precise.

❡ *eliminating blank lines in merge printouts*

Since the dawn of MailMerge, users have put up with the problem of blank lines in their mailing labels and merge letters. You set up fields for Title, Name, Company, Address, City, State, and ZIP, and the first thing you discover is that half your records have no company name associated with them. In many word processors, this leaves you with no option but to print the labels with a blank line where the company name would go. Officially, Word is no different, but there is a way around the problem.

very
hot
tip

Word's manual states that each ELSE statement must be enclosed with guillemets (which look like this: « »). But if you leave off the last », Word will not advance to the next line, and blank lines will be eliminated when the document is printed.

The official Microsoft approach shown below will leave you with blank lines if the title, name, or company field is empty:

```
«IF  title»«title»
«ELSE»
«IF  name»«name»
«ELSE»
«IF  company»«company»
«ELSE»
«ENDIF»«address»
«city»,«state»    «zip»
```

But the following Print Merge document will not leave blank lines, regardless of whether or not the title, name, or company field is empty:

«IF title»«title»
«ELSE
«IF name»«name»
«ELSE
«IF company»«company»
«ELSE
«ENDIF»«address»
«city»,«state»   «zip»

✿ *preserving ThinkTank indentation in Word*

When you convert a ThinkTank document to Word, the first thing you'll notice is that all the indentation is gone. Here's what to do to restore the indentation:

• search for all occurrences of '.head 0 +' and '.head 1 ?' and delete

• search for all occurrences of '.head 2 ?' and change them to '^t' (which creates a single tab)

• search for all occurrences of '.head 3 ?' and change it to '^t^t' (which creates a double tab)

• and so on for '.head 4?' and as many other levels as you have.

Chapter 7

Number crunching and data handling

General spreadsheet tips
(Unless otherwise indicated, all the tips in this section
refer to version 1.00 of Excel and version 1.1 of Multiplan.)

⚫ *escaping from cells with invalid formulas*

Neither Excel nor Multiplan will let you close a cell until the formula in it meets the program's formatting rules. You'll keep getting a message that says your formula is wrong and you'll be put right back in that cell. This can be maddening when you're working on a complex formula and can't seem to get it right.

very
hot
tip

To escape, just remove the equal sign at the beginning of the formula. Excel will now treat the entry as text and thus won't analyze it for correctness, allowing you to move on to another cell. After a little while away from the troublesome formula, you may be able to go back to it and spot your mistake.

⚫ *suppressing printout of blank rows and columns*

Both Excel and Multiplan print a whole page of rows and columns, even if your spreadsheet only takes up a few cells. But you can force them to print just the cells you want. All you have to do is select the cells you want to print and then choose:

in Excel: Set Print Area from the Options menu.
in Multiplan: Set Print Selected Cells from the Print menu.

✦ printing large worksheets

When you're printing a very large worksheet, use forced page breaks to divide it into sections of related data, rather than just letting the program insert page breaks arbitrarily. This makes the printout easier to read, since logically related information is grouped together on the same page, without irrelevant information to distract you. It also lets you print out selected portions of the spreadsheet simply by specifying the pages you want in the Print dialog box.

✦ protecting the structure of worksheets

If you're designing a worksheet that will require the repeated input of varying data, you'll want to protect the cells that contain text or formulas, so they don't get accidentally changed during the data-entry process. Here's how to do it (in both Excel and Multiplan):

Choose Protect Document on the Options menu. Then, in Excel, use the Cell Protection command on the Format menu to unlock only those cells where data is to be entered. (The dialog box will come up with the Locked box checked; just click on it to uncheck it.) In Multiplan, use the Remove Cell Protection command on the Option menu.

✦ saving time by turning off Automatic Calculation

shortcut

When working with large worksheets in either Excel or Multiplan, you can often save a great deal of time by turning off Automatic Calculation. In Excel, choose Calculation from the Options menu and click on the Manual option when the dialog box comes up. In Multiplan, choose Manual Calculation from the Calculate menu.

Now you can choose when you want the calculations to take place. The simplest way to do that (in either program) is to hit COMMAND- = (COMMAND-equal sign).

❡ *rounding*

As with most other spreadsheets, Excel and Multiplan store numbers as precisely they can, regardless of how you ask to have them displayed. Say, for example, that the result of a calculation is 31.89624. If you request that the number be displayed without decimal points, it will appear as 32; if you request that it be displayed with two decimal points, it will appear as 31.90. But it will continue to be stored as 31.89624 and that's the value that will be inserted into other calculations if you reference that cell in a formula someplace else on the worksheet.

This can be confusing. Imagine multiplying two cells that display 3 and 6 but have actual values of 2.51 x 5.62. If you ask for the result without decimal points too, you'll get 14 instead of the expected 18. Normally, of course, you want the precision, regardless of the confusion, but if you don't, both Excel and Multiplan can be told to use the displayed value—rather than the more precise, stored value—in calculations. In Excel, choose 'Precision as displayed' from the Options menu; in Multiplan, use the 'Round' function.

Excel tips
(Unless otherwise indicated, all the tips in this section refer to version 1.00.)

❡ *learning Excel* *(Arthur)*

Like many of Microsoft manuals, Excel's is maddeningly bad. But the program's help screens are pretty good, so use them instead of the manual to learn the program. You'll still have to look things up in the manual (a *very* frustrating—and usually fruitless—task), but the less time you spend with it, the happier you'll be.

⬤ *bird's-eye view of worksheets*

Large Excel worksheets can get really complex, and it's easy to lose the forest for the trees. To regain your sense of the overall structure, try viewing the worksheet in 4-point type (using the Font command on the Options menu). Go back to this bird's-eye view whenever you feel lost (you can't actually work on the spreadsheet when the type is 4-point).

⬤ *suppressing extra pages in printouts* (Paul Hoffman)

very
hot
tip

Sometimes when you've done a bunch of editing in Excel, you'll get extra pages in the printout that contain nothing but some borders. These are rows that were pushed right—or columns that were pushed down—during your editing. Even if you delete them using COMMAND-K, Excel will continue to print them. To keep them from printing, you have to not only delete them, but also save the document, close it and then reopen it.

⬤ *Excel's insistence on certain formats* (Paul Hoffman)

very
hot
tip

Excel can be maddeningly insistent on how a date, say, or a percentage, should be formatted. To get around this, start your entry with an OPTION-space. This will force Excel to treat the entry as plain text.

⬤ *outlining cells*

Although it's right there in the Border dialog box (on the Format menu), many Excel users don't realize that they can outline any group of cells they've selected simply by clicking on Outline. This is a lot easier than going back repeatedly to click on Left, Top, Right and Bottom, even if you're only outlining one cell.

❡ *hiding part of the worksheet*

You may want to hide part of an Excel worksheet, either because you have sensitive data in it that you don't want to be visible on the screen while you work, or so you can move from one column to another without having to use the scroll bar.

To do that, just set the width of the columns you want to hide to zero. Your data will still be there, but it won't be displayed. The only indication that there's a column hidden will be a jump in the letters at the top of the screen that identify each column.

To open up a hidden column, select the columns on either side of it, then choose Column Width... from the Format menu. All three columns will assume the width you specify (which means you may have to adjust them back where you want them after the hidden column is revealed).

❡ *Previews of printouts*

One of Excel's nicer features is the ability to preview on the screen what printouts will look like on paper (you do that by checking the Preview box in the Print dialog box). The text is too small to read in the Preview window (unless you're using giant type), but you can zoom in on any part of it by clicking the magnifying-glass pointer. Click again and you're back at the overall view of the page.

very good feature

You can move around in zoom mode by holding down the OPTION key. This turns the pointer into a little grabber hand (as in MacPaint) that you can use to move around while keeping the text at a readable size.

very hot tip

❡ *linked worksheets and recalculation speed*

Excel lets you link worksheets, a feature that can be very useful for complex models. That's the good news. The bad news is that linking worksheets can dramatically increase recalculation time, so only do it when it's absolutely necessary.

● *special characters in titles*

Excel won't print out certain symbols—like the ampersand (&)—in the titles of documents. They'll appear in the box in the Page Setup window when you type them in, but on paper there'll be nothing there.

● *font of titles*

When you print an Excel worksheet, the title appears in the same font as the rest of the worksheet. But when you print an Excel chart, the title is always in Geneva—or in Helvetica if you're printing on the LaserWriter and have Font Substitution on (see the next entry for why you'd better leave it on in that case).

● *printing Excel charts on the LaserWriter*

important
warning

Whatever you do, always leave Font Substitution on when printing an Excel chart on the LaserWriter. Because the chart title always stays in Geneva, no matter what you do to the rest of the chart, the program won't be able to print the title if you turn Font Substitution off, and will crash.

The window on the opposite page shows the best settings for printing an Excel chart on the LaserWriter.

● *easy worksheet navigation*

Navigating around large Excel worksheets can become tiresome. One way to make things easier on yourself is to break the worksheet up into logical parts and use the Define Name function from the Formula menu to define each part. Then you can use the Go To... command from the Formula menu to go directly to any part of the worksheet that you've defined. (You can also use the Border command under the Format menu to draw boxes around the Named Ranges to make them easier to see.)

very hot tip

LaserWriter			v3.1	[OK]

Paper: ◉ US Letter   ○ A4 Letter   Reduce or [100] %   [Cancel]
        ○ US Legal   ○ B5 Letter   Enlarge:

Orientation   **Printer Effects:**
                           ☒ Font Substitution?
                           ☒ Smoothing?

Page Header: [SETTINGS FOR BEST PRINTOUTS OF EXCEL CHARTS]

Page Footer: [   ]

Left Margin: [0]   Print Width: [10.5]

Top Margin: [0]   Print Height: [6]

○ Screen Size ◉ Fit to Page

The best settings for printing Excel charts on the LaserWriter

using Excel on a single-drive Mac

You can run Excel on a single-drive 512K Macintosh if your worksheets are relatively small. The best method is to create a RAM disk of about 220K and Copy a System Folder containing the System, Finder, and ImageWriter files it. Then set up a floppy with only Excel on it (you can add the Help file, if you like). There'll be plenty of room left on the floppy for all but the largest worksheets.

Excel and the Mac Plus keyboard

If you work extensively with Excel worksheets and are using the old keyboard, one of the best productivity investments you can make is to buy the new Mac Plus keyboard for $130. The numeric keypad makes entering numbers much easier, and the arrow keys are very useful for navigating around the worksheet.

bargain

⌘ *importing worksheets from the Mac XL*

If you import an Excel document created on a Mac XL to a regular Mac with a 9" screen, the spreadsheet's window will probably be larger than the screen, and you won't be able to resize it because the size box will be off the screen. The solution is simple: just double-click on the title bar, and the window will automatically resize to fit the Mac's screen.

⌘ *converting Jazz worksheets to Excel*

Jazz has no built-in ability to export files to other applications other than as plain ASCII text. But there is a way to convert a Jazz worksheet to Excel. Save each column of the Jazz worksheet individually as an text (ASCII) file, then load the files, one at a time and in order, into the new Excel worksheet. One drawback with this method: no formulas will be transferred, just the data in each cell.

⌘ *the world's most obscure Excel bug* (Steve Michel)

This bug is so strange I'm going to tell you how to duplicate it, so you can see it for yourself. Open a new worksheet, and into one of the cells, enter the text '=#REF!'. This is what Excel puts into a cell if there's a reference error in a formula, but the bug can be duplicated whether Excel puts it there or you do.

Make sure the cell with =#REF! in it is selected. Now make the text in that cell bold (using the Style command on the Format menu) and change the worksheet's font to 10-point Geneva (using the Font command on the Options menu). Now go through the steps of setting the size to 10-point again (even though it's already set on 10-point). Notice anything funny?

Every time you set the font size to 10-point, Excel makes all the columns in the worksheet narrower! After doing it half a dozen or more times, you'll find that they've all gotten very, very narrow.

This is a particularly pernicious bug because it's so time-consuming to fix. Unless you're using a standard width for all your columns, you'll have to go back and reset each one separately. I lost a lot of productive time trying to find the source of this bug, and I hope this tip helps you avoid it.

♦ *a very simple template for balancing your checkbook*
   (Arthur)

The mathematics involved here are pretty elementary (so elementary, in fact, that I debated leaving this tip out of the book), but I simply can never remember whether you add the outstanding deposits and subtract the outstanding checks, or vice versa. Now that I've put this template together, I balance my checkbook every month and actually look forward to doing it. Granted, I won't win the Nobel Prize for this template, but it makes my life a bit easier, and it might do the same for yours.

	A	B
1	balance shown on the statement you get from the bank ››	*copy from statement*
2		
3	deposits and other credits that haven't cleared the bank yet ››	*add up and put total here*
4	*(they're in your checkbook but aren't on the statement.)*	
5		
6	checks and other debits that haven't cleared the bank yet ››	*add up and put total here*
7	*(they're in your checkbook but aren't on the statement.)*	
8		
9	your checkbook should show this balance (if the bank is right) ››	=B1+B3–B6
10		
11	actual final balance shown in your checkbook ››	*copy from checkbook*
12		
13	add (or subtract) this amount from checkbook balance ››	=B9–B11
14		
15	*This assumes that the bank is right and that you made a mistake*	
16	*in your checkbook. Before correcting the balance, I always recheck*	
17	*the checkbook with a calculator to see if I can find the mistake.*	
18	*(The first time you do this, you just have to assume the bank*	
19	*is right and accept the balance on the statement as a starting point.)*	
20		

To set up your template, just type in the plain and boldfaced text; the stuff in italics is all comments and explanations. You can, of course, rewrite the text any way you want, and lay things out differently. Just make sure the formulas refer to the same numbers as they do in the example above.

Since you'll be looking at the template every month, you'll might want to pretty it up a bit. I'll assume you've already boldfaced as I have above. The next thing I'd do is select Column B (by clicking in the box at the top of the screen with **B** in it), then go to the Format menu and set Number for rounded dollars. (The window below shows you what that command looks like in Excel's brain-damaged system of symbols.)

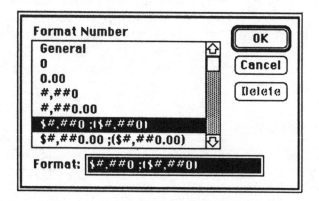

Excel's number format window

Next, select Column A and set Alignment—which is also under the Format menu—Right. And that should pretty much do it.

You can, of course, use another part of the worksheet to create a check and deposit register (a duplicate of the one in your checkbook), and plug totals from that into the template shown above. This saves you having to add up outstanding debits and credits on a calculator, but it means you have to type in each check. Both systems work fine; it's just a question of which you prefer.

⚫ *Time and Date functions*

Use the NOW( ) function to retrieve the current date and time from the system clock and enter it into a formula as a serial number. Use the following functions to convert the serial number to the format you need:

DAY
WEEKDAY
HOUR
MINUTE
MONTH
YEAR

For example, the formula =FORMULA("=HOUR(NOW())") gives you the current hour.

Multiplan tips
(Unless otherwise indicated, all the tips in this section refer to version 1.1.)

⚫ *improving the appearance of printouts* ·

Like most other spreadsheets on the Mac (except Excel), Multiplan's ability to highlight certain areas of your report is extremely limited. One way around this problem is to paste the worksheet into a graphics program like MacDraw or MacPaint and then use its tools to add some graphic interest.

⚫ *cursor movement on numeric keypad*

The arrow keys on the numeric keypad that was sold as an option for the original Mac keyboard are fully functional in Multiplan.

shortcut

♦ *converting Multiplan files to Jazz*

very bad
feature

Jazz support of the SYLK file format is...uh, spotty. Specifically, if you try to convert special formats along with your document when importing SYLK files to Jazz, you'll find yourself waiting *forever*. You may even get a bomb message.

So remove all of the special formatting before you save the SYLK file. Now the conversion to Jazz will merely take an excruciatingly long time—which you can profitably spend planning how to restore the special formatting to the document in Jazz. (The SYLK import feature in Jazz is a good answer to the question, "When is a feature not a feature?")

General database tips (Steve Michel)

♦ *duplicate database files before working on them*

important
warning

It's good practice to keep at least two copies of any database file, and three of any active one. But if you're too lazy to do that, at least do yourself the favor of duplicating a database file before launching the application to work on it. Most databases keep their files on disk, and constantly update them while you work. So the file you had on disk when you began to work is not the file you'll return to when you're done.

This constant, automatic saving to disk is a good feature, since it means that you don't have to worry about losing any appreciable amount of work if the system crashes. But if you make some changes you later want to discard, you're stuck—unless you made a copy of the file before you started.

Some programs also let you save a file under different names in the course of a long session (for example, Helix has a Backup As command). Other programs, like OverVUE, keep the entire file in memory while you're working on it, so the file remains unchanged until you deliberately save it (but, here again, the only safe course is to keep *at least* two copies of the file on different disks).

✦ *keep written notes as to what does what*

One of the drawbacks of most Mac databases is that they don't give you a good way to document what you're doing as you do it. For simple files, this isn't much of a problem. But for more complex ones, particularly in Helix and Omnis, it's easy enough to forget what a particular report, sort, calculation is supposed to do. I have one file I use at least three times a week, but recently when I went to make some changes to it, I lost a couple of hours work because I hadn't made extensive notes while I was designing it.

Keeping notes is particularly important if you're designing an application for someone else to use, even if it's just a mailing list. They'll help you to explain it to the person using it, and to yourself when you go to modify it weeks or months later

It's most convenient to make the notes in a desk accessory. I use Mockwrite or miniWRITER, which are nice text editors. Another good choice is Acta, the outlining desk accessory.

✦ *use a hard disk*

A hard disk greatly improves the performance of just about every type of software, but for databases the difference is really incredible. Not only do things speed up, but most databases let you create files as large as the available space on your disk; with a hard disk, this means files can be at least ten times larger than they can on a floppy.

Microsoft File tips

(Unless otherwise indicated, all the tips in this section refer to version 1.02.)

shortcut

⚫ *speeding up data entry*

Users of Microsoft File are familiar with the delays that occur when an entry is completed and File redraws the screen. You can minimize this delay by keeping the window as small as possible. The less File has to redraw, the less time it takes doing it.

⚫ *changing the field type after entering data*

File doesn't let you change field types in a database after you've started entering data. The way to get around this limitation is to copy the entire data file to the Clipboard, then Quit. At this point File will ask you if you want to save the data in the Clipboard as formatted or unformatted. Choose unformatted. Now you can open File, change the problem fields, and Paste the data from the Clipboard into the corrected form.

There are some disadvantages to this solution: you lose any pictures in the database, plus any information in hidden areas of the form. And the technique isn't risk-free. To minimize the chance of losing data, be sure you have at least one backup of the file. File's reference manual contains a section detailing the ins and outs of using the Clipboard, and it's worth reading.

very
hot
tip

⚫ *entering carriage returns within a field*

File uses a carriage return (generated by pressing the RETURN key) to move to the next field in a record. This can cause a problem if you need to use a carriage return within the field (as you would if you wanted specific pieces of information to fall on separate lines). The solution? OPTION-RETURN. It gives you a line break and keeps you in the same field.

🍎 *more info on File than the manual gives you*

File's manual does an excellent job of covering all the program's features, but it leaves practical applications to your imagination. For those, you need *Microsoft File: Organizing Your Business on the Apple Macintosh*, by Nancy Andrews, which is full of real-world small-business examples. There aren't many books about File available, so it's nice that one of the few is a good one.

Helix tips (Steve Michel)
(Unless otherwise indicated, all the tips in this section refer to version 2.0r7)

🍎 *make the Abacus icons simple*

When you first begin using Helix, there's a tendency to create large Abacus icons, with all the calculations hardwired in. But it's much smarter to make small icons that only do one thing. For one thing, small icons makes the Abacus easier to figure out (which is particularly important if you go back to modify something months after you created it). For another, small Abacus icons make Helix run faster. Here's why:

When a particular Abacus icon is used on a form, the results of its calculations are kept in memory—if Helix has to do the same calculation elsewhere on the form. These saved results speed up subsequent calculations, especially of the subtotal and lookup tiles. And the simpler an Abacus icon is, the more likely it is that there'll be another one like it somewhere on the form.

❡ using text tiles for data transfer

The text tiles in the Abacus icon are very handy for handling data transfers. For example, if you want to transfer a list of names and addresses into Microsoft Word for print merging, you'll need to put quotes around any field with a comma in it (because otherwise the comma will be interpreted as separating one field from another). It's easy to build an Abacus that uses the "followed by" tile to put the quotes around the field, and then to create a separate form for exporting the data.

❡ index judiciously

Helix lookups are much more efficient when done on indexed fields. But indexes slow the system down when you're entering (or deleting) data, and take up a lot of room on disk. So examine your indexes often and delete any that aren't being used.

❡ make backups often

This is elementary, but bears repeating. Helix data does not always survive system crashes very well (although this seems to be improving as Helix—and the Mac—mature).

❡ document your database

Here's another tip that bears repeating. Documenting what goes on inside a Helix program isn't easy. As I mentioned in one of the general database entries above, I use MockWrite or Acta to keep notes about my applications, but with Helix, it's also important to keep a paper record of all your Abacus icons. If you're deleting an Abacus or an index, it helps to have a paper copy the entire database, so you can find out where everything is used before deleting it.

OverVUE tips

❡ *stalled printouts in OverVUE*

OverVUE 2.0 won't print a character it doesn't recognize—like a dash; when the printout gets to such a character, it stalls. The solution is simply to go back into the document and change the troublesome character to a standard one (in the case of a dash, you can use two hyphens).

❡ *nonstandard COMMAND-Z*

In every piece of Mac software in the world but one, COMMAND-Z is equivalent to the Undo command. That one totally nonstandard piece of software is OverVUE—where COMMAND-Z shifts a column of data up one row!

important
warning

Since hitting COMMAND-Z gets to be second nature when you use the Mac a lot, you'll find yourself messing up a lot of OverVUE files—with little hope of retrieving your data unless you catch the mistake immediately (i.e. before the next keystroke or mouse click). Arthur found this to be so much of a problem that he stopped using OverVUE for that reason alone.

Chapter 8

Graphics

❡ *note on terminology*

Neither MacPaint nor FullPaint is an object-oriented program—that is, they both treat what you draw as a collection of dots, not as discrete objects the way MacDraw and MacDraft do. Nevertheless, when you select a bunch of dots with either the Lasso or the Marquee, they behave temporarily like an object (for example, they move together as a unit). The proper name for this collection of dots is the "selection," but we've found it less confusing to refer to it at times as the "object"—although that's technically incorrect.

MacPaint tips—tools

(Unless otherwise indicated, all tips in the following sections refer to version 1.5.)

❡ *double-clicking on tools*

Double-clicking on certain of the icons in MacPaint's tool palette (on the left side of the screen) produces some handy

shortcut

double-clicking on:	lets you:
Paintbrush	change the shape of the paintbrush
Pencil	enter FatBits
Grabber (hand)	enter Show Page
Eraser	erase the entire document window
Marquee	select the entire document window
any pattern box	change that pattern

● *SHIFT key effects*

Holding down the SHIFT key when using certain MacPaint tools produces the following effects:

very good
feature

SHIFT + :	lets you:
Pencil	draw perfectly straight lines (horizontal or vertical)
Eraser	erase in perfectly straight lines (horizontal or vertical)
Grabber	move in perfectly straight lines (horizontal or vertical)
Rectangle	create perfectly square rectangles
Circle	create perfectly round circles
Paintbrush	create some nifty borders (experiment and see)

● *quick FatBits*

The standard way to enter FatBits is to choose it from the Goodies menu. A quicker and more precise way in is to select the Pencil tool, hold down the COMMAND key, and then click in the document. The FatBits window will come up centered precisely on the point where you clicked.

shortcut

● *quick Grabber (hand)*

The standard way to select the Grabber (also known as "the hand"), is to click on its box in the tool palette. This can be annoying when you're moving around the document a lot, because you have keep going back to the tool palette every time you want to move, and then back to it again to select whatever tool you're using to actually do your work.

shortcut

If the Pencil is what you're using, there's a much more convenient approach. Just hold down the OPTION key and the pointer will turn into the Grabber. When you're done moving, it will turn back into the Pencil.

✎ quick Lasso

shortcut

You don't have to draw a complete loop around an image with the Lasso to select it. MacPaint will automatically complete the loop with a straight line between where you started and ended.

✎ quick Undo

shortcut

The standard ways to undo the last thing you did are to choose Undo from the Edit menu or to use the keyboard shortcut COMMAND-Z. MacPaint offers a third alternative that only requires one key—the tilde (~) key in the upper left corner of the keyboard. Hitting it has the same effect as the other two methods.

gossip/
trivia

How did the tilde key come to have this function? Most pre-Macintosh computers have a key called ESCAPE in the upper left corner of the keyboard which is used to exit from, or interrupt, whatever you happen to be doing.

✎ alternate erasers

When you're erasing unusually shaped images, it's often easier to use the Lasso than the Eraser, which wasn't designed for fine, detailed work. Just surround the image with the Lasso (thereby selecting it) and hit the BACKSPACE key. Everything within the shimmering area will be deleted.

shortcut

When you're erasing large areas, it's often easier to use the Marquee (also known as the Selection Rectangle) than the Eraser. Just use the Marquee to select the area to be erased and hit the BACKSPACE key.

very
hot
tip

When you're erasing very small details, it's often easier to use the Paintbrush than the Eraser. Pick a small brush size (with Brush Shapes on the Goodies menu), make white the current pattern (on the pattern palette at the bottom of the screen), and paint out what you don't want.

¢ *changing your choice of Brush Shapes*

If you're an advanced user, you can use the system utility ResEdit to change the size and shape of the Paintbrush choices offered you by Brush Shapes (on the Goodies menu). If you're not an advanced user, you can experiment with it. In *either* case, make sure you work on a *copy* of MacPaint.

Launch ResEdit, open the copy of MacPaint, and then scroll through the list of resources that are displayed until you get to the FONT resources. Double-click on 12. You'll find the Paintbrush shapes near the end of the displayed box. Edit the shapes with the standard FatBits techniques.

MacPaint tips— images and patterns

¢ *moving objects without the background*

When you select something with the Marquee and then move it, a rectangular chunk of the background moves with it. One time this looks particularly bad is when you're laying one object on top of another. To get just the object and not the background, use the Lasso instead of the Marquee.

If you're having trouble getting just the portion of the picture you want, because of other things near it, go into FatBits and use the Lasso there.

¢ *precise positioning of Lassoed objects*

To move a Lassoed object, you need to point to it, and that normally means the pointer will be on top of it—obscuring some part of it—when you move it. If the object you're moving is small and needs to be positioned exactly, this can make it difficult to place the object exactly where you want.

To avoid this, move the Lasso down to bottom edge of the window. It will change into an arrow pointer. Click at that point and you'll be able to move the selected object without the pointer obscuring any part of it.

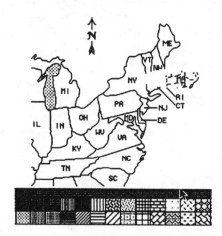

Moving a portion of a Lassoed map without obscuring any part of it

♦ *making a single copy of something*

You can duplicate objects in MacPaint by Copying and Pasting them, but there's an easier way to do it. First, use the Marquee or the Lasso to select the part of the picture you want to duplicate, then hold down the OPTION key while dragging it. Instead of moving the original, you'll peel away an exact copy. When you have it where you want it, just release the mouse button.

♦ *making multiple copies of something*

very good feature

To make multiple copies of a selected portion of a MacPaint document, use the Marquee or the Lasso to select the part of the picture you want to duplicate, then hold down the COMMAND and OPTION keys while dragging it. Instead of moving the original, you'll deposit one exact copy after another, until you release the mouse button. (We call this the "deck of cards" effect, or a "slur," but the picture below will probably give you a better idea than any words.)

The faster you drag, the less the multiple images overlap. You can also change the rate at which the multiple images are generated by—now get this—*changing the line width*. (This has to be the most bizarre command in MacPaint.) The thicker the line you select, the slower the multiple copies will be generated (and thus the less overlap there'll be at any given speed at which you drag the mouse). In other words, to get little overlap, select a thick line width and drag fast; to get a lot of overlap, select a thin line width and drag slowly.

If you want the copies to stay in a straight line, hold down SHIFT, OPTION and COMMAND at the same time.

very good
feature

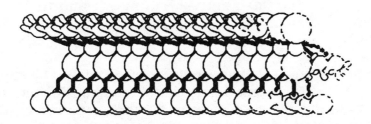

Making multiple copies in a straight line with SHIFT-OPTION-COMMAND

⚘ stretching things

To stretch something, select it with either the Marquee or the Lasso, hold down the COMMAND key, point to one of its edges and drag. You can create some dramatic effects with the distortion that results.

If you don't want distortion, hold down the SHIFT key as well as the COMMAND key when you drag (see illustration on next page).

very good
feature

Object stretched with SHIFT-COMMAND

🍎 *Bill Atkinson's "three-finger stretch"*

When you've mastered the basic stretching techniques described in the last entry, you may want to try what MacPaint's creator, Bill Atkinson, calls the "three-finger stretch."

Create a filled rectangle, circle or other shape, by choosing a pattern on the pattern palette and then choosing one of the filled icons on the tool palette. When the object is drawn, select a portion of it with the Marquee. Now hold down the SHIFT, OPTION and COMMAND keys and drag the image. The selected portion will stretch as you drag it, creating some

Object stretched with Bill Atkinson's three-finger stretch

strange and interesting effects as the pattern distorts.

If you don't want the pattern to distort, choose Grid on the Goodies menu before stretching. This is useful for stretching already created objects that aren't exactly the size you want them.

⚫ *resizing images*

Resizing things in MacPaint is quick and easy. You just select the area you want to resize with the Marquee or the Lasso, and then Cut it. Next you draw a Marquee rectangle that's the size you want the image to be. Then Paste the image, and it will be resized to fit the Marquee.

very good
feature

One problem with this technique is that it distorts patterns. But with images composed of lines, or black or white objects, it works fine.

⚫ *making images much smaller* (Dennis Klatzkin)

MacPaint images can be reduced in size simply by using the "stretch" feature (draw a Marquee around the image, hold down the COMMAND key, and drag a corner of the rectangle inwards). The rectangular proportions can be maintained ("constrained") by holding down the SHIFT key at the same time as the COMMAND key.

very
hot
tip

There's a major drawback to this technique: if an image is greatly reduced in size, it becomes dark, blurred, and indistinct. Here's a step-by-step approach to avoid that pitfall:

1. Have the image to be reduced in the MacPaint window by itself. If necessary, copy the image to a new MacPaint document.

2. Double-click on the Marquee icon. This will select the entire screen.

3. Choose Invert from the Edit menu.

4. Choose the Filled Rectangle icon from the MacPaint tool gallery.

5. Choose the fifth pattern from the left in the top row of the pattern palette.

6. Holding down the COMMAND key, draw a rectangle that completely covers the image to be reduced. This action will produce a "mask" effect over the inverted image.

7. Double-click on the Marquee icon once again (thus selecting the entire screen) and again choose Invert from the Edit menu. Your original image will now appear as if you were viewing it through a screen.

8. Now use the "constrained stretch" technique to shrink the image. Draw a Marquee rectangle around the image, hold down both the COMMAND and SHIFT keys, position the pointer at the corner of the rectangle, hold down the mouse button, and drag the rectangle inward.

9. As your image shrinks to different sizes, its resolution will vary. There is one point at which the image is half its original size, and at this point its resolution will be very good.

(This may seem strange to you, but it really works. Try it and see.)

⬤ *enlarging pictures to full page*

It's easier to enlarge a picture to full-page size in MacWrite than to try to do it in MacPaint. You just Copy or Cut the picture from MacPaint, Paste it into a MacWrite document, and then enlarge it by dragging on one of the little black "handles" that appear at the bottom of the picture. (If the handles aren't there, click on the picture to select it.)

⚫ *creating objects with no borders*

You can create filled objects without having to have a black border around them. Just choose the dotted line at the top of the lines palette. Any shape you draw until you change the line width will be borderless.

Same object with and without border

⚫ *creating dotted lines and outlines*

To create a dotted line, choose one of the larger line widths, then choose one of the smaller dots as a brush shape. Put a dot on the screen with the Paintbrush, Lasso the dot, and drag it while holding down COMMAND and OPTION. With some practice, you can learn to draw dotted circles and other shapes with this technique.

Two sample dotted lines

⚜ *shadowing images*

The Trace Edges command (on the Edit menu) is a lot of fun (You can also get it with the keyboard shortcut COMMAND-E.) Play with it a bit and then try the undocumented variation we call *shadowing*. Just hold down the SHIFT key while Tracing Edges. The results look like this:

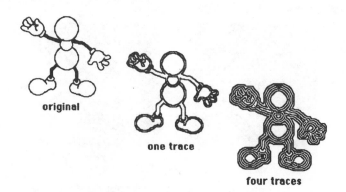

Examples of Trace Edges

⚜ *tracing pictures*

very
hot
tip

Here's a simple technique for transferring pictures from the real world into the Mac that doesn't cost as much—or work as well—as buying a digitizer. Buy some sheets of clear film at an art supply store, and trace the image onto one of them with a light-colored pen (the kind that's used for writing on overhead transparencies). Then tape the film onto the Mac screen, with the image centered where you want it, and trace the image carefully with the mouse.

Choose a thin Brush Shape (on the Goodies menu), but one that's thick enough to be visible behind the trace lines. If the combination you're using isn't working, try tracing the original again with a thinner pen.

❤ transparent images

To create an image you can see through—in other words, a "wash" effect like you get with watercolor paints—hold down the COMMAND key while you draw over an existing image with the Paintbrush, Paint Can, Spray Can or any of the filled shape tools. The new image will appear to be almost transparent, allowing the patterns and images underneath it to show through.

gossip/
trivia

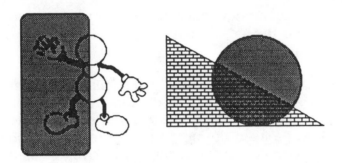

The wash effect

❤ creating new patterns

MacPaint offers two ways to change the patterns in the pattern palette. The better-known method is to edit an existing pattern by selecting Edit Pattern from the Goodies menu. But you can also select any part of a MacPaint image and install it as a pattern on the palette.

To do that, simply double-click on a pattern on the palette that you don't want to keep, then click on the part of the screen that contains the pattern you want to install in its place. (You can also select the pattern on the palette, choose Edit Pattern from the Goodies menu, and then click on the screen, but why bother?)

shortcut

very
hot
tip

⚫ *saving custom patterns*

When you change the patterns in the pattern palette, the new patterns are associated with the document you're working on, not with MacPaint itself. So if you quit MacPaint without saving the document, they'll be lost.

The easiest way to keep track of the new patterns is to use Save As... to store the document with a name like 'new patterns 5/12/87', and then erase the contents of the drawing window (double-clicking in the Eraser box is the easiest way) so that the document takes up less room. You now have a template with the edited patterns installed that you can use again and again.

As always with a document you're using as a template, be sure to save your new pattern document under another name immediately after opening it, so it will remain untouched on your disk to be used the next time. In fact, it's a good idea is to lock the template, so you can't save over it using the same name (use Get Info on the Desktop to do that). Finally, don't forget to copy the template to a backup disk.

Dealing with text in MacPaint

⚫ *using ENTER to manage text*

When you change the font, size or style of text in MacPaint, all the text you typed since the last mouse click changes to the new setting. This is unlike word processing programs, where the change only affects text you type after you make it. To make this happen in MacPaint, you have to click with the mouse to start a new text block. But then you have the problem of lining up the old line of text with the new, which is complicated by the fact that they're in different fonts and/or sizes and/or styles.

very good
feature

Fortunately, an answer to this problem is built into MacPaint. Hitting the ENTER key stops font, size and style changes from being retroactive. It's as if you clicked the mouse and laid down a new insertion point at the place where you hit the ENTER key, but the lines of text line up perfectly. You can press the ENTER key as many times as you need to make further changes.

♦ *formatting text from the Note Pad*

Another way around MacPaint's habit of treating text as just a bunch of dots after you've clicked the mouse or hit the ENTER key is to use the Note Pad to enter the text you want in your document, then Paste it into MacPaint. The newly Pasted text will appear in a Marquee.

As you resize the Marquee⁻(position the pointer within the Marquee, then hold down COMMAND and drag), the text will be reformatted to match the new Marquee's size. As long as the Marquee is active, you can format the text with any of MacPaint's text options.

♦ *formatting text from the Scrapbook*

When you Paste text from the Scrapbook into a MacPaint picture, all font and style attributes are lost; the text appears as 12-point Geneva.

The solution to this problem is to take advantage of the font and style control available in MacPaint. Information Pasted into MacPaint appears in a Marquee rectangle, and therefore can be changed. If you hold down the COMMAND key and point to the Marquee, you can resize the text to any shape or font you like. Also, you can select from the menu any of the text formatting options that MacPaint offers.

♦ *transferring formatted text to MacPaint*

If you use the standard method of copying text from MacWrite (or any other word processing program) to

MacPaint—that is, if you Cut or Copy it from the word processor and Paste it into MacPaint—you'll lose the formatting (font, type style, type size, etc.). Here's how to transfer the text with the formatting intact:

**very
hot
tip**

Take a screen shot of the MacWrite text (by putting it up on the screen and hitting COMMAND-SHIFT-3). This will create a MacPaint document named Screen0. Go to the Desktop and double-click on the Screen0 document (which opens MacPaint as well as the document). Select the desired text with the Marquee or the Lasso and Copy it to the Clipboard. Close the Screen0 document, open the MacPaint document where you want to put the text, and Paste.

NOTE: The first screen shot you take with COMMAND-SHIFT-3 is called Screen0, the next on the same disk is called Screen1 and so on up to Screen 9 (or until the disk is full).

✦ *keyboard shortcuts for formatting text*

The keyboard shortcuts below change the font and size of text in MacPaint:

shortcut	effect on text
COMMAND->	next larger size
COMMAND-<	next smaller size
COMMAND-SHIFT->	next font listed on the Font menu
COMMAND-SHIFT-<	previous font listed on the Font menu

shortcut

Remember that you can only change text entered since your last mouse click. When you click the mouse or press the ENTER key, MacPaint forgets that your words are text and treats them as just another pretty picture.

✦ *thinner outline text*

The outline type style makes text wider than plain text, and sometimes that makes it hard to fit it into a given area of a MacPaint document. An alternative is to enter the text in plain or bold style, then select it with the Marquee and choose Trace Edges (on the Edit menu). This gives you outline text that's no wider than the original plain or bold text.

very
hot
tip

Chicago

Chicago

Chicago

Plain text, regular outline text, and plain text with Traced Edges

🍎 *bolder than bold*

To create characters in your MacPaint documents that are bolder than bold, type them in outline and then fill them in with the Paint Can (make sure the black pattern is selected).

very
hot
tip

Cupertino
Cupertino
Cupertino

Regular, bold, and very bold text

🍎 *making a font chart in MacPaint*

The easiest way to make a font template is to use either MacWrite and MacDraw (see chapter 3 for more details on how to do that). But if you want each character to appear in its keyboard position and don't own MacDraw, you may have a use the following, somewhat tedious method for creating a font chart in MacPaint.

Select Shortcuts from MacPaint's Goodies menu. A drawing of the keyboard will appear. Take a snapshot of the screen (COMMAND-SHIFT-3); it will appear on the Desktop and in the list box as Screen0 (if it's the first one on the disk, Screen1 if it's the second, etc.). Open it in MacPaint, or a desk accessory like Art Grabber + or Artisto, and Copy it.

Now open a blank MacPaint document and give it an appropriate name, like Cairo Font Chart. With the Marquee, create an area large enough to contain the keyboard picture, and Paste it in. Carefully erase the key legends that appear in the keyboard. Now type a few characters in the desired font, Lasso them individually, and drag each one to the proper key. Repeat this procedure to complete the keyboard.

Making charts like this for the fonts you often use will allow you to remove the Key Caps desk accessory and free up some space. But remember that MacPaint won't print out laser fonts, so these charts will only be useful for ImageWriter fonts.

MacPaint tips—miscellaneous

❡ printing multiple copies of a single document

MacPaint doesn't give you the option of printing more than one copy of a single document, which means that you have to manually select Print for every copy you want. Here's a way around that tedious procedure:

Any Macintosh document can be printed from the Desktop (you just select it and choose Print on the File menu). You can also select more than one document and print them in the same manner. So if you duplicate the MacPaint document you want to print (using Duplicate on the File menu or the keyboard shortcut COMMAND-D), select all the duplicates and choose Print, you'll get as many copies as you made duplicates. (This technique is a bit tedious too, but at least you can walk away from the computer once you've set it up, instead of having to sit there and issue one Print command after another.)

One limitation on this technique: Since each copy of the document takes up space on the disk, it will only work on a disk with enough free space.

⬤ *free disk space required*

If MacPaint tells you that it can't create a new document because there isn't enough room, check the available space on your document disk. MacPaint is one of the many applications that uses temporary files that you never see because it closes them when you exit. It needs at least 25K of free space on the document disk for these temporary files.

⬤ *freeing up disk space*

Since MacPaint's a lot of fun, most users end up with a lot of MacPaint documents on their disks. If you find that you're running out of space, remove the ImageWriter driver (just drag the icon labeled ImageWriter from the System Folder to the Trash and then choose Empty Trash from the Special menu). This will save you 30K and won't cost you anything, since MacPaint bypasses the ImageWriter driver when it prints.

very
hot
tip

If you need to save still more space, try combining two or more documents into one. You'll save about 2K per document you combine, and even 2K can make the difference between a floppy having or not having enough room for one more document—particularly if you're using 400K disks.

✦ *Print Catalog*

The names of the documents on a MacPaint disk often don't provide enough information to remind you what the pictures actually look like. For more of a reminder, enter MacPaint and choose Print Catalog from File menu. You'll get a one-page catalog with tiny representations of every MacPaint document on the disk. The little pictures in the catalog will, of course, lack most of the detail of the originals, but they're usually adequate to remind you of what the picture is.

✦ *quick quit—don't use it*

important
warning

You can exit MacPaint quickly and restart the system by holding down the COMMAND key while choosing Quit from the File menu, but it's not a good idea. Quitting like that can scramble the directory on the disk, which means you'll lose all the information on it.

FullPaint tips

(Unless otherwise indicated, all the tips in this section refer to version 1.0.)

✦ *similarities to MacPaint*

very good
feature

FullPaint incorporates 95% of the features of MacPaint, and almost all of them function exactly the same way. So if you're familiar with MacPaint, you can start using FullPaint without missing a mouse click. This also means that virtually all the MacPaint tips described above also apply to FullPaint. The tips that follow cover a few of the things that are unique to FullPaint.

✦ *moving the tool and pattern palettes*

One of the nice features of FullPaint is the ability to move the tool and pattern palettes to get them out of the way. To do that, place the pointer along the edges of either palette. When it changes to a hollow cross, you can use it to drag the palettes anywhere on the screen that you want.

A even quicker method is to hold down the OPTION key when pointing to either palette; this changes the pointer to a hollow cross without your having to worry about exact positioning.

shortcut

♦ *quick select with the Lasso* *(David Goldman)*

Double-clicking on an object with the Lasso selects it.

very good feature

♦ *shrink-wrapping with the Lasso and the Marquee*

Holding down the COMMAND key when encircling an area with the Lasso makes it automatically shrink to the edges of the image being Lassoed. Holding down the COMMAND key when surrounding an area with the Marquee makes it automatically shrink as close to the edge of the selected image as it can while still remaining a rectangle.

very good feature

♦ *reverse Paint Can*

Normally the Paint Can fills the area where the tip of the pouring paint points. If you hold down the OPTION key, everything *outside* of that area will be filled instead.

♦ *editing the Paintbrush*

Creating a custom Paintbrush in FullPaint is incredibly easy. Hold down the COMMAND key while double-clicking on the Paintbrush icon in the tool palette. This will put you in FatBits mode.

Once you're there, you can move the pointer anywhere on the screen and click. The brush pattern will assume the shape of whatever you're pointing to, and you'll be able to edit the pattern.

MacDraw tips

(Unless otherwise indicated, all the tips in this section refer to version 1.9.)

♦ font limitations

very bad feature

One of MacDraw's biggest drawbacks is the limitation it places on the number of fonts you can use. Because it places the font size commands at the bottom of the Font menu, instead of on a separate menu where they belong, there's only room for eleven fonts above them. By the time you read this, this problem may be solved, but maybe not; it's been annoying people for so long, it's amazing it hasn't been solved already.

♦ preventing pointless saves

If you try to save a file that hasn't been changed since the last save, MacDraw gives you a message that reads: "there haven't been any changes since the last save." This is a nice touch, and should be a part of every Mac program.

♦ selecting just-drawn objects

Normally when you draw an object in MacDraw, the tool you're using changes back to the arrow pointer the moment the object is drawn. If you want to use the same tool to draw several objects without having to go back to the tool palette again and again, hold down the COMMAND key while drawing. The tool will persist from one object to the next (to get back to the arrow pointer, just release the COMMAND key).

♦ quick reselection of last drawing tool

To quickly reselect the last drawing tool used, hold down the COMMAND key while clicking the mouse button. This is easier than reselecting the tool from the tool palette, and is particularly useful when you're using the same tool repeatedly.

● *drawing perfect squares and circles*

It's easy to draw perfect squares and circles in MacDraw. Just hold down the SHIFT key while drawing with the circle or rectangle tool.

● *using Smoothing to draw curves*

When you use MacDraw's freehand shape tool (second from the bottom of the palette) to draw curves, you may not be very happy with the results. Instead, try drawing an angular approximation of the desired image with MacDraw's polygon tool (last one on the palette), then use the Edit menu's Smooth command to curve the edges. This usually produces a better effect.

very
hot
tip

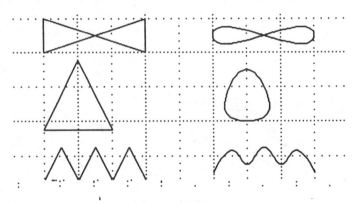

Before and after Smoothing by MacDraw

● *nonstandard text sizes*

If you want text in sizes other than the standard 9-, 10-, 12-, 14-, 18-, 24-, 36- and 48-point, import it from Microsoft Word. Word lets you type in any size you want, from 4 point to 127 point in 1-point increments. Be aware that the results will only print properly on the LaserWriter. Scaled type on the ImageWriter usually looks terrible.

❡ *putting text in a rectangle*

The MacDraw manual can be confusing when it describes how to draw a rectangle to use as a border around text. You may think from reading it that you should draw the rectangle, select the text tool, place the insertion point and then type. This method doesn't work.

Instead, draw the rectangle and just start typing, without bothering with the text tool and the insertion point. The text you type will word-wrap within the rectangle.

❡ *more precise images while dragging*

When you move an object around on the page, MacDraw normally represents it as a rectangle, regardless of its actual shape. If you want to see an outline that corresponds more precisely to the actual shape of the object, hold down the OPTION key while dragging.

❡ *embellishing Chart/Excel graphs*

When you've done all you can to a graph in Microsoft Chart or Excel, Paste it into MacDraw, where you can resize, rotate and shade every element of the chart separately, and do lots of other things besides.

Another advantage of putting the finishing touches on in MacDraw: it lets you print out on a number of different plotters that you can use to create overhead transparencies.

❡ *adding patterns to MacDraw*

MacDraw lacks the easy pattern-editing features of MacPaint, but you can use ResEdit to create new patterns in it. Open a *copy* of MacDraw with ResEdit and open the resource PAT#. Then open the box that contains the MacDraw patterns. Double-clicking on a pattern allows you to edit it in FatBits mode.

When you have the patterns you want, save and close ResEdit. If you need to use many different patterns, you can keep separate copies of MacDraw on separate disks. If you use this approach, be sure you use the appropriate copy of MacDraw with each document, because MacDraw assigns patterns based simply on where there are on the palette.

◉ *white stripes in LaserWriter printouts*

If you created an image in MacPaint, copy it into MacDraw, rotate it and then print it on the LaserWriter, narrow, parallel white stripes will probably appear in the image. The solution is to rotate the image in MacPaint (using T/Maker's Click-Art Effects) or in FullPaint before copying it to MacDraw.

◉ *Laserprinting small white text*

You may sometimes have problems printing a MacDraw document that contains small white text on the LaserWriter. The solution is to type the text in Outline, fill in the background (with any pattern you want), stretch the entire document to double its original style, then print with 50% reduction. Not an elegant solution, but it usually works.

Digitizer tips

◉ *what type of camera to use*

Less expensive black-and-white video cameras with high-quality lenses will provide much better images on camera-based digitizers like MacVision than the more expensive color cameras.

bargain

⚫ *creating depth with camera-based digitizers*

When using a camera-based digitizer like MacVision, you can give the image dramatic depth by angling the object slightly. Be careful though—just a little is enough.

⚫ *ThunderScan output on the LaserWriter*

very hot tip

Since the ThunderScan digitizer reads a picture on the ImageWriter, printouts on the LaserWriter often look no better than 72-dpi MacPaint document. But there's a way around this. Scan the image at 400 percent, then print it at 25 percent. That will give your image a resolution of 288 dots per inch (dpi).

But be prepared to wait a while. Scanning a whole page at 400 percent takes over an hour.

⚫ *avoiding stair-stepping on the ThunderScan*

very hot tip

One way to improve the quality of a ThunderScan image is to make sure you insert the original into the ImageWriter as straight as possible. If it contains horizontal lines, try to align them with the roller shaft. You can test the alignment quite easily—if the horizontal lines in the digitized image are slightly "stair-stepped," the alignment is off.

⚫ *vertical lines on the ThunderScan*

very hot tip

If the image you are digitizing with ThunderScan contains lots of vertical lines, put it in the ImageWriter sideways (but see the previous entry about aligning it precisely). You can then use MacPaint's Rotate command to properly orient the digitized image.

Chapter 9

Communicating with other computers

♦ disabling Call Waiting

Many phone companies offer their customers a service called Call Waiting that interrupts calls with brief signals that someone else is calling. You can then easily switch between the two calls. Unfortunately, these signals disrupt data transmissions, thus forcing modem users to choose between giving up the convenience of Call Waiting or gambling on an interrupted connection.

But help is on the way. As local phone companies upgrade their systems by installing electronic switching exchanges, they offer their customers the option of temporarily disabling Call Waiting for the duration of any outgoing call. You just precede the number you're dialing with *70 (on a tone phone) or 1170 (on a pulse phone). When the call is over, Call Waiting automatically comes back.

very
hot
tip

To see whether you can do this on your phone, just try putting the appropriate code in front of a number you're dialing. If the service isn't available, you should get a recorded message that the call can't be completed as dialed.

If you're using an autodial modem (if you don't know, the odds are you are), you have to instruct it to pause briefly between the Call Waiting disabling code and the number you're dialing. Two or three seconds is sufficient. The following command will cause a Hayes-compatible modem to give the code *70, then pause two seconds, then dial the number 555-1212: ATDT*70,555-1212 (needless to say, you should substitute whatever number you're dialing for 555-1212).

☀ *useful Hayes commands*

There are a slew of powerful and convenient commands in the Hayes manual. For example, putting ATM1DT in a dialing command turns on the speaker of any Hayes-compatible modem; ATM0DT turns it off. See the Hayes manual for dozens of others.

Communicating with MS-DOS machines

☀ *trading with the enemy* (Arthur)

If you use a personal computer at work, it probably isn't a Mac. No, the ugly reality is that most personal computers are IBM PCs or clones thereof (Compaq, etc.)—known generically as DOS (dawss) machines because the operating system they share is called MS-DOS (or PC-DOS on IBM PC itself), or simply as PCs.

WARNING! HYSTERICAL RANT AHEAD.

gossip/
trivia

There's an ignorant trend afoot to call all personal computers—presumably even Macs!—PCs, as if there were something wrong with the simple and straightforward word "computers." (The people who use "PC" in that way tend to be the same ones who talk about "software programs"—as if you needed the word "software" to distinguish a program running on your computer from, say, a television program or a drug rehabilitation program.)

Maybe they feel that the "P" in "PC" helps make it clear that you're referring to a personal computer and that without that qualification, you might ask someone what kind of computer they use at home and get an answer like, "Do you mean my *personal* computer, or the Cray I keep in the basement?"

This is all by way of saying that—in this book—"PC" refers to an IBM PC or clone, not to a real computer like the Mac.

END OF HYSTERICAL RANT. RESUME NORMAL READING.

Where were we? Oh, yes—the PC you have in your office. Although there's no way around the wrenching feeling in your gut you have to endure every morning when you travel back into the preMac stone age of computing, you can at least transfer data back and forth between the office machine and your Mac at home. The tips below tell you how.

⚫ *transferring files directly*

Transferring files back and forth between a Mac and a PC can be relatively simple, particularly if you can arrange to wire the two machines together directly. The cable that connects the original Imagewriter with the original Mac sockets (that is, the nine-pin sockets on the back of 128K and 512K machines) is the only hardware you need. Simply connect it to the modem port on the back of the Mac and to the serial connector on the PC. (If you're using a Mac Plus with the mini eight-pin connector, ask your dealer for a Mac-Plus-to-original-Imagewriter cable. They're not exactly common, but they are available.)

Next, you'll need a communications program for each machine. For the DOS machine, either PC-Talk or ProComm is an excellent choice. They operate at up to 19,200 baud and both support the error-checking file-transfer protocol called *Xmodem*. Both are shareware and can be obtained

shortcut

from most computer bulletin boards, commercial services such as CompuServe, or from PC users groups.

On the Mac you should run software that will transfer at 19,200 baud and that will allow you to disable MacBinary (a special kind of Xmodem file transfer protocol) when you're doing the transfer. Most communications programs for the Mac meet both requirements—although the otherwise excellent TermWorks doesn't allow you to disable MacBinary.

shortcut

With both machines set to 19,200 baud, data moves quite fast, and files of average length will be transferred in just a couple of minutes.

♦ *transferring files over the phone*

Lugging machines around can be tedious, so you may prefer to transfer files over the phone. The only differences from the method described above are that you need to add a modem at each end, and that data transfer will be slower. If at all possible, use a modem that supports at least 1200 baud—or, even better, 2400 baud.

In this example, we'll assume that you have a DOS machine at the office and a Mac at home (the opposite is a bit hard to imagine), both with 2400 baud modems. Before you leave the office, turn on the PC (if it isn't already on), start your communications program and set it to answer an incoming call. (ProComm is particularly well suited for phone transfers since it has a special option called Host Mode that gives you full access to the files on any disk when you connect remotely, while at the same time providing for extensive password protection so that only you and people you authorize can access the computer.)

When you're ready to access the office PC from your Mac at home, start your Mac communications program and tell it to dial the number of the PC. When you've connected with the PC, it will ask you for your password, then provide you with a menu of files available for transferring ("downloading") to your Mac.

Select the file you want to receive, then tell your Mac to get ready to receive a file (the command is usually called something like Waiting to Receive File). This process is no different than connecting to another Mac or a commercial service such as CompuServe. When you've transferred all the files you want, just tell the communications program on the Mac to hang up.

When you've finished working with the file, you can call the remote machine and sent it back, or set the Mac up so you can call it from the PC during the day.

🍎 *what gets lost in the translation*

If you use both a PC and Mac on a regular basis, you know that they are quite different animals. As a result, there are some limits to what the Mac can do with files transferred from DOS machines.

One program that imposes very few limitations is Microsoft Word. Word is available for both PCs and Macs, and the Mac version comes with a utility that converts Word files from one format to the other. This lets you work extensively on documents on both machines and send them back and forth with little or no loss of formatting.

very good
feature

If you're using another DOS word processing program, you may only be able to enter and edit text; you'll have to remember to save the document as a text file, and all your formatting will be lost in the transfers between the machines. (One way around this limitation is to find a word processing program on the PC that offers a conversion utility to Microsoft Word format.)

Spreadsheet users are in better shape, thanks to some standards in the industry and the flexibility of Excel, the most popular spreadsheet on the Mac. The standard spreadsheet in the PC world is Lotus 1-2-3, and you can read 1-2-3 files directly into Excel. After you've worked on the files in Excel, you can save them in 1-2-3 format and transfer them back. (The main limitation is that macros written in one product won't work with the other.)

very good feature

Database files also transfer fairly easily, if the PC program uses the Mac standard format of tabs between fields and carriage returns between records. The most popular PC database is dBASE III and dMAC III from Format Software lets you read and alter dBASE III files with no conversion. In fact, dMAC III is nothing less than dBASE III on the Mac, complete with cryptic commands and meaningless prompts.

The publishers of dBASE III, Ashton-Tate, have also come up with a Mac version of the program called dBASE Mac; it was due to ship late in 1986. Preliminary reports are that it can read and write dBASE III files but that it won't allow you to actually write dBASE III programs on the Mac. For that, you should use dMAC III.

All this transferring and modifying files can get to be a lot of work. If you're fortunate enough to have Macs at work as well as PCs, you should investigate one of the more direct—and expensive—solutions like TOPS, which is described below.

Connecting PCs and Macs with TOPS *(Eric Alderman)*

With mass quantities of IBM-compatible computers currently installed in corporate America and a growing number of Macintoshes wriggling their way through the back doors, the ability of these two considerably dissimilar computers to chat with one another is becoming—for many—a practical necessity.

Even if you don't have a pressing business need to transfer documents between a Mac and an IBM PC or compatible machine, the time will almost certainly come to pass when you wish you had a way to do it. Until recently there were only a few methods for accomplishing this feat, none of them very fast or efficient:

1. You could retype your documents.

2. You could use two modems to transfer the documents over phone lines between the two computers.

3. You could hard-wire the computers together using a serial cable that is connected directly to each machine.

(See the section above on communicating with MS-DOS machines for more information on how to do 2 or 3.)

All of these methods work fine if you have only an occasional need to transfer documents, but for any regular use they are tedious, slow, and a pain in the disk drive. A much better solution by far is to connect the machines onto a common network that has the ability to transfer a file from one computer to the other as easily as copying it from one disk to another. TOPS (from Centram Systems West in Berkeley, California; see Appendix C for their address) is a networking system that lets you do just that.

♦ *how TOPS works*

TOPS (the name stands for "transcendental operating system") uses the Appletalk network that's built into every Macintosh to effect this communication. To allow PCs to join the network, you insert an Appletalk interface card into one of their available slots. A standard Appletalk Connector kit for the original Macintosh (from Apple) plugs right into the 9-pin connector on the Appletalk card.

Once the machines are physically connected, the TOPS network software completes the union on an intellectual level.

When you "publish" a volume (a disk drive, directory or folder) onto the network—that is, when you make it available for others to use—you become a Server. When you "mount" a Server's published volume—that is, when you indicate that you want to use it—you become a Client. Any computer attached to the network can act as a Server, a Client, or both at the same time. The same software is loaded on each machine, regardless of whether it's intended to be a Server or a Client.

very good feature

One of the nice features of TOPS is that PC users continue to use the PC interface—they don't need to learn a lot about Macintosh terms like "icon" and "folder." And Mac users continue to use the Mac interface—they don't need to learn a lot about PC terms like "DOS prompt" and "subdirectory."

When you mount a published volume (which could be on a machine right next to you or up on the 12th floor), your computer treats it as if it were simply another disk drive attached to your system. On the PC, this means that you have another drive letter to use for saving and retrieving files, or performing any normal DOS command. On the Mac, it means another disk icon appears on the Desktop. When you open the window for this icon, you'll see the mounted volume's files. From the Open and Save As list boxes within an application, you simply click on the Drive button to access the new volume.

The fact that the volume you're using is not actually attached to your system is almost completely transparent to you, since your computer acts exactly as if you were using a local volume (for example, an external disk drive).

With TOPS, file transfer is as simple as copying a file between a local volume and remote volume. For example, let's say you're using a Macintosh and you've mounted a remote volume from a PC Server. To transfer a document from your Mac to the PC, you simply drag the file's icon from your Mac disk window to the PC volume icon. Got that? I know it's a bit tricky, so let me repeat it one more time. You drag the file's icon to the PC volume icon.

very good
feature

If you're on the PC side, you transfer a document to a Macintosh simply by copying it to the drive letter that represents the remote Mac volume. Folders on the remote volume will appear to your PC as subdirectories, so you can navigate around the Mac disk using the normal DOS subdirectory commands before copying the file.

Actually, in many situations you won't even need to copy your files between computers. Instead, you can simply access files directly from within your applications.

very good
feature

For example, Microsoft Excel reads and translates Lotus 1-2-3 worksheets automatically. Normally, you would first transfer the worksheet onto your Macintosh disk using one of the communication methods discussed above, and then you would load the file. With TOPS, you could leave the file in place on the PC's hard disk. While in Excel, you would click on the Drive button to access the 1-2-3 files on the remote PC disk, and then retrieve one—straight into Excel, right across the network.

Another common use for TOPS is to transfer word processing documents between the Mac and the PC. If you use Microsoft Word on both machines, you would use Word Convert, a program that comes with the Macintosh version of Word. This program converts documents between the Macintosh and PC Word formats, and works very well on a TOPS network.

A program called MacLinkPlus (from Dataviz; see Appendix C for the address) can translate documents in WordStar, MultiMate, and DCA format over the network and put them in MacWrite format (which Mac Word can also read), and vice versa. It can also perform many spreadsheet translations—for example from the DIF format common on PC spreadsheets to the SYLK format used by Multiplan and Excel.

⬥ *TOPS pro and con*

One disadvantage of TOPS is that, like many networking programs, a large portion of it resides in memory. On the Mac, TOPS takes up about 70K of RAM. On the PC, where memory is even more precious, TOPS takes up from 118K-130K of RAM. You should definitely be running with a full 640K complement of memory on your PC to offset this large RAM requirement.

TOPS is truly a revolutionary networking product. It does what didn't seem possible—it enables two very different computers to finally put aside their differences and come to speaking terms. Even if the two computers are still not software-compatible, they can at least transfer data between them with relative ease.

TOPS for the PC sells for $390, which includes an Appletalk card and software. TOPS for the Mac sells for $150. You need a package for each computer on the network, regardless of whether it will be used as a Server or a Client. You'll also need to get a $50 Appletalk connector for each computer.

Connecting Macs with MacServe
(Chris Belec)

If you have two or more Macs connected to a LaserWriter and a hard disk connected to one of the Macs, you should seriously consider buying MacServe (from Infosphere; see Appendix C for their address). It can change your present setup to a fast and convenient information-sharing environment in which all the Macs can share hard disks, LaserWriters and ImageWriters.

MacServe lets you spool print jobs, rank them in order of priority, and protect selected portions of the shared hard disk with passwords. All of these features operate without a dedicated disk server or printer server.

very good
feature

♠ *hardware requirements*

MacServe requires each Mac, LaserWriter and ImageWriter on the network to have an AppleTalk connector, and at least one of the Macs needs to be connected to a hard disk. Any Mac that's connected to a hard disk that other Macs on the network can use is called a "disk server" or "network host." Other Macs on the network are called "network users." You can have up to 30 network users on a MacServe network (plus the network host), but only 16 network hosts.

MacServe requires that each network host be created from a separate copy of MacServe, but no such condition applies to the network users. Therefore if you want to have three network hosts serving the needs of fourteen users, you'll only need to buy three copies of MacServe.

bargain

MacServe doesn't place a limit on the number of hard disks on the network, only on the number of network hosts. But the hard disks of network users can't be accessed by other Macs on the network.

♠ *setting up MacServe*

MacServe is easy to install. Only one file on the MacServe program disk is copy-protected. Called Installer, it puts the networking information onto the startup disks of both the network hosts and network users—a process that takes no more than two or three minutes for each Mac.

Before you install the network host software on a hard disk, you have to give a lot of thought to how you're going to distribute various application programs around the network. This is the tricky part.

To install itself on a hard disk, MacServe needs to initialize the disk. This is, needless to say, a problem if you've already been using the disk and have it organized just the way you want it. Unfortunately, MacServe forces you to alter this organization in order for the disk to be shared. Chances are that you, like me, haven't backed up your entire hard disk for some time. This is as good a time to do it as any.

You partition the hard disk into MacServe volumes using MacServe's Manager program. Up to sixteen volumes can be created on a hard disk, although for 20-megabyte disks, six to eight volumes seems quite adequate. These MacServe volumes define the portions of the hard disk that can be made available throughout the network. Each one is given a name, size and file structure (HFS or MFS) by the network host. You can protect any volume with a password that prevents other network users from nosing around in it.

very good feature

To access an (unprotected) volume on the network, you call up the MacServe desk accessory and click on the Servers button when the dialog box comes up. Once "mounted" (accessed by) your Mac, the volume takes on all the characteristics of a Mac disk: it has an icon on your Desktop, you can clear it off the Desktop by throwing it in the Trash, files can be copied to and from it, and it can be write-protected.

The number and the size of the MacServe volumes is determined by how many users there are on the network and the nature of the tasks that each of them will be doing. For example, let's say Tom, Dick, and Harriet each have a Mac on the MacServe network. Harriet, the supervisor of the group, has a Mac with a 20-meg hard disk and an ImageWriter connected to it, while Tom and Dick only have external floppy drives connected to their Macs.

Harriet is the network host and keeper of the passwords. She can create, delete, alter, and temporarily block access to the MacServe volumes (partitions) on her hard disk. She can also make changes to the printer queues, pushing aside low priority jobs and temporarily denying the others access to the print spooler.

Her first task, after initializing the hard disk, is partitioning it into three 2-megabyte sections, one for each user. Tom, Dick and Harriet then each choose a password for their private volume to prevent any non-authorized changes or access to the files in their volume.

Harriet then creates two public, or shared, volumes, which can be mounted on all Macintoshes on the network at the same time. Files can be added to shared volumes by any user, but the files already there can only be altered or deleted by the network host.

Harriet calls the first volume News. Tom mounts it on his disk, copies a Word document of his own to it, and then unmounts it. The News volume can then be mounted by Harriet and Dick, and they can copy the file to their private volumes. This type of information interchange makes particular sense when the network's users are far apart.

Harriet calls the second public volume Library, and onto it she copies all the application programs that the three of them will share. Each user then copies applications from the Library volume to their private volumes as needed.

Obviously, two users can't work on the same file at the same time, so there has to be some sort of communication between them. This can be verbal, or it can take place over the In-Box electronic mail program.

✎ a personal testimonial

very good feature

MacServe's greatest feature has to be its stability. It just doesn't crash! It doesn't even lock up network users when the network host suffers a system crash. Other network software (like StarLAN for PCs) goes to pieces if the network host is taken off-line. I was expecting the same from MacServe, but once the MacServe host restarts, all the network users can continue right where they left off. It's really incredible to watch.

At the computer store where I used to work, there was a person who had a knack for destroying system files on the Macintosh. To make things worse, when she didn't know how to quit from an application program, she would simply turn off the Macintosh and turn it on again to reset the system. MacServe survived her abuse every time.

The first occasion was when I was using Microsoft Word on a Mac that was set up as a network user. Our shock-tester was trying to do something (who knows what) on the Mac that was running as network host. I hadn't yet bothered to save the page and a half of text I had created when I heard the power switch on her Mac click twice and the reset tone rang out.

A dialog box appeared on my screen and told me that my Mac had temporarily lost contact with the network host and that it would try to reestablish communications. I was cursing both myself for not having saved any of the text to disk, and you–know–who for her irresponsible use of the system. To my great surprise and relief, my Mac reestablished contact with the network host and I was able to continue exactly where I'd left off.

MacServe also performs flawlessly when the reset button on the network host is hit, and it prevents the network host from choosing Shut Down from the Special menu if any of the users have one of the host's hard disk volumes mounted, or if there are print jobs in the host's printing queue.

✎ sharing printers

Non-AppleTalk ImageWriters can be shared over the network if they're connected to the modem port of a network host (MacServe and AppleTalk use the printer port). Thus you can have as many shared ImageWriters as you have network hosts. (ImageWriters connected to network users can only be used by that Mac.) Making an ImageWriter available to the network and setting up a queue for it takes a few seconds, using the MacServe desk accessory.

very good feature

The MacServe manual suggests you remove the Chooser desk accessory, since the MacServe desk accessory provides the same features, but we don't recommend doing this, since you'll need Chooser when you aren't on-line with MacServe.

To make it easier to locate your printing jobs in a long stream of fan-fold paper, MacServe puts a page at the beginning of each job that lists the network user's name, the name of the document, the print job number, the size in bytes, and the time of day it was printed.

MacServe provides print spooling for shared, non-AppleTalk ImageWriters. (As of release 2.0, MacServe doesn't support spooling for the LaserWriter or for the Imagewriter with the AppleTalk option installed.)

A problem you can run into with the spooler is insufficient room on the network host's hard disk for the files the spooler creates. You won't be able to tell if this is the problem from the cryptic error messages, but all you have to do is make more room on the disk and things work fine. Still, a message like "Not enough room on the host's disk to print job" would be a nice improvement.

MacServe provides a very convenient way to share printers. Several users can add jobs to a print queue at the same time, and print jobs are processed without tying up the Macintosh the printer is connected to. Added to this is the convenience with which information can be shared and the economy of sharing expensive printing and storage devices. Given all these advantages, I have trouble imagining an office with multiple Macs that wouldn't profit from having MacServe.

Connecting to Tandems
with MacMenlo *(Brad Bunnin)*

The Macintosh is a wonderful machine. Most mainframe and minicomputer terminals are not. Connecting a Mac to a mainframe—if done with skill and grace—can make your life as a user better than it would be if you had access only to the Mac or only to the mainframe, but not both.

very good feature

Tandem computers are especially favored by users who can't afford to lose data, because each Tandem is really two computers in one, each containing two separate CPUs and memory banks. Since it's *extremely* unlikely that both will crash at the same time, and since data is regularly and automatically saved between them, data loss is virtually eliminated.

very bad feature

Unfortunately, the terminals that come with Tandem systems aren't of the same quality as the computers themselves. They're cursed with a poor screen display and so many function keys that you spend most of your time trying to remember what they all do. Word processing is particularly difficult, because the software is line-oriented (an antique approach that's not even worth explaining here) and some of the commands are weird even for a line editor.

But thanks to a program called MacMenlo (from Menlo Business Systems; see Appendix C for the address), you no longer have to use the wretched Tandem terminal to communicate with the superb Tandem computer; instead, you can use a Macintosh.

MacMenlo lets you choose how you want to use your Mac: you can turn it into a super Tandem terminal, with standard Mac menus replacing clumsy function keys, or you can transfer files from the Tandem to the Mac, use standard Mac programs like MacWrite, Word and Excel to edit them, and then send them—or new files you've created on the Mac—back to the Tandem for storage. With another Menlo product, called Max, you can even preserve Mac formatting commands through the transfer. File transfer is menu-driven and slick.

very good
feature

You can customize MacMenlo to delight your heart—and your fingers: it makes the Mac's keyboard and Tandem menus fully configurable, so you can assign whatever functions you want to whatever keys you want. You can even do things with MacMenlo you simply can't do at all on the Tandem terminal, like selecting and copying tabular data without losing the tab settings you've chosen.

very good
feature

The first version of the MacMenlo manual was somewhat disorganized, repetitive and incomplete, but because this is a responsive company, many of these failings were corrected in the new manual (though it could be even better).

MacMenlo isn't cheap; it costs $400, plus $40 a year for updates. But that's a small price to pay to preserve your eyesight and sanity, both of which are threatened by the regular Tandem terminal.

MacMenlo comes with a 30-day money-back guarantee and—in my experience, at least—support has been just a phone call away. All in all, MacMenlo displays a remarkable degree of civility and intelligence, and stands as a model for what terminal emulation software can and should be.

very good
feature

MacTerminal tips

⚹ *MacTerminal keyboard shortcuts*

shortcut

The following keyboard commands are useful for navigating around within MacTerminal:

keystrokes	*effect*
COMMAND-H	backspaces cursor one space
COMMAND-I	moves cursor right to next tab
COMMAND-J	moves cursor down one line
COMMAND-K	moves cursor down two lines
COMMAND-M	moves cursor to beginning of line

Here's one that doesn't move the cursor:

COMMAND-G	sounds tone

⚹ *MacTerminal keyboard commands*

very
hot
tip

The following MacTerminal keyboard commands are mostly undocumented:

to send:	*press:*
break	ENTER (VT100 mode)
enter	ENTER (3278 mode)
escape	` (accent grave)
`	COMMAND-` (accent grave)
~	COMMAND-SHIFT-~ (tilde)
^A thru ^Z	COMMAND-A thru COMMAND-Z
^(	COMMAND-(or ` (same as ESCAPE)
^\	COMMAND-\ (backslash)
^)	COMMAND-) (close bracket)
^^	COMMAND-6 (no SHIFT)
^_	COMMAND-? or COMMAND-/ (slash)
delete	COMMAND-back space

⚫ *MacTerminal and the Radio Shack Model 100*

The first version of MacTerminal (1.0) was unable to convert incoming carriage returns to carriage return/line feeds. This caused a lot of problems for Radio Shack Model 100 users.

The solution is to give the Model 100 a POKE command in BASIC. You bring up BASIC on the 100 by pressing ENTER while the main menu is displayed. Type 'POKE 63066,255', followed by ENTER. This will force the 100 to issue a line feed with every carriage return.

This "patch" stays in effect until you cold boot the 100. If you need to reverse the POKE but want to avoid a cold boot of the 100, enter the BASIC statement POKE 63066,0.

Red Ryder (Dennis Klatzkin)

⚫ *politics, religion and communications programs*

Some people say that telecommunications will be seen as the single most important advance of the personal computer revolution of the 1980s—the innovation with the most profound effect on the way we live and work. Whether this is true or not, no other aspect of computing seems to generate as many unyielding opinions. You can no more tell someone which is the "best" telecommunications program than you can tell him or her which is the best religion or the best political party.

It's not clear why this should be. Maybe it's because people use communications programs for personal rather than business purposes, or because they use them almost every day, and for a broad spectrum of highly specific tasks.

Some users care more about ease of use and adherence to the standard Mac user interface. Others care more about support for different file-transfer protocols and specialized graphics standards; authentic emulation of different types of terminals; the ability to customize operations with function keys, macros, custom menus and automated procedures; and, of course, speed. But these power/ease of use conflicts exist for all kinds of software; why should people have such strong opinions about communications software?

gossip/
trivia

Well—who knows? For whatever reason, feelings run strong, and at the center of the controversy is a program called Red Ryder. (It's unclear where the name came from. Red Ryder was the name of a BB gun sold in the 50's, and there's also a play called *When Ya Comin' Home, Red Ryder?*, about a Vietnam vet who cracked up. But if anyone knows for sure, they're not talking.)

Many people have Red Ryder on a disk somewhere. Yet, in some circles, saying that you actually use it and like it is tantamount to admitting that you have to move your lips to read, or still have training wheels on your bike, or don't yet have indoor plumbing.

Red Ryder, in its many incarnations, has been around for almost as long as the Mac itself, and has matured and grown considerably. Back in the days when MacWrite represented the peak of sophistication of Mac software—and Apple had not yet released MacTerminal—MacTep and Red Ryder were introduced (as BASIC programs) to allow Mac users to enter the age of telecommunications.

very good
feature

The program has been through at least a dozen revisions and is now a stand-alone application (compiled in C) that doesn't require a BASIC interpreter. The development of Red Ryder is still continuing under the direction of Scott Watson, and it is distributed as a shareware product by his company, FreeSoft.

Watson's dedication to continually revising Red Ryder has actually been criticized by some people. Too much change may be unsettling for some, and each release has had its flaws, but Watson has shown a true commitment to improving his product. How many commercial software products can make that claim?

Red Ryder deserves praise not only for being in the vanguard of Mac communications software, but also because of its contribution to the success of shareware as a concept—thanks both to its popularity and to Watson's effective, consciousness-raising shareware reminders.

Red Ryder is popular both because it's good and because Watson continually upgrades it. So what's all the controversy about?

Well, for one thing, if program "leanness" is important to you, Red Ryder—approaching 200K in size—will probably give you apoplexy. Red Ryder tries to satisfy everyone, and only in some categories does it succeed. Even so, dollar for dollar Red Ryder offers a better and fuller mix of features—most of which at least approach the best of their class—than its competitors.

If you divide users of communications software into two groups—those who use it as a work tool and those with the old-time hacker's spirit, for whom the act of logging on (to almost anything) is an adventure in itself—Red Ryder definitely appeals to the latter group.

why I love *Red Ryder*

The most recent release of Red Ryder (version 9.4 as of this writing) provides what is perhaps the most powerful procedural language in any communications program on any microcomputer. Even nonprogrammer types can design automated sequences to perform just about every conceivable series of maneuver.

very good
feature

Other communications programs for the Mac, notably SmartCom and Microphone, allow the creation of command procedures in a more visually attractive manner, sometimes taking "Mac-ness" to its cutest extreme. But their procedures lack the flexibility Red offers, and they insulate users from the true power of their computers in a way that can only be described as user-condescending.

Red Ryder's commands give more of a flavor of what programming is really like, and the excellent documentation makes them quite accessible to everyone. For those without the expertise to dish up a serving of C or Pascal or assembly language, it's a real thrill to have a medium in which to write a bit of code for the Mac that actually does something useful!

❖ programming Red Ryder

The program below (called a "procedure listing") gives you a sampling of Red Ryder's command language. The comments on the right (after the semicolons) are for explanation only, and wouldn't be allowed in an actual program.

Procedure listings are text files and can be created with any text editor, including MacWrite, Word or the MockWrite desk accessory. Red Ryder even has a feature, aptly named "Write a Procedure For Me," which will watch your activities and responses during a telecommunications session and write the procedure file for you as you work. I used it to create the procedure listing on the next page, and then enhanced, tested and tweaked a bit.

It's an auto-log procedure that will dial CompuServe and automatically navigate you to one of the Mac forum's data libraries. The listing of newly uploaded files will be browsed and the listing saved to a text file on disk. When you press the '@' symbol (I chose the '@' symbol because it is seldom used on CompuServe), the disk file will be closed and you'll be logged off of the network.

```
COMM  1200-N-8-1-FULL        ;  Set several telecommunications
                             ;  parameters
REDIAL ATDT 956-4281         ;  Keep dialing until a successful
                             ;  connection is made
PAUSE                        ;  Let Red Ryder catch its breath
TYPE ^C                      ;  Type a control-C
                             ;  to wake up CompuServe
PROMPT User ID:              ;  When CompuServe asks for
                             ;  the User ID...
PAUSE                        ;
TYPE 12345,678^M             ;  ...Red Ryder types in the
                             ;  number and a carriage return
PROMPT Password:             ;  Likewise for the password
PAUSE                        ;
TYPE my-secret^M             ;  ^M (control-M) is the equivalent
                             ;  of a carriage return
PROMPT !                     ;  When CompuServe sends the !
                             ;  (ready for input) sign...
PAUSE                        ;
TYPE go macus^M              ;  ...RR sends the command
                             ;  to go to the Mac forum...
PROMPT Function:             ;
PAUSE                        ;
TYPE dl1^M                   ;  ...and from there to
                             ;  Data Library #1...
PROMPT !                     ;
PAUSE                        ;
TYPE bro^M                   ;  ...and then issues
                             ;  the "Browse" command
BELL                         ;  Now RR rings the bell 3 times
BELL                         ;  to let you know that you're
BELL                         ;  starting to browse the listings
RECA RR Disk:CIS Goodies     ;  The text file "CIS Goodies"
                             ;  is opened to record the listings
(BROWSING)                   ;  This is a label, used here
                             ;  as a place marker
ALERT1 @/JUMPTO (LOGOFF)     ;  RR is alerted to jump to the
                             ;  LOGOFF label if it sees @
TYPE ^M                      ;  Here starts a loop in which RR
                             ;  will send a carriage return...
```

```
PROMPT !                        ; ...wait for the ! prompt...
PAUSE                           ;
JUMPTO (BROWSING)               ;  ...and jump back to the BROWSING
                                ; label to repeat the loop
                                ;
(LOGOFF)                        ; If you type a @, Red will jump here...
CLOSE                           ;
                                ;  ...the file will be properly closed ...
TYPE off^M                      ;
                                ;  ...and the goodbye command will be
                                ; sent to CompuServe
```

very good feature

This is a simple procedure that can be put together in almost any communications program that has a procedure language. Red Ryder's command set goes far beyond these basic features, supporting such advanced concepts as strings; numeric and time variables; flags; decision-making; user-defined alerts; dialog boxes; pull-down menus; and more. Red Ryder's procedure language is where it leaves the others in the dust—it's truly a "communications program construction set."

⬛ *Red Ryder pro and con*

But it's not in the area of power that people fault Red Ryder. Aside from its bulk and department-store variety of features, it has been criticized for its design. Some find the program's user interface less direct and intuitive than the Mac allows. While this may be true, in a larger sense Red Ryder approaches Apple's design philosophy more closely than many other programs, certainly including Apple's own MacTerminal.

It's a principle of good Macintosh software design that Mac programs should employ as little functional modularity as possible. Translated into English, this means that, as much as possible, all options should remain available at all times. There should be as few modes (areas of special or limited options) as possible.

Most communications programs flout this principle. They require that the parameters (phone number, baud rate, etc.) used to access different remote systems be saved in external files which are only available one at a time. So in order to jump from your Dow Jones News Retrieval settings to those for CompuServe, you must exit the first set and load the next. For some users, such "modularity" is not much of an inconvenience; for others, it's quite irksome.

Red Ryder, however, lets you jump between system settings to your heart's content, without having to open and close parameter files, simply by changing those settings with user-defined macros generated by its powerful command language. This facility is unique in its class, and the result is that Red Ryder provides easy, all-in-one-window operation while you're on-line.

One of the best things about Red Ryder is that you can try it out for free. It's available on the major on-line networks like GEnie and CompuServe, and on many Mac bulletin board systems. Under FreeSoft's shareware agreement, you can try out Red Ryder for 45 days before the moral imperative to pay for it comes to bear upon you. When it does, the program will cost you $40 (the address to send it to is in the program). Or you can just order it directly from the author (his company name and address are in Appendix C.)

bargain

The program's documentation (available on-line as a group of MacWrite files) is both an excellent guide to using Red Ryder and an intelligent, understandable and witty examination of some of the general principles of telecommunications. Few others have been able to demystify telecommunications' esoteric terminology so successfully.

Future versions of Red Ryder will break new ground in Mac communications software when the so-called "Nautilus driver" is implemented. Despite the sophistication of the Mac, current communications programs generally employ standards that evolved in the days when teletypewriters were technological wonders. You may now have a screen full of

things to come

menus and buttons, but you still communicate your choices to the host system by pressing R for 'read' and Q for 'quit', or by typing such meaningful phrases as "GO MACUS." The details are still sketchy, but presumably the Nautilus driver will attempt to better integrate telecommunications into the familiar Mac user interface. It's a pioneering effort and will doubtless have its problems and its detractors, but it's an idea that's worth trying.

You may decide that one of the more expensive, commercial communications programs better suit your special needs. Or you may find one of the less full-featured shareware programs, the "lean and mean machines," more to your taste. But at virtually no cost you can test-drive this fully-loaded sedan and see how it feels. And for $40 more, you can park it in your driveway and call it your very own.

Chapter 10

Desktop publishing

PageMaker tips
(Unless otherwise indicated, all the tips in this section refer to version 1.2.)

🍎 changing page view sizes quickly

PageMaker offers several COMMAND-key shortcuts for moving between different page sizes. For example, when using the arrow tool, experiment with holding the COMMAND key down while clicking. This will toggle you back and forth between Actual Size and Fit in Window. If you're viewing the page in 200% mode, COMMAND-click will return you to Actual Size.

shortcut

COMMAND-OPTION-click will shift you to 200% actual size. The 200% view will be centered on the place where you clicked, so be sure to click near the middle of the area you want magnified.

🍎 getting to the hand quickly

PageMaker's scrolls very slowly when you use the scroll bars, so most users prefer the hand (known officially as "the grabber")—particularly when moving diagonally across the page. To change the text tool or the arrow pointer to the hand, just hold down the OPTION key without clicking.

shortcut

♦ *ems and ens*

To create an em space (which is as many points wide as the font you're using is high), use OPTION-SHIFT-hyphen. To create an en space (which is half the width of an em), use OPTION-hyphen.

♦ *summary of PageMaker keyboard shortcuts*

shortcut

placing documents

COMMAND-D	place a document (equivalent to Place... command)
COMMAND-click (with text icon)	place text with original line breaks
click (anywhere on page)	stop text flow

using tools

OPTION (while dragging)	use hand (grabber)
COMMAND-G	show/hide guides
COMMAND-R	show/hide rulers
COMMAND-W	show/hide toolbox

changing views

COMMAND-F	to Fit in Window
COMMAND-A	to Actual Size
COMMAND-click (at new center)	to Actual Size
COMMAND-click (at new center)	to Fit in Window (from Actual Size)
COMMAND-OPTION-click (at new center)	to 200% size

changing graphics

SHIFT (while dragging)	resize proportionally
SHIFT-click (on graphic handle)	return 'placed' graphic to original proportions
SHIFT-click (on rectangle handle)	change rectangle to a square
SHIFT-click (on oval handle)	change oval to circle

selecting text

double-click	select word
triple-click	select line
COMMAND-click	select paragraph
COMMAND-double-click	select text block

special characters

COMMAND-hyphen	discretionary hyphen
OPTION-SHIFT-3	page number marker

⚫ *maximizing disk space*

If you're using PageMaker on a floppy-based system, you can free up a significant amount of space on your work disk by removing the Quick Tour and Help folders, and either the ImageWriter driver or Aldus Prep file (depending on which printer you're using). Also remove any fonts or desk accessories you don't need.

⚫ *a do-it-yourself eraser*

You can get around PageMaker's lack of an eraser tool by making one of your own. Select the None command from the Line menu and the White command from the Shades menu, then use either the box or the circle tool to draw an object large enough to hide the area you want to erase.

⚫ *augmenting PageMaker's drawing features*

Just as you can enhance PageMaker's limited text manipulation capabilities with Microsoft Word, so you can enhance its limited drawing capabilities with MacDraw and MacDraft. MacDraw can give your drawings curves, polygons, freehand shapes and the like. MacDraft can add object rotation and scaling.

MacDraw drawings can be Cut and Pasted into PageMaker directly if they are saved in PICT format. MacDraft drawings can also be Cut and Pasted if they are first saved as MacPaint documents.

Another nice use of MacDraw is to embellish headline type. Use a laser font to print out the headline in MacDraw, and save it in PICT format. When you put it into a PageMaker document, eight handles will surround it. You can use them to stretch or compress the text for dramatic effect. (For some examples of what this looks like, see the Text on the LaserWriter section of chapter 11.)

♦ *don't mix Cut and Paste tools*

important
warning

Be very careful when using Cut and Paste with PageMaker 1.2. If you Cut with one tool and Paste with another, you'll probably generate a file corruption error. Proceed with caution until this bug is fixed.

♦ *smoothing MacPaint graphics on the LaserWriter*

MacPaint pictures have a resolution of 72 dpi and the LaserWriter prints out at 300 dpi. This difference in resolution results in distortion. To avoid it, choose the Smooth command from the PageSetUp menu. This tells the LaserWriter to fill in the jagged edges resulting from the difference in resolution.

very
hot
tip

Because 72 doesn't divide evenly into 300, the Smooth command is most effective when you reduce the Scaling to 96%. (96% of 300 is 288, and 72 divides into 288 exactly four times.) This makes for a much nicer picture.

♦ *using lots of fonts on the LaserWriter*

After PageMaker prints a block of text, it flushes the fonts it used out of the LaserWriter's memory. This means you can have as many fonts in a block as most applications let you have in a whole application. But it also slows down printing, since the fonts have to be downloaded to the LaserWriter anew at the start of each block.

● *font bug on the LaserWriter*

Under some circumstances, PageMaker 1.2 prints text in Chicago instead of the correct font. To make it use the correct fonts, go back to the text selection box (COMMAND-T) and click on the name of the font you're using. You don't have to select any text; just clicking in the text selection box will do the trick.

● *documents imported from Word*

PageMaker 1.2 has trouble importing documents from Word 1.05. It sometimes strips out the information that indicates what font the text is in. The only solution is to select the text and change it back into the right font.

Ready,Set,Go! tips
(Unless otherwise indicated, all the tips in this section refer to version 3.0.)

● *retrieving the end of a document*

There are two ways you can lose the end of a document in Ready,Set,Go! One is by not allowing enough blank pages before you Get Text. The other is by adding enough to an already existing Ready,Set,Go! document to drive the end of it off the last page. Whatever the cause, the problem is easy to fix.

very
hot
tip

Select the last page of the document and choose Insert Page(s) from the Special menu. Click on Duplicate Current Page (instead of the default, which is Insert Blank Page).

Choose as many pages as you'll think you need (let's assume you only need one) and click on OK.

When the inserted page appears, delete the text that already appears on the page you duplicated and the end of the document will magically flow up onto the new page. (If you've inserted more than one page, just go to each page in order and delete the text you already have on earlier pages until the end of the document flows up onto the page you're on.)

⬤ *speeding things up with shallow windows*

shortcut

If you're just checking something at the top of each page (like a page number or a header), you can speed things up considerably by making the window very shallow. Since Ready,Set,Go! will have less to draw, it will bring up each page much more quickly.

This technique also works if you're checking things at the bottom of each page, but you have to click in the scroll bar as each page comes up, to take yourself to the bottom of it. Still, you'd have to do that anyway, and a shallow window stills speeds things up.

Drawing copyright © 1984 by Esther Travis.

Part III—

Maximizing hardware

Chapter 11

Printers

ImageWriter tips

✦ *the original Imagewriter vs. the ImageWriter II*

Because the first model of the Imagewriter spelled its name without a capital W, and was never called the Imagewriter I, we refer to it as "the original Imagewriter." The main difference between the two printers is that the ImageWriter II is faster, quieter, supports color printing and has a great (optional) sheet feeder.

It's easy to tell the machines apart: the original Imagewriter is beige and rectangular, while the ImageWriter II is white and looks sort of like a flattened version of R2D2 doing pushups.

✦ *stopping printouts*

very
hot
tip

If you need to stop printing from within an application and clicking on the CANCEL button doesn't work (or if the application you're using has no CANCEL button to stop printing), try COMMAND-period (COMMAND- .).

If even that doesn't work, you can always just turn off the ImageWriter. Most programs will continue for a while as if they were still sending output to the printer, then realize it's no longer responding and give you the opportunity to exit from print mode.

⚫ *best quality text*

When you select Best print quality from an application's print dialog box, the Mac looks for a font size double the one you've specified and then reduces it 50% to create a high-quality image. If the double-size font isn't installed, the print quality won't be much better than Faster quality. So for the highest quality printouts, make sure that a font twice as large as the one you've requested is installed either in the system file or the application.

very
hot
tip

⚫ *lubrication*

The manual for the original Imagewriter recommends lubricating the shaft on which the print head travels with a light machine oil that doesn't contain rust inhibitors. But you can ignore the warning about the rust inhibitors. The Imagewriter's original specifications called for a different type of metal than actually ended up being used. In fact, Apple itself recommends light sewing-machine oils, all of which contain rust inhibitors.

According to the manual for the ImageWriter II, no lubrication is required.

⚫ *proper ImageWriter switch settings for use with Macs*

The ImageWriter, whether the original or the II, was designed to work with the entire family of Apple computers, not just the Mac. Any ImageWriter you buy to use with a Mac should come with the switches set right, but here are the correct settings, just in case:

On the original ImageWriter, the switches are under the cover on the right. You can ignore the larger group of switches labeled SW1 since the Mac overrides these settings. The smaller group labeled SW2 should be set as follows:

                    1 - closed
                    2 - closed
                    3 - open
                    4 - open

On the ImageWriter II, the switches are under the front cover on the left. Again, you can ignore the group of switches labeled SW1, and set the SW2 group as follows:

                    1 - closed
                    2 - closed
                    3 - open
                    4 - open
                    5 - closed
                    6 - open

Because these switches are tiny, you may have trouble throwing them with your finger. One tool you can use to help is a ball-point pen. Never use a pencil point, an eraser, or anything else that might leave a residue of particles on the switches.

❤ inexpensive extension cables

bargain

If you need an extension cable for your ImageWriter, go down to Radio Shack and pick up one of their joystick extension cables (part number 276-1978) for about $4. It plugs into the back of any 128K or 512K Mac, and will work with either model of the printer. Unfortunately, this cable won't work with the Mac Plus, which uses different jacks (unless you also get an adapter cable from your Apple Dealer).

❤ self-tests on the ImageWriter II

Unlike the original Imagewriter, the ImageWriter II will print self-test documents in all printing modes—draft, standard, and high.

For a self-test in draft mode, turn off the printer, hold down the 'on/off' and 'form feed' buttons, then turn the printer back on and release both buttons simultaneously (which will also turn the printer back on).

Once the printer is doing a self-test in draft mode, you can check it out in standard mode. Press the 'line feed' button (which pauses the printout), then press the 'print quality' button (which puts the printer into standard mode). Now press the 'line feed' button again, and you'll get a self-test in standard mode.

Once the printer is doing a self-test in standard mode, you can check it out in high-quality mode. Press the 'line feed' button (which pauses the printout), then press the 'print quality' button (which puts the printer into high-quality mode). Now press the 'line feed' button again, and you'll get a self-test in high-quality mode.

To end the self-test, simply turn the printer off (by pressing the 'on/off' button).

✎ *print spoolers designed for the original Imagewriter*

Print spooler software (for background printing) developed before the introduction of the ImageWriter II may not work with it. Because the II works a little differently from the original Imagewriter, it sends a message back to the Mac announcing that it's a II. The original Imagewriter doesn't send such a message, so software designed only to work with the original Imagewriter often gets confused when it receives this unexpected identification.

If your print spooler software doesn't work with an ImageWriter II, contact the publisher. By the time you read this, just about every print spooler should have been updated to support the ImageWriter II.

⚫ alternative ribbons

From time to time your local supplier may run out of ImageWriter ribbons. This will probably happen late Saturday afternoon, just before you plan to begin a marathon weekend of printing to meet Monday morning's deadline. But don't panic: ImageWriter ribbons are completely interchangeable with ribbons for the C. Itoh 8510, the NEC 8023, and DEC LA50 printers. You shouldn't have any trouble finding one or another of these ribbons.

⚫ draft printing on the original Imagewriter

The spacing between the words on documents printed in draft mode on the original Imagewriter is usually quite irregular. You can avoid that by changing the font of the entire document to Monaco (which is a monospaced font). For this technique to work, you have to convert the whole document; if any line of text includes more than one font, or if there are graphics in the document, spacing will be irregular.

⚫ print-head overheating on the original Imagewriter

important
warning

Printing documents that are more than 25% solid black can cause the print head on the original Imagewriter to overheat and fail. Replacing the print head is not only expensive but a major hassle, since many dealers don't stock adequate spare parts. So—never print more than one page of a document that contains large black areas without giving the print head a chance to cool.

This precaution isn't necessary with the ImageWriter II, because it has built-in protection against print-head overheating.

⚫ making ditto masters on the ImageWriter

Teachers! Here's how to use your ImageWriter (either model) to make perfect ditto masters. Just remove the ribbon and set the paper thickness level (under the cover on the far right side) to 2. Then print out your document at standard quality (sometimes called "faster").

❖ *print quality with ImageWriter driver 2.2*

When using version 2.2 of the ImageWriter driver, graphics print darker in standard quality ('Faster') printouts than they do in high-quality ('Best') printouts—just the opposite of what you'd expect.

❖ *bug in ImageWriter driver 2.2*

Version 2.2 of the ImageWriter driver occasionally forgets how to recognize the ImageWriter II. This bug was fixed in version 2.3 (the version released with Finder 5.3).

Basic LaserWriter tips
(and tips on other PostScript printers and typesetters)

❖ *versions of software, models of hardware*

Unless otherwise specified, these tips assume you're using the following software and hardware: Finder version 5.3, System 3.2, LaserWriter 3.1, LaserPrep 3.1, HFS, regular LaserWriter (not a LaserWriter Plus) and either a Mac Plus or an Enhanced 512K Mac (or any other machine using the 128K ROMs). If you're running with older versions of software than those, you should definitely install the new ones.

You can find out what version of the LaserWriter driver you have by looking in the dialog box that comes up when you choose Print from the File menu (with every program but PageMaker). The number appears just to the left of the OK button.

how the paper feeds

The LaserWriter prints on the bottom side of sheets fed from the paper tray and on the top side of hand-fed sheets.

after installing a new printer driver

The first time you print from an application after installing a new version of a printer driver, choose Page Setup (on the File menu) before choosing Print. You don't have to change anything in it if you don't want to—you can just click OK as soon as the dialog box appears—but you do need to enter and exit Page Setup to activate the new driver.

where to put the LaserWriter

The LaserWriter's fan makes a fair amount of noise. It's nothing like the one on a PC XT, which sounds like a commercial jet testing its engines, but next to the wonderfully silent Mac it can be pretty annoying. (This is particularly true if you're lucky enough to have a quiet place to work. In the typical office environment, you may barely be able to hear the LaserWriter.)

One way around this problem is to put the LaserWriter in a closet. Since it's connected on AppleTalk, there's no problem with the cables not reaching, and most closets are large enough. According to the manual, you have to leave 7" between the rear of the LaserWriter and the wall, about 13" on each side and 16" to the front (where the toner cartridge is inserted). But you can cheat on the front dimension, because you can replace the toner cartridge with the closet door open.

We keep our LaserWriter in a closet with just 8" to the front, 7" to the rear and a couple of feet to each side, and we've had no problems with insufficient ventilation or heat buildup. Because closets usually have no windows, and often have no external walls, they tend to vary in temperature less than regular rooms.

If you're really worried about heat buildup, hang a thermometer on the closet wall and check it regularly. We do that, and ours has never registered above 80°—even on days when it was hotter than that outside and when the LaserWriter had been on for many hours (although, admittedly, it never gets *really* hot here in Berkeley; the average high temperature during the hottest month is just 72°).

The manual says the temperature of the air around the LaserWriter shouldn't get over 90°, which means that if you live in New Orleans or some other place where the sidewalks melt in the summer, you're going to need air conditioning to stay within their specs (which also call for humidity of 80% or less). But if you live in a place like that, the LaserWriter's not going to be the only reason you need an air conditioner.

There is, of course, one major disadvantage to putting the LaserWriter in a closet—you have to get up and walk over to it each time you want to look at the output. We don't find this bothersome, and enjoy the break and exercise (if walking ten feet can be called exercise). But it could get annoying, particularly if you're doing a lot of trial-and-error futzing with a document.

⚫ flashing messages and lights during printing

When the LaserWriter and the Mac are trying to figure out how to print your document, a message appears on the Mac's screen that lists its "status" as "processing job." Every five seconds or so, this message flickers. DO NOT PANIC (as Arthur, of course, did). The periodic flashing doesn't mean that the power pole outside your house is about to fall over, or that enemy aliens from Saturn are trying to destroy your Mac by sending power surges through the house wiring. It's perfectly normal, just a way of reminding you that the Mac is thinking.

The LaserWriter lets you know it's thinking by single-flashing its yellow light every two seconds. (Double-flashing indicates a "wait state," which usually doesn't last more than 30 seconds.)

When the Mac's role in the printing collaboration is done, the status message will disappear from the screen, but a page still may not have emerged from the LaserWriter. DO NOT PANIC (as Arthur, of course, did). The LaserWriter is still thinking on its own about how exactly to print the document (you know that because the yellow light is still flashing). You're free to continue editing the document, to close it, to quit the application, or whatever. The LaserWriter will print the document eventually, all in its own good time.

♦ *printing multiple copies*

shortcut

Because the LaserWriter takes a long time to figure out a page, and not very long after that to print it, it's *much* faster to ask for multiple copies of a document than to reprint it several times.

♦ *maximum image areas*

The maximum area a LaserWriter will print on a standard US letter-size (8.5 x 11) sheet of paper is 8 by 10.92 inches, centered on the page. The width limitation is the most significant; it means you must always have a margin of at least a quarter inch on each side. (The required .04-inch border top and bottom is, of course, trivial.)

What's more, few programs are capable of filling the entire area. MacDraw, for example, can only fill an area of 7.68 by 10.16 inches, and MacWrite requires a left margin of 1".

The image-size restriction is even more dramatic on legal-size paper (8.5 x 14). There the LaserWriter can only fill an area 6.72 inches wide by 13 inches deep, thus requiring margins of more than 7/8" on each side and 1/2" borders top and bottom. (There are similar restrictions for the common European paper sizes, A4 and B5.)

The reason for these limitations is the LaserWriter's memory. Even though it has 1.5 megabytes of RAM, that's only enough to image between 87 and 88 square inches of page (which is what both 8" x 10.92" and 6.72" x 13" amount to). To really process a page adequately with PostScript, a printer should have at least 2 megs of memory, and ideally 2.5. Many other PostScript printers and typesetters do have that much memory but the LaserWriter scrapes by with 1.5 megs.

One time it's important to remember these size limitations is when you're proofing something on the ImageWriter that will ultimately be printed out on the LaserWriter. Because the ImageWriter can print wider than the LaserWriter, be sure to leave adequate margins; otherwise your image will get cropped on the edges when you put it on the LaserWriter.

⁂ *how to get the right right margin*

There's something very screwy about the right margin when you use MacWrite on the LaserWriter. To get a right margin of 1", you think you'd set the right margin marker to 7-1/2" (8-1/2" minus 1"). But if you do that, you'll end up with almost no right margin at all. The setting that actually works is—for some strange reason—6-7/8". To get a right margin of 1-1/4", you set it at 6-5/8".

very
hot
tip

The rule seems to be: add 5/8" to whatever width you want the right margin to be, then subtract the total from 8-1/2" to get the correct setting.

⁂ *how to get rich, deep blacks*

You can't. Black areas of any significant size will contain small white splotches or streaks, regardless of where you put the *print density dial* (on the back of the machine). The Canon LBP-CX "marking engine"—around which the LaserWriter and many other inexpensive laser printers are built—simply can't do it.

This is only a problem with areas of black, not regular text—which tends to look good no matter how low you set the print density dial. And it's also only a problem if the LaserWriter's output is used at the final product. The film used by printers will almost always fill the black areas in, and you can usually even get the same result from a photocopy machine.

But if you aren't going to print or photocopy what comes out of the LaserWriter, it makes sense to follow the rules below:

1. Try to avoid graphics with black backgrounds or other dark areas.

2. If, like most people, you'll mostly be printing text, use a page of text, not a graphic image, as your sample when you're adjusting the print density dial.

3. Don't bother turning the dial all the way to high—you'll just be wasting toner for no purpose.

● *relative resolutions of various devices*

In a normal ImageWriter text printout (from a word processing program like MacWrite or Word), there are 80 dots per inch across and 72 down; if you choose Tall Adjusted, there are 72 x 72. So the resolution of an ImageWriter printout varies between 5760 dots per square inch (in a regular Tall printout) and 5184 dpsi (in a Tall Adjusted printout).

very good feature

The LaserWriter's resolution is 300 dpi, which amounts to 90,000 dpsi—about 16 to 17 times the ImageWriter's. But 90,000 dpsi is nothing compared to what regular typesetting machines can do. On the 1270-dpi Linotronic 100, for example, there are 1.6 million dpsi—about 18 times the resolution of a LaserWriter and almost 300 times the resolution of an ImageWriter. On the 2540-dpi Linotronic

300, there are 6.45 million dpsi—more than 70 times the resolution of a LaserWriter and well over 1000 times the resolution of an ImageWriter.

Text on the LaserWriter
(and on other PostScript printers and typesetters)

● *ImageWriter fonts on the LaserWriter*

If you turn Font Substitution on (in the Page Setup window), the LaserWriter converts four basic ImageWriter fonts to laser fonts when it runs across them in a document. The conversions are: New York to Times; Geneva to Helvetica; Monaco to Courier (they deserve each other); and Seattle to a modified version of Helvetica. But the character spacing produced with Font Substitution leaves a lot to be desired.

If you turn Font Substitution off, or use any ImageWriter fonts other than the four mentioned above, the LaserWriter creates special PostScript versions of the ImageWriter fonts it finds in a document. (Most people don't realize that PostScript can create *bit-mapped fonts* as well as *outline fonts.)*

These bit-mapped LaserWriter versions of ImageWriter fonts print more smoothly than the original fonts do on the ImageWriter, and they also scale *much* better. But rotation doesn't work too well (which means that they may not look great in italic, for example). Two other disadvantages of the PostScript versions: they take much longer to print, and they strip out most of the type style variations you get on the ImageWriter. (For more information, see the entries below titled "how fonts affect the LaserWriter's speed" and "type styles on the LaserWriter.")

✦ *two types of laser fonts*

The LaserWriter comes with four fonts (or, to use the traditional term, four font families) built into its ROMs—Times, Helvetica, Symbol and Courier (if that can be called a font). If you buy a LaserWriter Plus, or the Plus upgrade, you get an additional six fonts in ROM: Palatino, Bookman, Zapf Chancery, Zapf Dingbats, Avant Garde and New Century Schoolbook. As of this writing (late 1986), those are all the fonts you can get in ROM.

bargain

If you want other laser fonts, you have to buy them on disk and *download* (send) them to the LaserWriter. *Downloadable* fonts have some advantages over fonts in ROM. For one thing, there's a much greater selection of them. For another, they're much easier for the publisher to enhance, upgrade or update. And they tend to be cheaper, with some selling for as little as $30. But they do take longer to print and they do use up some of the LaserWriter's precious RAM (see the entries on those subjects below).

very bad feature

One final advantage of downloadable fonts is the very poor reliability record of the LaserWriter Plus upgrade. The Plus board has been plagued with problems, and Apple has not been very responsive about correcting them.

✦ *two ways to download fonts*

Laser fonts that reside on disk rather than in ROM can be sent to the printer two ways. You can "manually" download them to the LaserWriter before printing, or you can have them downloaded automatically during printing (you just use the screen fonts in your document and the Mac sends the fonts' print files to the LaserWriter as it runs across them). Automatic downloading takes about 5-15 seconds per font.

(Apple and Adobe refer to manual downloading as "permanent" downloading, which is pretty confusing, since the fonts only stay in the LaserWriter until you turn it off. "Manual"—which is obviously based on an analogy to automatic and manual transmissions in cars—isn't exactly the right word either, but we can't think of a better one.)

Manual downloading is done with a program that comes on the disk with the fonts, called Font Downloader, LW Download or some name like that. Automatic downloading only works with versions 3.1 (or later) of LaserPrep and LaserWriter (or with equivalent versions of PageMaker's LaserPrep equivalent, AldusPrep) and with compatible system software. Most, but not all, applications support automatic downloading.

The advantage of manual downloading is that the LaserWriter prints faster. The advantage of automatic downloading is that it's easier (manual downloading is an annoying chore, even though it only takes a few minutes) and that the fonts get flushed out after each printing job, making room for new fonts on the next printing job.

As a rule, manual downloading isn't worth the trouble unless you're going to be using the same font(s) in three or more short printouts (which might be the same document revised and reprinted three times). On the other hand, it almost always makes sense when you're printing from PageMaker, which flushes automatically downloaded fonts after each text block, rather than at the end of the printing job, and thus has to reload them for each subsequent text block.

very
hot
tip

❤ *where to store downloadable fonts*

If you're running under HFS, put the files for downloadable laser fonts either in the system folder (that's the best place for them) or in the startup disk's window (also known as the "root directory"). If they're stuck away in a folder anywhere else, the Mac won't be able to find them and they won't be downloaded to the LaserWriter.

important
warning

Why those restrictions? Because there can be so many files on a hard disk that the Mac could spend forever looking for the fonts, if it didn't limit its search to just those locations. (However, the public domain program Set Paths, by Paul Snively, lets you put printer files wherever you want them. For details, see the Utilities section of Chapter 14.)

The above applies only to the actual printer font files that get sent to the LaserWriter; screen fonts should, of course, be installed in the System file with the Font/DA Mover (version 3.2 or later).

important warning

By the way, don't change the names of those print files; the automatic downloading process depends on their staying the same. (Sometimes the icon for a print file will change when you copy it from the disk you get from the publisher, but don't pay any attention to that.)

⬥ *installing screen fonts*

You can install no more than 200 ImageWriter fonts or screen fonts in the System file. You may think you'd never need to have anything like that many fonts installed, but each different size counts as a different font; in other words, it's the listing in the Font/DA Mover window that counts (with the sizes alongside the names), not the one on the Font menu (where the sizes aren't listed). So if you have twenty fonts installed, each in 9-, 10-, 12-, 14-, 18- and 24- point, you're already up to 120.

Needless to say, you don't need to install every size of a font, unless you're going to be printing it out on the ImageWriter. Since the LaserWriter does its own scaling and doesn't depend on the screen fonts, you only need enough sizes installed to keep the screen display legible.

In our experience, performance begins to degrade significantly when you have anywhere near 100 screen fonts installed. Virtually anytime you try to install another font,

Font/DA Mover (version 3.2) hits you with a error message ("ID = -2, -108"). You *have* to go back to the Finder. If you still want to install the fonts, you then have to Shut Down too.

very bad
feature

This is a *very* frustrating bug which will hopefully have been fixed by the time you read this.

One way to keep the number of screen fonts down is to only install the ones for plain text, not bold or italic or whatever. If you have the 128K ROMs, choosing a plain text font and then making it bold (say) will produce exactly the same effect as if you choose the bold screen font. (For more on this, see the next entry.)

❖ special characters on the LaserWriter

As a general rule, laser fonts give you a much wider selection of special characters than ImageWriter fonts (for more details, see chapter 3). But many laser fonts borrow some of their special characters from the Symbol font. So if you want the full range of special characters, make sure Symbol's printer font file is in the System Folder on your startup disk.

important
warning

❖ type styles on the LaserWriter

On the Imagewriter, every font can be transformed into **bold**, *italic*, outline, shadow and any combination thereof—which comes to sixteen possible variations. On the LaserWriter, however, no font we've seen can produce all sixteen variations. For example, Zapf Chancery (from Adobe) only gives you three: plain, outline and shadow (bold, italic and bold italic print out as plain and all the other variations print out as either outline or shadow).

The LaserWriter's built-in fonts, Times and Helvetica, do much better. Although outline shadow looks the same as shadow, eliminating four possibilities, the other twelve variations are there. (We've yet to see a laser font that will make the distinction between shadow and outline shadow—

although with some type sizes in Word, characters are spaced farther apart in outline shadow than in shadow.) Adobe's Benguiat has the same twelve combinations, as does Casady's San Serif. Casady's Ritz provides eight of the possibilities—exactly half.

ImageWriter fonts lose most of their style variations when they're translated into PostScript bit-map fonts. For example, when printed on the LaserWriter, Chicago retains just five of the sixteen styles it has on the ImageWriter. The only way to tell what variations a particular font will give you on the LaserWriter is to try them out. (For an easy way to do that, see the description of font templates in the next section.)

All type styles on the ImageWriter are produced algorithmically—that is, by the application of a rule like 'increase the width 10%' (to create boldface) or 'slant right 15°' (to create italic). But on the LaserWriter, many fonts have their own separate *cuttings* for bold, italic and bold italic— that is, all the characters in those styles were individually designed, as if for a separate font.

If a font does have separate cuttings for certain styles, you'll have to load a separate printer font file in the system folder for each one. But, as a rule, you'll get better looking characters than with an algorithmically derived style. This isn't always true, however. For example, **there's a separate font file for boldface in the font you're reading now (ITC Benguiat)**, *while there isn't one for italic—it's algorithmic. But they both look pretty good—although, admittedly, the bold does seem* **more distinctive.**

You can always tell whether the style you're using is algorithmic by looking to see if there's a separate font file for it. (In some cases, you don't need to bother: for example, type styles called "oblique" rather than "italic" are almost always algorithmic.)

Fonts with separate cuttings usually come with screen fonts to match, but you can save room in your System file by not installing them. You can just select the type style you want from a style menu and PostScript will know to look for the font file before making the change algorithmically (at least it will on any machine that uses the 128K ROMs). But if you do install the special screen fonts, you'll get a cleaner representation of the characters on the screen.

Some fonts also have separate cuttings for variations with different names than bold, italic, outline or shadow (see the next entry for several examples). In these cases, you do have to install the screen font—unless the style is basically a variation on bold or italic. If it is, it will normally be "mapped" to the menu option. For example, "demi" type is bolder than regular, so selecting text set in Souvenir and then choosing Bold from the menu will give you Souvenir Demi.

Generally, font publishers try to do what makes sense; if a font comes with four variations, you can usually get them by choosing plain text, bold, italic and bold italic.

very good
feature

Although "oblique" is the only other name in common use for italic type (both are slanted, but italic letters are also redrawn in other ways), there are many names for various levels of boldness. The common ones are listed below, going from lightest to boldest:

very
hot
tip

Ultra Light
Extra Light
Light
Roman, or Book, or no adjective (just the name of the typeface)
Medium
Demi
Bold
Extra Bold, or Heavy, or Black
Ultra Bold

❡ special type styles on the LaserWriter

Some laser fonts offer exotic type styles far beyond the standard sixteen (only on the Mac could you call bold italic

very good
feature

outline shadow "standard"). In addition to all the different levels of boldness mentioned at the end of the last entry, there's condensed or "thin" (letters squeezed together and stretched vertically) and expanded or "fat" (letters spread apart and stretched horizontally).

Century's Special Effects use some really fancy algorithms—stack, fill, reflect, and so on. For samples of these, see the fonts section of chapter 14. (We'd show them to you here, but—given the software we're using and the LaserWriter's skimpy RAM—this document won't print out if we put any more fonts in it. For an explanation of why that is, see the entries below on RAM limitations and using lots of fonts. We've resigned ourselves to breaking chapter 14 into many small documents and pasting some of it up by hand, but we don't want to be doing that throughout the book.)

To get special type styles like condensed and expanded, stack and fill, you obviously have to install the screen fonts, since there are no menu items that correspond to them.

● *creating your own special typographic effects*

very good
feature

To distort a headline or other piece of display type for special effect, type it first in MacDraw or MacDraft. Then Paste it into MacWrite, Word or PageMaker, either through the Clipboard or the Scrapbook. Once it's there, select it and drag on the little handles to stretch the type horizontally, vertically, or both. It will look terrible on the screen but when you print it out, the characters will have the same crisp, clean edges that laser fonts normally do.

You can also use MacDraw to "drop out" ("reverse out") type—that is, to generate white type on a dark background. (But remember that black comes out streaky on the LaserWriter, regardless of where you set the print density dial, and you'll have to photocopy or photograph the output to fill in the blacks.) To drop out type, first create a solid shape filled with black (or gray or any other pattern you want for the background). Then, with that shape selected, choose the font and size you want, choose Outline from the Style menu, and start typing.

You can also combine both these techniques, creating white writing on a dark background and stretching it once it gets into your word processing program.

These typographic special effects also work on the ImageWriter, but you don't get smoothing and the results don't look anywhere near as good. On the LaserWriter, however, you can really produce some nice-looking stuff, as the four examples below may or may not make obvious:

Gloria Zarifa

Gloria Zarifa

Gloria Zarifa

Gloria Zarifa

(The first two samples are in Adobe's Benguiat and the last two in Casady's Calligraphy.)

✎ *how fonts affect the LaserWriter's speed*

The first basic rule is: the more fonts you use, the longer it will take the LaserWriter to print a page. (If you use too many, it won't print the page at all. For advice on what to do then, see the entry below about using lots of fonts.)

The LaserWriter processes some kinds of fonts much faster than others. Laser fonts in ROM are the fastest. Downloadable laser fonts are slightly slower (and, in addition, ones that are downloaded automatically take 5-1.5 seconds longer than ones that are manually downloaded, since that's about how long it takes to send them to the LaserWriter). ImageWriter fonts are far and away the slowest, because the LaserWriter not only has to download them but also has to create a PostScript version of them.

shortcut

So you'll get the very fastest speed out of the LaserWriter if you use just one built-in laser font in just one style—and, because scaling also takes time, in just one size. But that's quite a sacrifice to make for a little speed.

✎ *RAM limitations*

very bad feature

After the LaserWriter finishes imaging the page and doing other necessary tasks, it only has about 210K of RAM available for downloading fonts and other necessary information. To give you an idea of just how limiting that is, consider that PageMaker takes about 50K for its *header* (the PostScript instructions it gives to the printer) and that the necessary QuickDraw information takes another 90K. This leaves only 70K for your downloadable fonts, which usually require between 20K and 35K each.

(Fortunately, PageMaker flushes out the fonts after each text block, instead of at the end of the document, so the limitations are on fonts per text block rather than fonts per document. Other programs often have somewhat smaller headers, and thus leave slightly more room for fonts to be downloaded.)

In addition to the space the fonts themselves take up, another 10K or so has to be downloaded along with the first font. This *one-time hit* contains information that applies to all fonts.

In most applications, using the full image area only leaves you room to download three or four fonts; under some extreme circumstances, there may only be room for two. (Adobe's Font Downloader program has a menu item called Printer Font Directory that tells you how much RAM is left in the LaserWriter and what fonts—both downloadable and ROM-based—are already there. Casady and Century include similar programs on their font disks. All three companies also provide software for resetting the LaserWriter—that is, flushing its memory and making it generate a new startup page—without turning off the power.)

To get around this limitation, some applications use *note format*, which gives half-inch margins all around (on the assumption that you're not going to want to print anything closer to the edge of the paper than that). This gives you room for more fonts, theoretically as many as eight or ten. But don't count on it.

By the time you read this, Apple will probably have released a new LaserWriter driver that will automatically swap fonts in and out of the LaserWriter's RAM *during* a printing job, rather than merely flushing out all the ones that have accumulated at the end of each printing job. (Some laser fonts may have to be rewritten to take advantage of this new feature.)

things
to come

It's also possible, and devoutly to be hoped for, that future models of the LaserWriter will have more RAM available or, even better, that Apple or someone else will come out with a *font server*—a hard disk or other device that stores fonts and feeds them to the LaserWriter as needed (this probably would require laser fonts to be rewritten).

things
to come

In the meantime, you'll almost certainly find yourself overflowing the LaserWriter's RAM. For what happens when you do that, see the next entry.

⚫ *using lots of fonts on the LaserWriter*

**important
warning**

Don't. (We'll resist the temptation to make this the shortest entry in the book.)

You can usually get away with three or four fonts—but remember that if bold, italic, bold italic or some other style comes in its own *cutting* (that is, if it's been separately designed and comes as a separate font file), it counts towards the total just like a completely different typeface. (One exception to this are special cuttings labeled "oblique." They're usually derived algorithmically—that is, by the application of a rule—and take up much less of the LaserWriter's memory. For example, ITC Glypha Oblique only takes up 3K if you already have Glypha Roman loaded, since all that needs to be added are the PostScript instructions on how to tilt the letters.)

PageMaker offers you one way around the problem. With it, the limitations that normally apply to fonts per document apply to fonts per *text block*. And since you can have as many text blocks as you want in a document, you can also have as many fonts as you want (within reason, that is; things can get pretty tedious with dozens of text blocks on a page).

**very bad
feature**

If you use too many fonts, the Mac will show you one or more messages that tell you you're running short of memory. In a classic case of boneheaded design, these messages neither beep nor stay on the screen for very long. So if you happen not to be completely catatonic and have therefore chosen to get up and do something rather than to stare blankly at the screen for the five or ten minutes it takes the LaserWriter to print a document with a lot of fonts, you'll miss the messages. When you come back into the room, the LaserWriter will be humming innocently away ("What do you mean, 'Where's your printout?' What printout?"), with no indication on the screen of what happened.

(The above assumes your fonts are being automatically downloaded. If you're manually downloading fonts—sending them to the LaserWriter one by one with a downloading program prior to printing—and you overrun the LaserWriter's RAM, it will probably just restart itself and spit out a new startup page.)

If a document won't print, it's always worth trying to print it again; it often works the second time. If that doesn't work, try printing the document one page at a time. If *that* doesn't work, try breaking it into smaller documents.

very hot tip

If you're not sure that too many fonts is the reason the LaserWriter won't print your document, the easiest way to find out is to make a copy of it, change the entire copy to Times or Helvetica, and try printing that. If that works, your problem is almost certainly too many fonts.

All in all, the limitation on how many fonts you can use is one of the LaserWriter's most annoying shortcomings.

❡ *sticky header files*

Most Macintosh applications send *header files* of PostScript instructions to the LaserWriter at the beginning of each document to be printed. Sometimes these header files stay in the LaserWriter and force it to reset (and spit out a startup page) before letting you print a document from a different application. This is a bug. If you find the LaserWriter resetting every time you switch from a given application, contact the publisher of that application for a fix.

❡ *using downloadable fonts with 400K floppies*

If you're using 400K disks, you may not have enough room on your startup disk for both the screen fonts and the font

bargain

files you need in order to use downloadable laser fonts. (With ImageWriter fonts, you only need the equivalent of the screen fonts, so you can squeeze more of them on a disk.) The solution, of course, is to upgrade to an 800K drive—which, in our opinion, is worth every penny of its relatively modest cost.

⬤ *copy protection on Adobe fonts*

The only copy-protected laser fonts are those from Adobe Systems. When you install an Adobe font, you have to name the printer you want it to work with. From that point on it won't work with any other printer—and, needless to say, you only get to install each font once. (Adobe does offer a more expensive version of their fonts that can be installed on up to five printers.)

⬤ *laser fonts in MacPaint*

MacPaint, that bastion of bit-mapping, will not output laser fonts. What you get instead is the screen font, just the way you see it on the screen.

To get around this, use MacDraw or MacDraft or, even better, SuperPaint, which lets you combine bit-mapped and object-oriented graphics.

⬤ *incorrect character spacing with the old 64K ROMs*

When Apple introduced the 128K ROMs (for the Mac Plus and the Enhanced, but also available as a separate upgrade), they allowed for a new font resource, .FOND. Unlike the earlier .FONT resource, .FOND is much smarter about character widths in laser fonts, and virtually eliminates the problem of spacing on the screen being different from what you get on paper (but see the next entry).

The 64K ROMs don't know about .FOND and therefore can't look for it. So if you want precise character spacing with laser fonts, make sure you've got the 128K ROMs.

✦ different versions of Times, Helvetica and Courier

The 10- and 12-point sizes of the laser fonts Times and Helvetica and the 10-point size of Courier have been slightly modified to improve character spacing. As a result, a document that was perfectly formatted in an old version of one of them may have some unexpected line breaks and page breaks when printed with a new version (or vice versa, of course). The only solution is to go through and readjust things as needed.

Images on the LaserWriter
(and on other PostScript printers and typesetters)

✦ automatic reduction of some graphics

Some applications will scale bit-mapped images to 96% of their original size when printing them on the LaserWriter. That's because the Mac's resolution of 72 dpi doesn't divide evenly into the LaserWriter's resolution of 300 dpi. Reducing the image to 96% gives you 75 dpi, which goes into 300 dpi exactly four times. This helps with Smoothing.

(If the application doesn't do it for you, you can do it yourself, by simply putting 96% in the Reduce or Enlarge box in the Page Setup window.)

✦ halftoning on the LaserWriter

The LaserWriter handles text so nicely, it's tempting to use it to produce everything that goes on the page, including pictures. But certain kinds of images have to be processed before you can print them. Here's why:

All printed material is made up of either text or *art* (which is what every graphic element except text is called). There are two kinds of art—*line*, which contains no grays, and *continuous-tone*, which does (the name comes from the fact that the tones form a continuum, from black through gray to white).

Continuous-tone art presents a problem: Since printing ink is black (or whatever) and paper is white (or whatever), how can the grays be represented?

Far-and-away the most common solution involves putting a *screen* over the photograph. (It's called a screen because the original ones were made of fine metal mesh, although most screens today are sheets of plastic with dots printed on them.) The screen converts light grays to tiny black dots on a white background, and dark grays to tiny white dots on a black background. From a normal reading distance, these dots—in many different sizes—look like various shades of gray.

Once a continuous-tone image has been screened, it's called a *halftone*. If you hold a magnifying glass to a halftoned picture (virtually any printed picture will do), you'll see the little halftone dots, but you won't find them on a continuous-tone photograph like a snapshot.

If you use the traditional screen approach to halftoning, you won't be able to integrate your graphics with your text and print them both out on the LaserWriter at the same time; you'll have to leave a space for the graphics and add them at a later stage. To integrate halftones with text, you need a device called a *scanner* that can capture continuous-tone images and halftone them electronically.

Scanners vary in *sampling density* (how many times per inch they evaluate the picture) and in how many levels of gray they'll pick up. They also vary in quality and price. ThunderScan is an inexpensive scanner ($230) that can produce images suitable for use in an informal newsletter—

or better than that, if you really know how to use it. Microtek and Abaton, which scan at 300 dpi, cost about ten times as much; their software makes it easy to capture an image as a PostScript file. An even higher-quality scanner is the ImagiTex 1085.

Once the scanner has captured the image, you can use various programs—usually software that comes with the scanner—to play with it. But you might be better off simply capturing the image as PostScript data and letting the LaserWriter do the halftoning—if the scanner will let you do that. (For one way to turn MacPaint, ThunderScan and MacVision documents into PostScript files, see the next entry.)

PostScript has better halftoning algorithms than most scanners, and also has many commands for altering the image. (The second issue of *Colophon*—the newsletter of Adobe Systems, which developed PostScript—shows several samples of what it can do.)

The quality of a halftone depends on the *frequency* of the screen you use (how many lines per inch it breaks the picture into). The higher the number of lines, the better the photograph looks. The coarsest screen in general use is 65 lines per inch. Newspapers typically use an 85-line screen and magazines a 120-line screen. The finest screen in general use is 150 lines per inch.

Laser printers and typesetters each have a *default screen frequency* that the manufacturer has picked to produce the best output on that particular device. On the LaserWriter, it's 60 lines per inch (lpi); on the Linotronic 100, 90 lpi; on the Linotronic 300, 120 lpi. You can vary this frequency somewhat (using simple PostScript programming), but if you go too far from the default, the results may not look very good.

very
hot
tip

The LaserWriter's resolution of 60 lpi is just below the usual minimum standard for halftones, and you can't expect an image printed at that resolution to look like the ones in magazines and books. But the quality is good enough for many purposes, and can be quite impressive, as the pictures facing the part titles demonstrate.

✦ *converting images to PostScript files using LaserTools*

JustText is a powerful but complex text formatting and page makeup program that includes a useful set of utilities called LaserTools. One of these, Paint to PostScript, converts MacPaint files to PostScript image files, which can then be manipulated in many ways that aren't possible with MacPaint. LaserTools also includes utilities for converting ThunderScan and MacVision documents to PostScript.

Supplies for the LaserWriter

✦ *what kind of paper to use*

Laser printers put images down on paper in exactly the same way as photocopiers do; in fact, the guts of a LaserWriter (and of several other PostScript-compatible laser printers) are identical to those of many Canon copiers (all use the LBP-CX "marking engine"). So the kind of paper specifically designed for use in copiers—often labeled "xerographic"—is what you want for the LaserWriter.

Copier paper comes in more than one grade. When you're preparing originals for presentation, you'll naturally want to use a nice-looking, heavy, opaque paper. But for everyday use, and when you're preparing documents to be reproduced, use the cheapest kind you can find. Here's why:

very
hot
tip

When the humidity is high, pieces of paper tend to stick together. To help them separate more easily, paper manufacturers put powder between the sheets. This is called *dusting*, and the more expensive a paper is, the more dusting it tends to have. The problem with dusting is that particles of the powder tend to get bonded to the paper along with the image, producing a rough, uneven surface. So cheap paper, with little or no dusting, is best.

Cheap paper has another advantage: because of its low fiber content, it has a smoother surface than most expensive paper (except for some types specifically designed to be ultrasmooth). The smoother the surface, the more precise the image bonded to it will be.

If there's a discount paper supply house in your area that sells retail, you should be able to buy inexpensive copier paper for $2-$3 a ream (500 sheets). If there isn't (and you live on the West Coast), try a local Copy-Mat outlet. They sell the standard paper they use in their machines for $3.75 a ream. (We don't know if other copy shops also sell paper, but it's worth asking.) Copy-Mats also have a fairly good selection of other kinds of paper (colored, "parchment," "laid," etc.), although a paper supply house's stock will obviously be much more extensive.

bargain

But the best source for paper we've found is the Costco wholesale discount chain. You have to be a member (small businesses, independent professionals, government workers, organization members, etc. qualify) and be willing to buy ten reams at a time, but if you are, you can get plain 20-lb. bond for less than $2 a ream.

bargain

Except in an emergency, it makes absolutely no sense to go into a stationery store and pay $6-$7 a ream when you can get the same paper at half the price or less elsewhere.

❤ *getting the most from toner cartridges*

Before installing a new toner cartridge in a LaserWriter, you should rotate it gently from side to side (that is, lift the right side, then the left—it's roll you want, not yaw). If you don't do this, the images you get may not be dark enough. (You may also have to break in the cartridge by printing thirty pages or so.)

very
hot
tip

bargain

very good
feature

If you rock the cartridge whenever pages start to look light, and keep the print density dial set low until the cartridge is really on its last legs, you should easily be able to get 4000 pages and more from each cartridge, with perfectly acceptable quality (except, of course, for solid blacks, which you can't get even with a new cartridge).

The LaserWriter manual has an excellent section (chapter 4) on all aspects of setting up and maintaining a LaserWriter; it's clearly written and full of helpful illustrations.

♦ buying new toner cartridges

If you can't find an Apple-brand toner cartridge for your LaserWriter, the Hewlett-Packard LaserJet cartridge will work just as well. The cost to the dealer for both brands is the same, so your cost should be too. In theory, a toner cartridge made for any other laser printer that uses the Canon LBP-CX marking engine should also work, but we haven't tried them.

Miscellaneous LaserWriter tips
(and tips on other PostScript printers and typesetters)

♦ proofing on the LaserWriter before typesetting

The Macintosh and the ImageWriter use QuickDraw routines to create their images, while the LaserWriter and many other laser printers and typesetters use PostScript. Although a lot of brilliant work has been done to allow QuickDraw and PostScript to talk to each other, what you see on the Mac and on an ImageWriter is always going to vary somewhat from the output of a PostScript-driven device.

This means there's no substitute for hard copies. If you're planning to do final output on a PostScript-driven typesetter like the Linotronic, you definitely should proof your work on the LaserWriter. The differences between its output and the typesetter's will be negligible. (The resolution will, of course be higher on the Linotronic—that's why you're using it in the first place—but the position of all the elements, and the overall look of the page, will be the same.)

There are two exceptions to that rule. First of all, the Linotronic can print all the way to the edges of the roll of paper it's using (which can be either 8.5" or 11" wide) while the LaserWriter can't print wider than 8". Secondly, the Linotronic won't smooth bit-mapped images. If you want the images smoothed, print them out on a LaserWriter and then paste them manually over the equivalent unsmoothed images in the Linotronic output.

● *renting time on a LaserWriter (or other PostScript device)*

bargain

Businesses are springing up all over (particularly in big cities and near universities) that let you come in with your Mac disk and print it out on one or more kinds of PostScript-compatible printers. Renting time can be surprisingly inexpensive; there's a place near us that charges just $5 and hour and 15¢ a page.

If you can't find a place in the phone book, check with a local Mac user group (in fact, do that first; unlike the Yellow Pages, they can tell you which businesses know what they're doing, charge the least, and so on). If there's no user group in your area, or they don't know of a rental place, check out the entry below about remote typesetting services; many of those services also provide LaserWriter output.

● *getting your disks ready for a rented LaserWriter*

When you're planning to rent time on a LaserWriter, you might as well format your documents and set up your disks as completely as possible ahead of time, to cut down on the amount of time you have to pay for.

The first step is to make sure that the disk you bring with you has the software you need on it; the rental place will obviously have some software, but they may not have what you used to create your document (or the same versions of it). Call beforehand to make sure they have the laser fonts you want to use installed on their printer; if not, be sure that the System file on the startup disk you bring has the appropriate screen fonts installed, and that the System folder contains the font files you need for the printer.

If you haven't already done so, change the fonts in your document to laser fonts by selecting the text and choosing the screen fonts just the way you would any other font. (We're assuming you proofed your document on the ImageWriter.) Next, open Chooser (on the ⌘ menu) and select the LaserWriter icon. If you're using Chooser version 2.3 or later and System version 3.2 or later, you can do this without having a LaserWriter actually attached to your system—as long as you have the LaserWriter file in your System folder and have connected AppleTalk on the Control Panel.

(If you're using older system software and have Choose Printer instead of Chooser, you can select 'no printer' by clicking in the space just below the last printer listed. But why are you using out-of-date system software? The new stuff is free.)

Once you've selected the LaserWriter in the Chooser, go back into your application, open the Page Setup window (on the File menu), make any changes you want (or no changes) and click on OK. Now go through your document. ImageWriter page setup has different margins from LaserWriter page setup, and there are other incompatibilities, so there may be changes you need to make. When you've done that, you're ready for the shortest possible time rental on the LaserWriter.

⌘ *remote typesetting from Mac disks*

Let's say you've proofed your document on a LaserWriter until it's just the way you want it. Now you want to typeset it.

But your budget's a little tight and you can't afford to buy a Linotronic this month (it probably wouldn't fit in the closet anyway). Don't despair. There are several services that will accept your Mac disks and print out from them on their own PostScript-driven typesetters or laser printers.

The costs usually run from $5 to $15 a page (some places also have a one-time registration charge of about $50). Many of these services let you send data via modem—although if your document is at all long, it's going to take forever. Another advantage of mailing the disk (or, if you're in a hurry, sending it by Federal Express) is that you can send a printout along with it as a proof, so there won't be any questions about how you want the finished document to look.

bargain

Even if you send the document on the phone, you should send a message with it detailing exactly what you want. This is always a good idea, but with version 1.9 and earlier of MacDraw, it's an absolute necessity. MacDraw remembers fonts in the order in which they were installed in the system (other applications may do this too), and since the odds that the typesetting service will have installed the same fonts in the same order that you did are about one in a trillion, you'll need to tell them what fonts you want.

important warning

(This is not a problem with MacDraw drawings after they've been pasted into documents created by other applications—as long as the same System was used to create those documents as was used to create the MacDraw drawings.)

Here's a very incomplete list of some of the services that offer typesetting from Mac disks: Advanced Computer Graphics of Boston, MA; Desktop Publishing & Design of Boston, MA; Laser Designs Corp. of Cambridge, MA; Laser Printing Services of Southfield, MI; Macintosh Typesetting Club of Aptos, CA (Arthur has had good experience with these people); MacTypeNet of Livonia, MI; Typeline of Teaneck, NJ; and Typesetting Service Corporation of Providence, RI. (Their addresses and phone numbers are in Appendix C.)

For more current information, check out the various magazines on the Mac and on desktop publishing; they sometimes run updated lists of such services.

🍎 *suppressing the startup page*

Even time you turn on the LaserWriter, it spits out a rather attractive test page that tells you how many copies have ever been printed on the machine. It's possible to get into this constantly mounting total as a measure of your productivity, and therefore your general worth as a human being ("I've printed 3000 pages on my LaserWriter; I must be doing something useful with my life"), but it does cost you about 3¢ in toner, some fraction of a cent in paper, and some hard-to-figure but probably significant amount of wear and tear on the machine.

So it's sometimes nice to be able to turn off the startup page, at least for a while. Century Software has a pair of programs that do that. Called Start-up On and Start-Up Off, they...well, we're sure you can figure it out.

Here are two public domain programs that do the same thing. Just type them out as you see them below (only the last line is essential), save them as a text only file with a name that's easy to remember, and send them to the LaserWriter with a program like PostScript Dump, Font Downloader or LW Download (which come on laser font disks).

```
%Disable LaserWriter from Printing Startup Page upon Powerup
% John Monaco Compuserve 73317,3677 %%GEnie J Monaco %%EndComments
serverdict begin 0 exitserver statusdict begin false setdostartuppage
```

```
%Enable LaserWriter to Print Startup Page upon Powerup
% John Monaco Compuserve 73317,3677 %%GEnie J Monaco %%EndComments
serverdict begin 0 exitserver statusdict begin true setdostartuppage
```

One function of the startup page is to tell you exactly when the LaserWriter is ready to begin printing. If you turn off the startup page, you need to know the following:

When you turn the LaserWriter on, it tests itself; while it's doing that, the green light blinks. When the green light stops blinking, wait a few seconds and the machine is ready to use. In a cold room, this warmup and test procedure may take about a minute. If you've used the machine recently and/or the room is warm, it might take much less time than that.

✺ *printing custom stationery on the LaserWriter*

Access to a LaserWriter can not only save you the expense of buying stationery, it can allow you to modify your stationery as often you like. You can change the text, the fonts, the graphics, or the paper you print it on. (On the LaserWriter, it's just as economical to produce five sheets of letterhead with matching envelopes as it is to produce five hundred.) Custom stationery makes a wonderful present, particularly if you use you fancy paper and spend some time make the stationery match the recipient's personality.

bargain

There's no special trick to doing letterhead on the LaserWriter. (There are some general tips on the subject in the general word processing tips section of chapter 6; also see the entry below on special typographic effects). But envelopes can be tricky. You have to hand-feed them into the LaserWriter, face up and against the back edge of the manual feed guide (where the small brown label is). Certain kinds of envelopes don't feed very well—like ones made from "parchment"-type paper.

If you print your name and return address along the length of the envelope (that is, in the same direction as the name and address of the person you're sending it to), you'll only have to run the envelope through the Laserwriter once. If you want your name and address to run across the end of the envelope—which looks a lot snazzier—you'll either have run the envelopes through a second time, print labels and stick them on, or address the envelopes by hand. (For a tip on how to set up Word to print across the end of envelopes on the LaserWriter, see the Word section in chapter 6.)

Whichever direction you use for your address, you may find yourself frustrated by the LaserWriter's inability to print closer than a quarter of an inch to the edge of the envelope.

🍎 *Word on the LaserWriter*

Although Microsoft has given more consideration than most software publishers to optimizing their software for output on laser printers, they've gone about it in a nonstandard way. As a result, the performance of Word 1.05 on the LaserWriter is quirky when running under System version 3.1 and later (and you certainly don't want to use an earlier version of the System). This may also be the reason why some people say MacWrite prints out faster than Word on the LaserWriter.

There's no fix for this, but Word 3.0 deals with the problem.

🍎 *viewing PostScript code*

To see the actual PostScript code that gets sent to the LaserWriter, give the Print command, click OK when the print dialog box comes up, then immediately hold down COMMAND-F. (When you see the message that reads "creating PostScript file," you can let up on the keys.) The PostScript code generated to print the document will be placed in a file on disk, rather than being sent to the printer.

important warning

This file will be named "PostScript" and it's a good idea to rename immediately, because if you use COMMAND-F again, a new file named "PostScript" will overwrite the old.

Chapter 12

Miscellaneous hardware tips

the most important tip in this book

As wonderful a machine as the Mac is, it's far from reliable. Arthur had the power supply on his Mac replaced four or five times (it happened so often he lost count). Although the Mac's power supplies are notorious for failing, they're not the only components that cause trouble. So the most important tip in this book is this: take out a service contract on every piece of Mac equipment you own, and keep it in force for every second you own that piece of equipment.

very
hot
tip

Apple's service contracts go under the name of AppleCare; they provide the same coverage you get during the 90-day warranty period (free parts and labor for whatever goes wrong—unless, of course, you drop your Mac out a window or something like that). AppleCare isn't cheap—for example, a year's coverage for a 512K Mac cost $150 and for a LaserWriter $420 (as of the end of 1986)—but if you can't afford it, don't buy the machine or peripheral at all.

Tips on major components

protecting the phosphor on your screen

The phosphor that's painted on the inside of your screen and glows when the electron beam hits it can become exhausted from too much use. The exhausted areas show up as dark spots on your screen. So it's a good idea not to leave an image visible on your screen except when you're actually using the computer. But you don't want to be constantly turning the Mac on and off, because that's hard on the electronics.

There are desk accessories available that keep track of how long it's been since you hit a key or the mouse button and black out your screen automatically after a certain amount of time has passed (you can usually select how long that time should be). Hitting any key or the mouse brings back the image. Or you can just turn the brightness down when you get up from the Mac.

The brightness control is on the front of the machine, to the left, just underneath the Apple logo (🍎). Now don't feel that we're patronizing you by telling you something as basic as that. Arthur was once at the house of a (very intelligent) writer friend who uses her Mac extensively. He saw an image on the Mac's screen, so he casually walked over and turned the brightness down to black. She had no idea what had happened and totally freaked out. He showed her how to adjust the brightness, but she wouldn't calm down until he turned it back up and left it there. Even then she had the sneaking suspicion that he'd done some sort of subtle but irreparable damage to her machine.

🍎 screen brightness

It's nice that the Mac screen has dark characters on a light background, the way printed pages do. But this does increase the amount of flicker, and makes it harder to look at the screen for a long time.

One thing you can and should do to make the screen easier on your eyes is turn the brightness down. You want black on *gray*, not black on white. Another important step is to keep your room as dark as possible, and eliminate glare (reflections on the screen). If daylight does seep in, or if there are lights you can't turn off, turn the brightness up to compensate. But a dimly lit room and a black-on-gray screen are ideal.

🍎 *setting up a workstation*

If you put the Mac and its keyboard on the same surface, either the screen will be too low or the keyboard too high.

For comfortable typing, your wrists should never be higher than your elbows. Depending on your height and the height of your chair, this means the keyboard should be on a surface 24–27 inches off the floor. The screen should be 4-8 inches higher than the surface the keyboard is on, so that you can look at it comfortably without having to bend your head. And don't strain your eyes by putting it too close either—allow at least a foot between the back of the keyboard and the front of the Mac.

very
hot
tip

One way to put together a comfortable workstation is to use two tables—one a low typing table and the other normal height. Put them together with the low one in front, then put the keyboard on it and the Mac on the higher table in the back. A good swivel (like Ergotron's MacTilt) can help raise the Mac to where you want it, or just put it on a thick book or a sturdy box.

Another inexpensive approach is to find a used desk with a typing well in it. Fasten the well in the open position and use it for the keyboard, then build a higher platform behind it (it doesn't have to be anything fancy, just a piece of plywood and few boards) for the Mac to rest on.

🍎 *where to put an external floppy drive*

Don't put the external floppy disk drive on the left side of the Mac. The Mac's power supply is there and can interfere with reading and writing to disk. The best place for the drive is on the Mac's right side, either sitting flat on the table or

important
warning

sideways against the side of the Mac in a bracket like the one that comes with Ergotron's MacTilt (see chapter 13 for details).

You may also be tempted to put the external drive on top of the Mac, but don't. The Mac generates enough heat after an hour or two to expand the surface of a disk, and this can cause errors. Even if you don't get errors immediately, any information written to a disk that is warmer than normal might not be readable when the disk has cooled to normal temperatures. (If, in spite of this warning, you still insist of putting the external drive on top of the Mac, at least make sure it's right in the center, so it doesn't block the cooling vents.)

⚫ *putting hard disks where you can't hear them*

Hard disks are great, and once you have one you won't be able to understand how you lived without it. But even the ones without fans make a fair amount of noise. If you're sensitive to noise, and love the fact that the (standard) Mac is virtually silent, a hard disk is likely to bother you.

Fortunately, the solution is simple. Just attach a long cable to your hard disk and put it in a closet or some other place where you can't hear it (Arthur's are on a shelf outside—and above—the door to his work room).

SCSI drives are designed to accept cables up to 21 feet, or 7 meters, long (7 meters is equal to 23 feet, not 21, but don't blame us—we're just quoting from the AppleTalk box). Apple's HD20 isn't supposed to take a long cable, but Arthur's has been hooked up to a 12-foot extension cable for many months and he hasn't noticed any particular problem.

Since it seems unlikely that you can physically harm a drive by putting it on a long cable, it makes sense to at least experiment with one; if you do have problems, you'll only be out the price of the cable. (Since you *always* back up your work every fifteen minutes or half hour, you won't lose much data no matter how often the disk crashes—right?)

● *connecting SCSI drives*

The connector on the back of a SCSI drive is different from the SCSI connector on the back of the Mac Plus, because Apple chose to use a 25-pin connector instead of the standard SCSI connector. So there are two kinds of cables: SCSI-drive-to-Mac-Plus cables, and cables with standard SCSI connectors on both ends that you use for chaining SCSI drives together.

If you upgrade a 128K or 512K Mac with the 128K ROMs and have a third-party SCSI connector installed, you'll probably need the SCSI-drive-to-SCSI-drive cable with the standard connectors at both ends, because that's what third-party SCSI boards almost always use (that is, the connector on the back of your Mac will be the same as the connector on the back of the SCSI drive—not different as it is on a Mac Plus.)

To chain two or more SCSI drives together, you may have to open up one or more of them and throw a switch that tells the Mac which one to use as the startup drive. If you're squeamish about doing that, have your dealer do it for you.

● *actual disk capacities*

The amount of data stored on different brands of 20-megabyte hard disks can vary by more than a meg. For example, SuperMac's DataFrame 20 holds 20,792K while Apple's HD 20 only holds 19,476K. (Twenty megs is 20,480K, so the DataFrame holds 1.5% more than it claims and the HD 20 5% less.)

important warning

● *using UniDisk as an external drive*

Apple markets a double-sided 3-1/2" external drive called the UniDisk for the Apple // family of computers, and you can use it as a substitute for an 800K external drive. Why you would want to do this we don't know, but here's how:

Remove the screws to open the case to reveal the two circuit boards, one above the other. Disconnect the ribbon cable from the upper board, then disconnect the cable from the lower board. Now connect the cable you removed from the lower board to the upper board. Ignore the remaining cable.

This procedure bypasses the Apple // disk controller in the UniDisk, which is the only significant difference between the UniDisk and the Mac 800K external drive (the Mac drive has no built-in disk controller because the Mac uses its own internal circuitry to control it). Curiously, the UniDisk is priced either the same as or lower than the Mac drive.

The main limitation to using the UniDisk on the Macintosh is that you won't be able to boot from the external drive.

¢ *Haba 800K floppy drive*

important warning

The Haba double-sided drive doesn't work with HFS. It's also just about the noisiest drive of any kind, for any computer, that we've ever heard.

¢ *easy way to restart the Mac/XL*

shortcut

To restart the Mac/XL without having to reload MacWorks, hold down the ¢ key while you turn the power on and off. The machine will restart and return you directly to the Desktop.

Tips on minor components

¢ *worn mouse feet*

The two small feet on the bottom of the mouse will wear down eventually. You can extend the time this takes by moving your mouse on a surface softer than the average desktop—like a mouse pad (they're available for about $9 at just about any computer dealer).

But what if the feet on your mouse are already worn? One solution is to attach small pieces of Velcro (the loop—not the hook—type) on either side of the worn feet, with the fuzzy side facing down.

very
hot
tip

Another obvious solution is to buy a new mouse, which we only mention so we can tell you that authorized Apple dealers will charge you less for a new mouse if you trade in your old one.

￼ Dale's cheap mouse pad

Dale's favorite mouse pad is a sheet of heavyweight paper inside a good quality spiral-bound notebook. Unlike the cloth surfaces on commercial mouse pads, it doesn't attract dust and cat hairs, and it sells for a fraction of the cost. Best of all, when you want a new one, all you have to do is turn the page.

bargain

If you already have a commercial mouse pad, you can prolong its life by covering its surface with a piece of heavy paper cut to size.

￼ alternative AppleTalk cables

AppleTalk cables are sometimes in short supply. In an emergency, you can make your own. Order the connectors for the end of the cable from your Apple dealer (Apple part number #815-0878). For the cable itself, contact an electronics supply store. Ask for Belden 9999 (PVC) or Belden 89999 (Teflon).

Another approach is to use PhoneNET, a less-expensive AppleTalk substitute described in chapter 13. PhoneNET uses a combination of their own connectors and generic

bargain

telephone cable, which costs a *whole* lot less than AppleTalk cable. They make an adaptor for connecting AppleTalk hardware and PhoneNET hardware, so you won't lose whatever you have invested in your network.

❡ *alternative keyboard cables*

The Mac's keyboard cable looks just like a telephone cord, but it isn't—the wires in the Mac keyboard cable connect straight through from one end to the other, while in a telephone cord, they twist. So if you want a longer keyboard cable, you can't just substitute a phone cord.

Lon Poole recommends Your Affordable Software Company (see Appendix C for their address). They sell a 12-foot cable for $10 and a 25 foot cable for $13. (Why anyone would want to type 12 to 25 feet away from a 9-inch monitor is beyond us, but to each his own.)

❡ *what the Mac's battery does*

The Mac's battery provides power to a special area of memory called *parameter RAM*. It addition to keeping track of the date and time and running the alarm clock, parameter RAM remembers how the *serial ports* are configured. (The serial ports are the two sockets on the back of the Mac where you plug in modems, printers, AppleTalk connectors, and some hard disks; they're also known as the *printer port* and the *modem port.*)

So if your battery is getting weak, anything connected to a serial port may fail. The solution is to replace the battery, of course, but if you can't do that immediately, you can still continue to use your Mac. Turn the Mac off, take out the battery and, when you turn the Mac back on, reset the time and date and re-select the serial ports. (Use the Alarm Clock desk accessory to set the date and time and the Chooser to reselect the serial ports. You have to reset these parameters every time you turn on the Mac, until you replace the battery, but at least you can continue to use your computer.)

❖ *replacing the Mac's battery*

The battery in the back of the Mac will eventually run down and need to be replaced. (Usually the battery is good for about two years.) The proper replacement batteries are: DuraCell PX21, Eveready 523BP, Panasonic PX21, and Ray-O-Vac RPX21. They should cost about $5 and should be fairly easy to find.

❖ *don't mistake the SCSI connector for an RS232*

Although the SCSI connector on the back of the Mac Plus looks like the RS232 serial connector found on some older computers, it's not the same, and you can damage the Mac if you try to plug an RS232 cable into it.

important
warning

Keeping the Mac cool

❖ *fans, pro and con*

According to Apple, all Macs up through the Mac Plus can maintain an internal temperature of no more than 15° Celsius (27° Fahrenheit) higher than the room temperature without the help of a fan. (Although the Mac Plus has more memory chips than the 512K, its total chip count—and therefore its total heat output—is actually less than a 512K's.)

The Mac's fanless cooling is done by convection—the basic principle of which is that hot air rises. The Mac designers put this principle to work by placing hot components like the power supply near the vents on the top of the Mac case, where they create an upward flow of air that cools things below.

very good
feature

While a 15° C. difference is within Apple's guidelines, and normally won't present a problem, the cooler a computer runs (within reason), the better. So a fan certainly isn't going to hurt the performance of any Mac, and if yours has third-party additions (memory expansion upgrades and/or internal hard disks), a fan may well be a necessity.

Some fans for the Mac are external—they mount on top of the case and boost the Mac's normal convective cooling. Because they're relatively powerful, they also draw dust, dirt, and smoke particles into the Mac. So use them with caution if you're a smoker or work in a relatively dusty environment. They also tend to be the noisiest type of fan for the Mac.

very bad feature

You should definitely avoid any external fan that draws air in and forces it downward into the Mac's case. Since the power supply is the major source of heat in the Mac, and since it's near the top, these fans actually blow hot air down onto the delicate (and expensive) motherboard.

very good feature

Internal fans usually cost less than external ones. There are two kinds—rotary (blades twirling around) and piezo-electric (two thin plastic flaps that vibrate back and forth). Internal rotary fans (which usually come with internal hard disks and are seldom sold separately) are less noisy than external fans, and piezoelectric fans are quieter still, making only a slight, dull hum.

Dale recently installed a 2-megabyte memory upgrade in a Mac Plus. Since the clip-on board mounts directly over the Mac's 68000 chip, he was skeptical that the little piezoelectric "feather fan" provided would be adequate to expel the heat generated. But after using the newly upgraded system for about five hours, he felt the top of the unit and was delighted to find that it was barely warm to the touch, dramatically cooler than a fanless 512K Mac. This made him a piezoelectric fan fan.

Since all types of Mac fans are adequate at cooling the Mac, and since they're all relatively inexpensive, the real question comes down to noise. In this regard, piezoelectric fans are clearly superior, but they do still make some noise. In Arthur's opinion, the ideal solution is the MacChimney, a totally silent and very inexpensive device for cooling the Mac that's described by its inventor in the next tip.

If you do decide to get a fan, spend five minutes listening to it first, and make sure you have the right to return it. Many people find the noise from a fan much more annoying over hundreds or thousands of hours in a quiet home or office than they think they will when listening to it for a few minutes in a noisy computer store.

very
hot
tip

🍎 *silent cooling with the MacChimney* (Tom Swain)

It's said that Steve Jobs passionately disliked the concept of a fan-cooled Macintosh. So, like several other more notable design decisions that never made it to a committee, the fanless Mac was born. (Back then no one ever dreamed that people would soon be stuffing internal hard drives, floating point coprocessors or—for that matter, a megabyte of memory—into Apple's new baby.)

Well, the Mac has grown up, but it still has no fan to show for all its maturity. Do the 512K Mac and Mac Plus need some help? I believe so, especially in the summer months when the ambient temperature can already be high. However, when I followed conventional wisdom and installed a fan, my friendly unobtrusive workstation was transformed into a hissing and obnoxious desktop troll.

I started searching for an alternative and in the process acquired some information I'd like to pass on. Here's the lowdown on why heat is an enemy, what the risks are, and what you can do to eliminate or reduce them. I also describe a low-cost alternative I invented, which I call the Mac-Chimney.

Internal heat is an enemy of the Macintosh for two main reasons. First, cool chips last longer. For the techies out there, the statistical lifetime of a semiconductor device is a fourth order function of the operating temperature, assuming the device fails by thermally induced diffusion in the silicon wafer. What does this mean? If a chip is fated to die after one year of operation at 170° F., it would last two years at 80° F.

important
warning

Secondly, and I believe more importantly, the heat generated can warm and thermally expand the floppy disk in the internal drive. If a file is written to the disk in this condition—say on a hot summer afternoon after your machine has been on for several hours—this file can do an unpleasant disappearing act the next morning when you turn your machine on. The air is cool, and the read head on your internal drive is aimlessly searching for a track that moved a little during the night. (Incidentally, if this happens, the file can most likely be recovered by letting the machine—and therefore the disk—warm up for a few hours and then trying to reread it.)

very
hot
tip

An excellent qualitative test of the temperature inside your Mac can be made by leaving the machine on for at least an hour with a disk in the internal drive and then ejecting it. Immediately hold the top side of the disk's shutter mechanism to your face. The warmth (or lack thereof) will give you a good gauge of how effective any subsequent cooling strategy is.

The arguments for a cool Mac are clear enough. Unfortunately the existing alternatives offer their own set of problems. If the fan draws power from the Mac's power supply (as most of them do), then a power supply with an already questionable track record is being asked to do more work. You may also discover after installing your fan that a noiseless workstation is not only a blessing but instrumental in maintaining your sanity.

Furthermore, addition of a fan that pumps air through the Mac rather than simply circulating it internally can turn your machine into a dust trap. It has happened more than once that someone opened their case after six months of fan operation only to find that the innards looked like the lint sock on a dryer vent. This is a situation to be avoided, as disk drives are intolerant of dust.

Piezoelectric fans reportedly achieve a significant overall temperature reduction by mere internal circulation. Whether such a fan reduces the temperature of the internal floppy disk in addition to the circuit boards is not clear.

My solution to cooling the Mac is the MacChimney. It's primarily suited to people who generally keep their Macintosh in one place, prefer to leave it on much of the time, and are hesitant to plunge into the purchase of a fan that may violate their sense of environmental aesthetics.

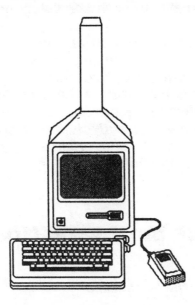

The MacChimney (all rights reserved by Thomas Swain)

The MacChimney exploits what in the lexicon of fluid mechanics is termed free convective laminar flow in a vertical duct. Basically it operates the same way a fireplace chimney works. Hot air rising up a vertical enclosure that opens to denser air acts as a buoyant mass that exerts a driving pressure proportional to the vertical height. Cool air enters the Mac in the bottom side vents and becomes heated by the electronics. The pressure differential generated by the buoyant mass of warmer air in the chimney has the same effect as a fan.

very good feature

Geometry is important. A long chimney (6') is functionally preferable but unaesthetic and unwieldy. If the cross section of the chimney is too large, then unstable cold air will spill down into the top and reduce the buoyant driving potential. Making its cross section too small is tantamount to blocking all the Mac's vents. Through the use of flow visualization techniques and fluid mechanics, the MacChimney's geometry has been optimized to allow about a 60% increase in airflow rate over a normal Mac, with absolutely no noise pollution.

bargain

(Note from Arthur: I'm so sensitive to noise that even a piezoelectric fan got on my nerves after a while. In desperation I turned to MacChimney and I love it. My Mac looks a little strange—sort of like the Tin Woodman in The Wizard of Oz—*but that gives it a certain charm. MacChimney cools the Mac very efficiently, is totally silent, costs only $15 and makes a great conversation piece. For ordering information, see Appendix C.)*

Advanced hardware tips

🍎 *how to open the Mac's case*

The original designers of the Macintosh never imagined that users would want to open their machines to add the hard disks, fans, and other goodies that many of us consider necessities. In fact, you need special tools just to open the case.

(There's a good reason for this. The Mac contains high-voltage components that can give you the shock of your life, and possibly even end it. Continue reading this tip only if you know where they are and how to avoid them. We provide this information because it's both useful and commonly available, and because many Mac owners do routinely open the case on their Macs. But we do *not* recommend this practice.)

The screwdriver used to open the Mac case needs to have a Torx T-15 tip and an 8" shaft. Apple sells this tool to dealers along with a "splitter" to pry apart the two parts of the case. The splitter is not commonly available. The next best tool is an architect's three-sided ruler.

To open the case, set the Mac on its face on a smooth surface. Use the long screwdriver to remove the five screws on the back. Two are deep in the handle (hence, the long shaft), two are just above the cable connectors, and the fifth is hidden behind the battery cover.

Then use the architect's ruler to gently separate the two parts of the case. An aluminum RF shield fits over the cable connectors and may come off when you remove the case. Just replace it before you replace the back of the case.

⌘ *modifying the Radio Shack joystick extension cable*

As mentioned above, Radio Shack's joystick extension cable (catalog #276-1978) is an excellent DB9-to-DB9 extension cable. (DB9 is the name of the connectors found on the original Mac 128K and 512K.) If you're handy with a soldering iron, you can also use it to make custom cables. The pinout code is:

1	Green
2	Yellow
3	Orange
4	Red
5	Brown
6	Blue
7	Black
8	Gray
9	White

Part IV—

Maximizing your purchases

Chapter 13

Recommended hardware

⌘ *when to buy hardware*

Because computer prices are always falling, people will often caution you to wait and buy later, when it will cost you less. While this sometimes makes sense, it isn't necessarily good advice. In the first place, if you followed it faithfully, you'd *never* own a computer. In the second place, it fails to consider the value of owning and using the equipment instead of just sitting around waiting for the price to fall.

Dale once upgraded a Mac for a client who had bought it when they first came out; in other words, he had paid $2500 for a 128K machine. The client mentioned how much it had cost him to be first on the block. But then he added, "Of course, I wouldn't have gotten my new job if I hadn't had two years' experience on the Mac."

Here's another example: A couple of months after Arthur bought the LaserWriter on which this book was typeset, its list price dropped by $1000. But in those two months he'd learned how to use it and had printed thousands of pages on it. Although it galls him bitterly to ever pay a nickel more for something than absolutely necessary, he has to admit that the use of the LaserWriter for that time was clearly worth more than $1000 to him.

very hot tip

In fact, neither of us has ever owned a computer that didn't give us more value in a single year than the total price we paid for it. So the rule is: if you have a use for a piece of hardware now, go ahead and get it. The benefits of having the tool will almost always outweigh whatever money you'd save waiting for tomorrow's lower price.

⌘ contact information

The products and companies mentioned in this chapter (as well as those mentioned elsewhere in the book) are listed in Appendix C. Company listings include addresses and, when we have them, phone numbers; some product listings also contain ordering information.

Models of the Mac

⌘ a short history of the Mac

The original 128K Macintosh was a marvel. Even though its slowness and seemingly insatiable appetite for disk swaps could really get on your nerves, it did things no affordable computer before it could even dream of, and did them with a grace, logic and affection for the user that was revolutionary.

Steve Jobs is generally given the credit for the main design decisions that led to this machine. Jobs envisioned an "appliance computer"—one you could buy, take home and use without having to read a book or even having to decide what type of monitor, how much memory or what additional options (hard disk, modem, graphics card, etc.) you wanted.

In addition to its 128K of RAM, the original Mac had 64K of ROM, one internal 400K floppy drive, a connector for one external 400K disk drive, and two serial ports for connecting a printer and a modem. It was a closed machine, which means you couldn't open it up and install add-on boards. In fact, you were warned not to open the case, and needed special tools to do it.

These specs seem a bit chintzy by today's standards, but that's just because the computer industry is evolving with such blinding speed. Many months pass from the time engineers make final decisions about a machine until it appears in stores. When the Mac design was frozen so production could begin, 128K was more RAM than most personal computers had, and even today 400K is more than most floppies can store.

But Mac software tends to require more memory than the software that runs on other computers. On a 128K machine, running an application as basic to the Mac as MacPaint could be quite tedious. For example, if you used Grabber (the "hand") to move the image, you had to wait while the Mac went to the disk and got the new portion of the image.

Even worse, external drives were not available for months, and the months seemed like years as users developed "disk swap elbow." Sometimes people simply shut off their machines rather than accede to yet another request to insert a disk that the Mac had already asked for 28 times.

Another problem with the original Mac was the lack of useful software. Apple offered MacPaint and MacWrite, and Microsoft came out with Word and Multiplan, but there wasn't much else.

In the fall of 1984, Apple introduced the 512K "Fat Mac" (which wasn't called the "Big Mac" to avoid a lawsuit from McDonald's). Software ran much faster; now you could move around a MacPaint image with virtually no delays at all. And suddenly it seemed that every week an exciting new application appeared that made use of the extra memory (Excel, PageMaker, Switcher, Omnis, Helix, etc.).

But other than the extra 384K of RAM, the Fat Mac was essentially identical to the original 128K machine. There were still no slots, no (official) way to expand the memory further, and no provision for either internal or external hard disks.

In fact, Apple seemed to do everything possible to discourage the use of hard disks on the Mac. The system software originally couldn't deal with much more than a couple of megabytes of storage (as opposed to the 10 or 20 megabytes of storage capability that was standard at the time on other machines). One drive manufacturer told us that Apple also mislead developers by advising them to design disks that ran off the serial connectors, rather than the much faster floppy disk connector, saying that they had future plans for the floppy disk connector.

After several external hard disks had come out, General Computer introduced HyperDrive, an internal unit that connected directly to the 6800 processor chip. This inventive approach yielded acceptable hard disk performance for the first time.

Apple finally realized that the complex applications being developed for the Mac required a hard disk. So they came out with a drive of their own, the Hard Disk 20. And they were smart enough not to follow their own advice; the HD 20 connected to the faster floppy disk connector rather than the slower serial connectors and was—until the SCSI drives came out—the fastest external drive on the market.

At the same time, Apple introduced new system software that both removed the limit to the number of files you could have on a disk and also let you organize them hierarchically (that is, on different levels), by nesting folders within folders within folders.

very good feature

In January, 1986, Apple released the third incarnation of the Mac. The Mac Plus looks a lot like previous Macs, but there are some differences that make it a real performer. It has an entire megabyte of memory, and because its 256K memory chips are on four, small, removable boards, they can be removed and replaced with 1-megabyte chips (when the price comes down on those)—thereby quadrupling the memory.

very good
feature

A new set of 128K ROMs replaced the original 64K ROMs, with the hierarchical file system (HFS) built right in. The internal floppy drive was changed to a double-sided 800K drive which, in addition to storing twice as much data as the older drive, is much faster and dramatically quieter. Apple also introduced an external 800K drive.

gossip/
trivia

Perhaps the most exciting addition Apple made to the Mac Plus is the SCSI connector on the back of the machine. SCSI is an industry-standard interface for hard disks and other devices; the name stands for "small computer system interface" and is pronounced 'scuzzy'. (The other contending pronunciation was 'sexy', which is not only much nicer but also closer to how the word "scsi" would actually be pronounced, but Cotton Mather and his gang apparently still haunt the consciousness of even the most technologically advanced in our society, and 'scuzzy' won out.)

very good
feature

Hard disks designed to work with the SCSI connector are dramatically faster than drives connected to the serial connectors or the floppy disk connector. In fact, most are even faster than internal drives.

very good
feature

But speed is only one of the advantages of the SCSI interface. While no substitute for slots, it does provide a simple, inexpensive solution to the problem of adding multiple devices to a closed machine. Up to seven SCSI devices can be daisy-chained to the SCSI connector. If each is a 20-megabyte hard disk, that gives you a total of 140 megs of storage. Tape backup units designed for the SCSI connector are already on the market, with other devices sure to follow.

⚫ *Mac Plus upgrade path*

If you're confused about the official Apple upgrade path from a Macintosh (with the 64K ROMs) to a Macintosh Plus, here's a simple explanation of the three steps involved:

1. *Upgrading to the 128K ROMs and the 800K drive.* You have to do this before either of the steps mentioned below, and you must have at least 512K of RAM to use the 128K ROMs and the 800K drive. Any Apple dealer can do this step, usually while you wait (if you call a few days ahead to make an appointment).

The two 64K ROMs on the Mac's motherboard (main circuit board) are removed and replaced by the 128K ROMs; the 400K internal disk drive is removed and replaced with the double-sided 800K disk drive. Your newly upgraded machine will now run more quietly (the 800K Sony drives are wonderful) and faster, because both the drives and the QuickDraw routines in the ROMs are faster.

very good
feature

This upgrade costs $300, including labor, which is a bargain.

bargain

2. *Upgrading the motherboard.* The original motherboard (main circuit board) is replaced, although the 128K ROMs from your original motherboard are put on the new one (you got them when you did step 1). This gives you an extra 512K of RAM. The rear portion of the Mac's case is also replaced to accommodate the SCSI port and the small, round, serial-port connectors.

This upgrade costs $600 if you're upgrading from a 512K Mac, or $800 if you're upgrading from a 128K machine.

3. *Getting a Mac Plus keyboard.* (You can do this without step 2, but not without step 1.) The Mac Plus keyboard has a built-in numeric keypad with four arrow keys and costs $130; you get to keep your old keyboard. Some people love the Mac Plus keyboard; other people can't stand how big it is, and the fact that some keys are missing and others are smaller.

The total cost for all three upgrades is $1230 if you're starting with a 128K Mac, $1030 if you're starting with a 512K Mac. When you've done all of them, the only thing you'll be missing is the Macintosh Plus logo that goes on the front of the machine.

⬢ *the future of the Mac*

As this book goes to press Apple has not yet announced its plans for 1987, but you can be certain that several new versions of the Mac will be introduced (all of which will be described in our first update). What follows is just speculation.

things
to come

One new model will look very much like the current Mac Plus, and you may be able to upgrade to it from a Mac Plus. But inside there will be several important changes. The processor will be a Motorola 68020 (a more powerful version of the 68000 processor that all Macs to date have used), running at 16 MHz. This means the new Mac will be very fast. Three-dimensional drawing programs like Easy 3D and Phoenix 3D will suddenly become much more usable. The machine will also have an optional math co-processor to further speed up some applications.

There will probably be one—or perhaps even two—internal 1.6MB floppy drives. This Mac is also expected to have one slot, which probably will be used for either a card that speeds up AppleTalk or one that lets you run MS-DOS software (whoopee).

things
to come

Apple is also expected to introduce the "slot Mac"—a new-looking machine with several internal expansion slots. Like the other machine, it will use the 68020 chip and will offer a math co-processor chip as an option. Two to four megs of memory will be standard, and you'll have a choice of monitors, one of which may be large enough to display an 8-1/2 x 11 page. A color monitor may also be available.

Hard disks

✺ *the four basic types*

Hard disks for the Mac fall into four basic categories, based on how they connect. There are those that plug into one of the serial connectors, into the floppy disk connector, into the SCSI connector, and those that connect (and are housed) internally. We'll discuss each category in turn.

✺ *disks that plug into one of the serial connectors*

The first hard disks available for the Mac connected to one of the two serial ports (modem or printer) on the back of the Mac. In the early days of the Mac, Apple told hard disk developers to forgo the faster floppy disk connector in favor of the slower serial connectors, and they all dutifully followed these marching orders. The result is that these drives are among the slowest available for the Mac.

In addition, serial-port drives all require a boot disk; that is, you have to start the system with a special floppy that tells the Mac there's a hard disk connected to it. For both these reasons, serial-port drives are not very popular since the introduction of the Mac Plus with its SCSI port, and hard disk drives that connect to it.

But if speed is of no great concern to you, you might be happy with a serial-port drive—especially if you want to save money, since they're the least expensive hard disks available for the Mac. One good one is Paradise Systems 20-megabyte Mac 20. We've seen it on sale by mail order for as little as $500.

✺ *disks that plug into the floppy disk connector*

This class of drives is limited to one model, Apple's 20-megabyte Hard Disk 20. While faster than serial-port drives, it's still much slower than the newer SCSI drives. The only advantage to owning an HD 20 is that you can get AppleCare for it. The HD 20 lists for $1200, but you should be able to get it for less than that, particularly if you're purchasing a Mac at the same time.

🍎 *disks that plug into the SCSI connector*

This is the type of drive creating the most excitement in the market today, and the one we recommend. To use a SCSI drive, you need to either have a Mac Plus or add a SCSI interface to your regular Mac. SCSI drives are relatively inexpensive and extremely fast.

very good feature

Many companies are scrambling to introduce SCSI drives, but the most successful so far seem to be SuperMac Technologies, MDIdeas, and PeripheralLand. All are good drives, but SuperMac's Dataframe has several advantages: a *two*-year warranty, a generally good record of reliability, and no fan. (SuperMac stood the drive on its side, so it could cool itself convectively the way the Mac does.) But you can still hear the platter spinning.

A DataFrame 20 lists for $1100, but you should be able to find one for under $900. In late 1986 SuperMac began shipping a 40MB DataFrame ($1800) and the XP series of 20MB ($1200) and 40MB ($2000) drives which are twice as fast as its regular models. You can upgrade an existing DataFrame 20 to an XP for $100.

The speed of the XP DataFrame is truly remarkable (and if you've ever put a computer to serious use, you know how important disk speed is). How SuperMac does it is beyond the scope of this book (translation: we don't understand it well enough to explain it to you), but we've seen it demonstrated and it works. While we can't recommend the XP yet because we have no idea how reliable it is, we've put our order in and will report the results in our first update.

⌘ *internal hard disks*

General Computer was the first company to devise a way to mount a hard disk inside the Mac and connect it directly to the processor chip. The major advantage of this method is that you don't have to lug a separate hard disk around when you're moving your Mac—although a Mac with an internal hard disk is both more fragile and heavier than a normal Mac.

But there are several disadvantages to this approach. Mounting a disk inside the Mac increases the demand on an already overloaded power supply, and it generates heat, requiring the use of a fan. And if the disk needs to be repaired, you'll be without your Mac for the interim.

The Micah AT is an updated variation on General Computer's HyperDrive. Rather than connect directly to the Mac's 68000 processor, the Micah AT is an internal SCSI drive. Its performance is very good, measurably faster than the HyperDrive, and users report few problems.

very good
feature

As an added advantage, this drive comes with an external SCSI connector that is installed in front of the battery compartment, so if you install the Micah AT in a Mac Plus, you'll have two SCSI connectors. Although you probably don't need two SCSI connectors (after all, you can daisy chain up to seven devices on one connector), it never hurts to have more capability than you really need.

Unfortunately, we can't recommend any internal drive. The HyperDrive had reliability problems throughout 1986 and Micah is currently in a financial reorganization that has left all of its customers without warranty service—temporarily, we hope. If you want an internally mounted drive, check with your local users group or a reliable dealer to see if the situation has changed.

important
warning

Printers

❡ *the two obvious choices*

very good
feature

Selecting a printer for your Mac is a relatively simple process. If you can justify spending $5000 or so on a LaserWriter (or if you're so rich you don't have to justify it), you'll be getting one of the most powerful and elegant printers ever devised for personal computers, and one that's designed specifically to maximize the Mac's many wonderful features. (See chapter 11 for more details.)

very good
feature

If you're about $4500 shy of the mark, get the ImageWriter II—one of the best medium-priced dot-matrix printers available, and one which is also optimized for the Mac. This is the only dot-matrix printer you should consider buying; nothing else will faithfully reproduce the Mac graphics and fantastic selection of fonts.

❡ *"letter-quality" printers*

"Letter-quality" was a name commonly given to formed-character printers before the advent of laser printers. Formed-character printers produce images the same way typewriters do—by pushing something the shape of a character against an inked ribbon and then into the paper. The something they push is a daisywheel or thimble containing all the available characters, very similar to the ball used on IBM Selectric typewriters.

Because formed-character printers work like typewriters, they're able to produce pages that look like they were typed on a typewriter. The question is: why would anyone want to work on a machine as sophisticated as the Macintosh and then try to fool the world into thinking the work was done on something as primitive as a typewriter?

Whenever you hear someone say that only a formed-character printer will do for their work, imagine you're back in the late 1800's. You've just suggested to the president of your company that he invest in a typewriter. His response: "What!? Send out a letter that isn't hand-written? Never!"

The ImageWriter can produce documents that are much more pleasant to look at than those from a typewriter or "letter-quality" printer (not to mention the LaserWriter, which simply leaves all three in the dust). Fortunately, most businesspeople and academics have finally come to realize this. In fact, thanks mostly to the Mac, expectations about the visual quality of documents have risen markedly in the last few years.

⌘ *the ImageWriter's sheet feeder*

Using fan-fold paper is a lot of trouble. You have to load it into the tractor feeder. If you're printing out long documents, it often gets jammed. And when the printing is done, you're faced with the task of removing the perforated edges with the holes in them, separating the individual pages, and collating them. (This is particularly true on the ImageWriter II, whose tractor feeder is not very good.)

A sheet feeder frees you from all that. You can use virtually any kind of paper you please, and change it as often as you want. When the printing is finished, the pages of your document are not only separated but also collated. Finally, regular 8-1/2 by 11 paper is both less expensive and easier to find than fan-fold paper.

very good feature

So why doesn't everyone use sheet feeders? Because they're usually expensive, complex and not very reliable. Fortunately, none of that is true about the one Apple sells for the ImageWriter II. It's inexpensive ($230), easy to install, and very reliable. In fact, next to a hard disk, it's just about the wisest addition you can make to a Macintosh system.

bargain

For some unaccountable reason, the ImageWriter sheet feeder is one of the best-kept Mac secrets, and many dealers don't even display the product. But don't let it stop you—if you use the ImageWriter more than just occasionally, find some place that sells the sheet feeder and buy one.

Miscellaneous hardware

⚫ networking

bargain

AppleTalk is an excellent, inexpensive local-area network but there's a substitute for it called PhoneNET that's even less expensive. PhoneNET connectors, which function just like AppleTalk's, cost $50 instead of $75, and PhoneNET uses regular telephone wire—available at hardware stores every- where—instead of AppleTalk cable ($7.50 a meter). If you have a network of any size, PhoneNET can save you a considerable amount of money. We use it ourselves and have never had a problem with it.

⚫ big screens

very good feature

The best of the screens that display a whole page or more of text seems to be the Radius ($2000), which has an excellent, steady image (in part because it refreshes 67 times a second instead of the Mac's 60) and lets you use the Mac's screen in addition to its own. It was designed by two Mac wizards, Burrell Smith (hardware) and Andy Hertzfeld (software).

If you're doing a lot of book or magazine work, you might also want to look into E-Machine's Big Picture ($2000), which will display facing pages.

♦ screen filters

Many people feel that it's important to put a glass or mesh filter over the Mac's screen to cut down on glare and on certain low-frequency radiation that may have harmful health effects. This is a big subject and we're not going to go into it here, but if you want to find out about it, write or call Ergonomic Computer Products in San Francisco. They sell excellent products at good prices and are extremely well informed. They also provide the best customer service that we've ever encountered anywhere.

very good
feature

♦ mounting the Mac

As we said in the last chapter, a computer screen should be 4–8" higher than the surface the keyboard rests on, so you can look at it comfortably without having to bend your head. Some people also like to be able to change the viewing angle during long sessions.

MacTilt is an ergonomic stand for the Macintosh that both raises the Mac 4" and lets you position it just about any way you can imagine. It tilts 15° forward and 15° back, and rotates 360°. You can adjust the Mac with the touch of a finger, and it stays where you put it. And MacTilt is built so tough you can stand on it.

very good
feature

This is one of the best tilt/swivel devices on the market; it costs $100, but it's worth it.

♦ cooling the Mac

There's a long discussion of this topic in the last chapter, and you should read it if you're interested in this subject. All we're going to tell you here is that MacMemory makes a piezoelectric fan called MaxChill ($50) and you can buy the revolutionary MacChimney for $15 from Tom Swain.

bargain

very good feature

♦ *covering the Mac*

To paraphrase an old saying, dust never sleeps, and the more of it that gets into your Mac, the worse off you are. Many people sell covers for the Mac, but the ones we like best are sold by Computer Cover Company (how's that for a straightforward name?). They come in several colors, are attractive and well made, and are available for the Mac, the keyboard, the ImageWriter, the external floppy drive and even the mouse. Best of all, they're made of high-quality woven nylon, instead of vinyl with its nauseating, carcinogenic fumes.

♦ *replacement mice*

Don't automatically buy another mouse from Apple if the original one wears out. For one thing, there are other devices for moving the pointer—like Personics' VCS (for "visual control system"). It looks like a pair of earmuffs without the earmuffs (or a pair of earphones without the earphones) and it lets you control the pointer with minute movements of your head. (We made a policy of no photographs in the book, but this is one place we could really use one.)

Although VCS allows you to keep both hands on the keyboard, and although we love the elegance of the concept, we weren't able to get comfortable using it. But some people swear by them—or by trackballs, another mouse substitute—and you should try out both products, if only for curiosity's sake, before buying a replacement mouse.

Even if you decide to stick with the mouse, companies other than Apple make them. And there are different kinds. For example, the optical mouse has no rolling ball in the bottom; instead, it reads a fine grid on the mouse pad you move it over. Since it has no moving parts, it lasts longer and moves more smoothly than the standard design.

Arthur's favorite mouse is the one that came with the original Lisa. He used it while writing a book about the Lisa and then when the time came to give the machine back to the publisher, he kept the Lisa mouse and gave them the one that came with his newly acquired Mac. (Not long after, Apple started using the same mouse for both machines.)

The button on the original Lisa mouse has a much lighter touch than the button on the standard Mac mouse, but they no longer make them. Arthur is still using his, but if it wears out and he has to start using a regular Mac mouse, he'll probably kill himself. So if anyone out there knows where you can still get an original Lisa mouse (with the flat, rectangular button, that doesn't curve down the front), please contact us c/o Goldstein & Blair, Box 7635, Berkeley CA 94707.

Chapter 14

Recommended systems software, utilities & fonts

✦ a note on terminology

Systems software is a catchall term for the basic programs that help computers work; it includes operating systems, programming languages, certain utilities and the like.

Utilities are programs that perform a relatively simple task—like searching for a specific file on a disk, setting an alarm, clipping a picture or counting the words in a document. Although some desk accessories are complex enough to be considered applications rather than utilities, most are utilities, and we've lumped them all together here for the sake of simplicity.

✦ contact information

The products and companies mentioned in this chapter (as well as those mentioned elsewhere in the book) are listed in Appendix C. Company listings include addresses and, when we have them, phone numbers; some product listings also contain ordering information. (In the case of some particularly deserving and inexpensive shareware programs, we break our general rule and give ordering information here as well as in Appendix C.)

Fonts

(For basic information about fonts, see pp. 45–53.)

⌘ *ImageWriter fonts*

Dubl-Click Software puts out a very nice collection of ImageWriter fonts. They go by the name of World Class Fonts; a three-disk set costs $40 and a six-disk set $60. The latter contains over *six dozen* fonts; at less than $1 a font, it's a terrific value.

bargain

World Class Fonts offer several foreign alphabets (Greek, Hebrew, Japanese, Russian) and a vast quantity of unique special characters that are hard—or impossible—to find elsewhere. There are Macintosh symbols (everything from the ⌘ key to the MacPaint's spray can and paint bucket), chess pieces (a black set and a white set), postal labels, religious symbols (34 separate crosses, among much else), two fonts of architectural symbols and three fonts of border designs.

very good feature

But the ImageWriter fonts we use the most come on a two-disk Fluent Fonts set from Casady ($50). In addition to fonts of architectural, astronomical, astrological, biological, chemical, electronic, mathematical, meteorological and even a few yachting symbols, it includes some of the most useful and beautiful ImageWriter typefaces we've seen. Our personal favorites are Oblique (a great substitute for—and improvement on—Apple's Athens), Nordic, Chubby Shadow, Slim, Dream, Vines and Borderline (a font of borders).

very good feature

It isn't worth doing a whole template of Slim—beautiful as it is—so here's a sample of what it looks like in 24-point and 18-point.

THE SAME GOES FOR

CHUBBY SHADOW (THIS IS 24-POINT).

You'll find brief samples of Dream and Vine on page 52; that leaves Oblique, Nordic and Borderline. Templates of the first two, and a chart by categories of the last, follow (see chapter 3 for more information about the template and the decisions that went into it).

very good feature

We'll print them out the ImageWriter and Paste them in, because a lot of the type styles get dropped in LaserWriter printouts. But for straight text, particularly in scaled sizes (which look dreadful on the ImageWriter), the LaserWriter can't be beat. For example, here are some scaled LaserWriter samples of 12-point and 24-point Oblique (which is supplied only in 18-point).

12 point: 1234567890 abcdefghijklmnopqrstuvwxyz
ABCDEFGHIJKLMNOPQRSTUVWXYZ

24 point: 1234567890
abcdefghijklmnopqrstuvw
ABCDEFGHIJKLMNOPQRST

font: Oblique   from: Casady

9 point: 1234567890 abcdefghijklmnopqrstuvwxyz
ABCDEFGHIJKLMNOPQRSTUVWXYZ

18 point: 1234567890

abcdefghijklmnopqrstuvwxyz

ABCDEFGHIJKLMNOPQRSTUVWXY

unshifted symbols: ` - = [ ] \ ; , . /
shifted symbols: ~ ! @ # $ % ^ & *
( ) _ + { } | : " < > ?

option keys:

` ¡ ™ £ ¢ ∞ § ¶ • ª º – ≠
œ Σ ´ ® † ¥ ¨ ^ ø π " ' «
å ß ∂ ƒ © □ ∆ □ ¬ …
æ Ω ≈ ç □ ∫ ~ µ ≤ ≥ ÷

shift-option keys:

🛑 ← → ↑ ↓ ← → ↑ ° ↓ □ – ±
Œ □ È □ ©1985 Casady Co. □ □ □ ø π " ' »
Å □ □ □ □ □ □ □ □ □ Æ
□ □ Ç ◇ □ □ □ □ □ ¿

This is bold. *This is italic.* This is
outline. This is shadow. *This is
bold italic.* This is bold outline.

This is bold shadow. *This is italic outline. This is italic shadow.* This is outline shadow. *This is bold italic outline, bold italic shadow* and bold outline shadow. *This is italic outline shadow and bold italic outline shadow.*

---

font: Nordic   from: Casady

8 point: 1234567890 abcdefghijklmnopqrstuvwxyz
ABCDEFGHIJKLMNOPQRSTUVWXYZ

12 point: 1234567890 abcdefghijklmnopqrstuvwxyz
ABCDEFGHIJKLMNOPQRSTUVWXYZ

18 point: 1234567890

abcdefghijklmnopqrstuvwxyz

ABCDEFGHIJKLMNOPQRSTUVWXYZ

unshifted symbols: ` - = [ ] \ ; ' , . /

shifted symbols: ~ ! @ # $ % ^ & *
( ) _ + { } | : " < > ?

option keys:

` i ™ £ ¢ ∞ § ¶ • ª º – ≠

œ Σ ´ ® † ¥ ¨ ^ ø π " ' «

å ß ∂ ƒ © □ ∆ □ ¬ … æ

Ω ≈ ç √ ∫ ~ µ ≤ ≥

shift-option keys:

©Casady Co. 1984   POB 223779 Carmel CA. 93922   □ ° □ □ — ±

Œ □ □ □ □ □ Ø π " ' »

Å □ □ □ □ □ □ □ Æ

□ □ Ç ◇ □ □ □ □ □ ¿

This is bold.   *This is italic.*   This is outline.   This is shadow.   *This is bold italic.*   This is bold outline.   This is bold shadow.   *italic outline and italic shadow.*   This is outline shadow.   *This is bold italic outline and bold italic shadow.* **This is bold outline shadow.** *Italic outline shadow* & *bold italic outline shadow.*

font: Borderline   from: Casady

(Key to be struck, followed by Borderline character)

arrows and arrow-like patterns

amerindian patterns

asian patterns

z ♥♥♥   Z ♠♠♠   X 🕌🕌🕌🕌   #

corners

Q   1   5

c   v   3   4

human artifacts

a   + 📦📦📦   ] ♣◇♠◇♥◇♣

m   P   e |||

7   b 1010011010100110101001100   ^

intricate patterns (round)

* ◎◎◎   . ⚙⚙⚙   ~

9   —

intricate patterns (square)

d ▰▰▰   f ▰▰▰   t ▦▦▦   r ▦▦▦

& ✦✦✦   ? ▨▨   , ◇◇◇◇◇   g ▨▨

) ▨   h ▨▨▨   : ▨

lines

D ┄┄┄┄   A ▬▬   R ▤▤   U ═

W ▬▬   Z ═   6 ▬   ' ▬▬▬

{ ■ | or OPTION + almost any key ▮   K ▨▨

nature (miscellaneous)

B ⛰⛰⛰   M △△△   N ⛰⛰⛰⛰⛰

V ▲▲▲   O ○○○○○○

! ☁☁☁   @ ☁☁☁   J ☁☁☁

8 ⟪⟪   y 🍃🍃🍃

simple patterns

S ⋀⋀⋀ Y ⋈⋈⋈ T ▨ L ▥

(▦ s ▓ / ▤ u ◇◇◇◇

C ⋯ F ⦀ H ▸▸▸

waves and wave-like patterns

q, W 🌊 G 〰〰 E ⫯⫯⫯

$ 〰〰〰 % 〰〰〰

Apple's laser fonts

The LaserWriter comes with two fonts and two semi-fonts built in. The two fonts are Times (the classic, standard serif typeface) and Helvetica (the classic, standard sans serif typeface). The semi-fonts are Symbol (which supplements the other fonts and doesn't contain an alphabet of its own) and Courier (here's your chance to make the LaserWriter look like a typewriter—what a brilliant idea!).

With the exception of the space wasted on the graceless, useless Courier, the fonts were wisely chosen, and Adobe did a nice job of implementing them. Here's a template of Times:

<u>*font*</u>: **Times**   <u>*from*</u>: **Apple**

<u>*9 point*</u>: 1234567890 abcdefghijklmnopqrstuvwxyz
ABCDEFGHIJKLMNOPQRSTUVWXYZ

<u>*10 point*</u>: 1234567890 abcdefghijklmnopqrstuvwxyz
ABCDEFGHIJKLMNOPQRSTUVWXYZ

<u>*12 point*</u>: 1234567890 abcdefghijklmnopqrstuvwxyz
ABCDEFGHIJKLMNOPQRSTUVWXYZ

<u>*14 point*</u>:   1234567890 abcdefghijklmnopqrstuvwxyz
ABCDEFGHIJKLMNOPQRSTUVWXYZ

<u>*18 point*</u>: 1234567890
abcdefghijklmnopqrstuvwxyz
ABCDEFGHIJKLMNOPQRSTUVWXYZ

<u>*24 point*</u>: 1234567890
abcdefghijklmnopqrstuvwxyz
ABCDEFGHIJKLMNOPQRSTU

<u>unshifted symbols</u>: ` - = [ ] \ ; ' , . /
<u>shifted symbols</u>: ~ ! @ # $ % ^ & * ( ) _ +
{ } | : " < > ?

<u>option keys</u>:
` ¡ ™ £ ¢ ∞ § ¶ • ª º – ≠
œ ∑ ´ ® † ¥ ¨ ^ ø π " ' «
å ß ∂ ƒ © ˙ ∆ ˚ ¬ … æ
Ω ≈ ç √ ∫ ~ µ ≤ ≥ ÷

<u>shift-option keys</u>:
Ÿ / ¤ ‹ › fi fl ‡ ° · — ±
Œ „ ‰ Â Ê Á Ë È Ø ∏ ” ’ »
Å Í Î Ï Ì Ó Ô   Ò Ú Æ
Û Ù Ç ◊ ı ^ ˜ ¯ ˘ ¿

This is bold. *This is italic.* This is outline.
This is shadow. ***This is bold italic.***
This is bold outline and bold
shadow. *This is italic outline.* ***This is***
italic shadow. This is outline
shadow *and bold italic outline.*

bold italic shadow and bold outline shadow. This is italic outline shadow and bold italic outline shadow.

⬢ laser fonts from Century

Century Software offers a wide selection of laser fonts that are both very inexpensive ($35-$45) and loaded with features. For example, they've remapped the keyboard to provide you with all the accents you need to type in more than thirty languages—including Polish, Czech, Turkish, Hungarian and Esperanto.

bargain

Even better, the keys that normally produce square brackets [ ] and, when shifted, curly brackets { } produce true single quotes ' ' and, when shifted, true double quotes " " in Century Fonts (the brackets are shifted to the OPTION and SHIFT-OPTION positions). If, like most people, you use quotation marks more often than brackets, this is great. Their remapped keyboard also gives you commas and periods when the SHIFT key is down, as well as when it isn't.

very good feature

All Century fonts offer a strikeout character and some arrows ➡ ⇨ and boxes ■ □; some of their fonts have other useful symbols like ⌘, ✔ and △. But they do have one drawback—they take *forever* to do outline and boldface.

Another great Century product is Special Effects—unusual style variations on the LaserWriter's two built-in fonts. There's

S̶t̶a̶c̶k̶ ̶T̶i̶m̶e̶s̶,̶ ̶S̶t̶a̶c̶k̶ ̶H̶e̶l̶v̶e̶t̶i̶c̶a̶,̶

Shadow Times, Shadow Helvetica

very good feature

bargain

and ten others. Because they're algorithmic, Century's Special Effects hardly take up any of the LaserWriter's precious memory and, on top of everything, they only cost $2.50 each! At this price, we recommend them to virtually any LaserWriter user.

Century laser fonts are named after rivers (rather than cities, as was the convention when the Mac first came out). One of our favorites is Thames (a template of it follows). We don't have room to show you others, but you should definitely send for their catalog. At $35-$45 a pop, Century fonts are very hard to resist.

<u>font</u>: *Thames*   <u>from</u>: *Century*

<u>9 point</u>: 1234567890 abcdefghijklmnopqrstuvwxyz
  ABCDEFGHIJKLMNOPQRSTUVWXYZ
<u>10 point</u>: 1234567890 abcdefghijklmnopqrstuvwxyz
  ABCDEFGHIJKLMNOPQRSTUVWXYZ
<u>12 point</u>: 1234567890 abcdefghijklmnopqrstuvwxyz
  ABCDEFGHIJKLMNOPQRSTUVWXYZ
<u>14 point</u>:   1234567890 abcdefghijklmnopqrstuvwxyz
  ABCDEFGHIJKLMNOPQRSTUVWXYZ

<u>18 point</u>:   1234567890
  abcdefghijklmnopqrstuvwxyz
  ABCDEFGHIJKLMNOPQRSTUVWXYZ

<u>24 point</u>: 1234567890
  abcdefghijklmnopqrstuvwxyz
  ABCDEFGHIJKLMNOPQRSTU

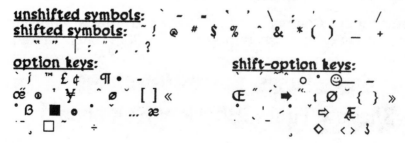

<u>unshifted symbols</u>: ` - - ` \ ' /
<u>shifted symbols</u>: ~ ! @ # $ % ^ & * ( ) _ +
  " " | : " , . ?

<u>option keys</u>:   <u>shift-option keys</u>:

This is bold. *This is italic.* This is outline. This is shadow. ***This is bold italic.*** This is bold outline. This is bold shadow. *This is italic outline.* *This is italic shadow.* This is outline shadow. *This is bold italic outline.* *This is bold italic shadow.* This is bold outline shadow. *This is italic outline shadow.* *This is bold italic outline shadow.*

● *laser fonts from Casady*

Richard Ware, the man responsible for Casady's beautiful Fluent Fonts for the ImageWriter, also designed their line of laser fonts. One of those, Monterey, is particularly classy; you can see a sample of it in the letterhead on page 101. Another Fluent Laser Font is called Calligraphy; there's a sample of it on page 52.

Fluent Laser Font disks (each of which contains one or two fonts in one to four styles) cost $70. Here again, you really should send for their catalog; at those prices, you can afford to be tempted.

very good feature

bargain

● *laser fonts from Adobe*

Adobe's fonts typically cost $185 (which is much more than the competition) and they're copy-protected so that even at that price, you can only use them on one printer (although you can pay more for a version that will install on up to five printers).

Before we actually used Adobe fonts, we couldn't imagine how they could possibly be worth the extra trouble and expense. Now we know and you see the result: this book is set in Adobe's ITC Benguiat, with headers in their ITC Zapf Chancery.

(The ITC you see before the names of various fonts stands for the International Typeface Corporation of New York City, a powerful force for excellence and innovation in typography. They've been responsible for many beautiful new fonts, and for tasteful redesigns of classic old fonts like Garamond as well.)

very good
feature

We haven't made a side-by-side comparison of each Adobe font with each of its competitors, but our subjective impression is that—at least for the most part—Adobe's fonts simply look better. The difference in quality may not matter all that much to you, or you may not be in a position where you can afford to let it matter. Or you may prefer to spend your money on a lot of fonts rather than a few very fine ones. But there is an argument to be made for quality versus variety and price, and that's an argument we think Adobe wins.

gossip/
trivia

We've already printed out a complete template of Benguiat (pages 50-51) but we'd like to tell you a little about the man who designed it. Ed Benguiat (BEN-gat) is a jazz drummer, a pilot, and the designer of more than 500 typefaces, including classics like Bookman, Souvenir, Korinna, Tiffany and Charisma. He says, "my feeling has always been that in designing an alphabet, each letter should almost be like a painting, or a piece of sculpture—that is, beautiful within itself." This approach is evident in all his typefaces, but nowhere more than in the one he put his name on.

We're not going to print out a template of Zapf Chancery, partly because it only has three styles—plain, outline and shadow (no bold, no italic, etc.), and partly because samples of it are at the top of almost every page. Instead we'll show you another one of Herman Zapf's fonts, Optima—which is one of the prettiest sans serif faces ever designed.

font: *Optima*   from: *Adobe*

9 *point*: 1234567890 abcdefghijklmnopqrstuvwxyz ABCDEFGHIJKLMNOPQRSTU

10 *point*: 1234567890 abcdefghijklmnopqrstuvwxyz
ABCDEFGHIJKLMNOPQRSTUVWXYZ

12 *point*: 1234567890 abcdefghijklmnopqrstuvwxyz
ABCDEFGHIJKLMNOPQRSTUVWXYZ

14 *point*: 1234567890 abcdefghijklmnopqrstuvwxyz
ABCDEFGHIJKLMNOPQRSTUVWXYZ

18 *point*: 1234567890
abcdefghijklmnopqrstuvwxyz
ABCDEFGHIJKLMNOPQRSTUVWXYZ

24 *point*: 1234567890
abcdefghijklmnopqrstuvwxyz
ABCDEFGHIJKLMNOPQRST

unshifted symbols: ` - = [ ] \ ; ' , . /

shifted symbols: ~ ! @ # $ % ^ & * ( ) _ +
{ } | : " < > ?

option keys:
` ¡ ™ £ ¢ ∞ § ¶ • ªº – ≠
œ ∑ ´ ® † ¥ ¨ ^ ø π " ' «
å ß ∂ ƒ © ˙ ∆ ˚ ¬ … æ
Ω ≈ ç √ ∫ ~ µ ≤ ≥ ÷

shift-option keys:
Ÿ / ¤ ‹ › fi fl ‡ ° · , — ±
Œ „ ‰ Â Ê Á Ë È Ø ∏ " ' »
Å Í Î Ï Ì Ó Ô Ò Ú Æ
Û Ù Ç ◊ ı ˆ ˜ ¯ ˘ ¿

This is bold. *This is italic.* This is outline.
This is shadow. ***This is bold italic.*** This
is bold outline and bold shadow.
This is italic outline. *This is italic*
shadow. This is outline shadow.
This is bold italic outline. ***This is***
bold italic shadow. This is bold

outline shadow. *This is italic outline shadow. This is bold italic outline shadow.*

Desk accessories

(For basic information about desk accessories, see pp. 69–70.)

🍎 *public-domain and shareware DAs*

There are hundreds of desk accessories available, and most of them are either shareware (you get to try them out before paying) or in the public domain (i.e., free). The ones listed below are some of the best, and are often more powerful than their commercial competitors. (Some good commercial DAs are described below as well.)

You can get shareware and public-domain DAs from information services like CompuServe and GEnie and from many bulletin boards (for a list of a few of the best, see Appendix B). If you don't have the modem (or the patience) you need to access a BBS, most user groups also sell disks full of DAs. For example, BMUG (the Berkeley Macintosh Users Group) has more than 75 DAs on their disks.

Finally, you can always order a shareware DA directly from its publisher (who is usually also its author). Of course this means you have to pay for it before you're sure you like it, but the price is typically so low that it hardly makes a difference.

very hot tip

Shareware and public-domain desk accessories are certainly the greatest bargains there are on the Mac. So make sure you always pay for any shareware program you end up using. Be selfish—keep these people writing software.

● *DiskInfo*

Most people familiar with this little gem agree that if they were stranded on a desert island with only one DA, DiskInfo is the one they'd want to have. Here's why they feel that way:

From within any application DiskInfo will tell you how much memory and how much disk space you have available, and the name, size, type and creator of any file on any disk (even ones you've ejected), including files that are invisible on the Desktop.

But DiskInfo has another capability that alone makes it worthy of a DA slot in your system file—it will locate any file on a disk (even on a disk you've ejected). This can be handy on a floppy, but on a hard disk—where you may have literally thousands of files—it's indispensable.

very good
feature

You can search for a file by its full name, by the beginning of its name, or by any part of its name. Even expensive commercial packages don't offer search options as flexible and powerful as this.

DiskInfo's publisher (Maitreya Design, Box 1480, Goleta CA 93116) only asks $10 for the program—an incredibly low price for any useful program, much less for DiskInfo, which we consider the most useful DAs you can own.

bargain

Maitreya, by the way, is the name of the next Buddha to arise (according to the traditional doctrine, there are many Buddhas, and we're due for one more in this cycle). Now, we ask you—what other book on the Mac goes behind the scenes to give you this kind of in-depth information?

gossip/
trivia

● *Other...*

Other... does just what its name implies—it allows you to run other DAs than the ones you have installed in your system file or application. Other... is also useful for sampling new

DAs to see if you like them, without having to go to the trouble of installing them.

very good feature

When you choose Other... from the ￼ menu, it gives you a list box like the one you get when you choose Open... from the File menu. You then use it to locate and open any uninstalled DA on your disk. From that point on, the DA you've opened acts just as if it were installed and you chose it from the ￼ menu. When you're finished using the DA, you just quit Other... and you're back in your document. Nothing could be simpler—or more useful.

bargain

Other... is even more of a bargain than DiskInfo (if that's possible). Its author, Loftus E. Becker, Jr. of 41 Whitney Street, Hartford CT 06105, asks that you send him $5 if you like the program. This is ridiculous. If the program is worth anything at all to you, send him $10, so it's worth it for him to open the envelope.

￼ QDial

shortcut

If you've ever been frustrated by trying to connect to a busy bulletin board, QDial is a DA that you won't want to be without. It continues to dial the number in the background and lets you use your Mac in the meantime (the only thing you can't do is use another communication program).

very good feature

Once you've told QDial what to do, the only indication that it's working is a small icon of a telephone that appears to the left of the ￼ Menu each time it dials. When a connection is made, QDial notifies you with an unmistakable honking you've probably never heard your Mac make before. You then choose QDial again from the ￼ menu and click on the Cancel button. QDial holds the connection long enough to start your regular communication program.

QDial works with Hayes and most Hayes-compatible modems, and will store up to five numbers in its dialing directory. You can use standard Hayes dialing commands to control the number of seconds between retries.

QDial is free (although it's not technically in the public domain, because the author retains the copyright). You can get a copy of it from many bulletin boards, including the two that the author of the program, Léo Laporte, operates in San Francisco—MacQueue I (415/661-7374) and MacQueue II (415/753-3002).

bargain

⌘ *MockWrite*

MockWrite is another favorite desk accessory of ours. If you've ever needed to take a note or two during a database or spreadsheet session, or needed to compose a message off-line for uploading to information services that charge by the minute (CompuServe, etc.), this is one of the first DAs you should get.

MockWrite provides all the standard Macintosh editing functions (Cut, Copy, Paste, etc.). The MockWrite documents you create can be printed and saved. About the only thing the program lacks is the ability to change fonts (everything is displayed in boring 12-point Monaco).

very good feature

MockWrite is another great shareware bargain—it only costs $30 to register the entire MockPackage, which also includes MockPrint, a print-spooling utility, and MockTerminal, a somewhat limited communications desk accessory. If you don't have access to a BBS, an information utility or a user group, you can get the MockPackage directly from CE Software, 801 73rd St., Des Moines IA 50312 (515/ 224-1995).

bargain

⌘ *Artisto*

If you deal with a large collection of clip art and often find yourself searching for just the right picture, you'll really appreciate the flexibility that Artisto provides. This desk accessory allows you to open any MacPaint or FullPaint document on any disk, Copy all—or any portion—of it to the

very good feature

Clipboard (using a standard selection rectangle), and Paste it directly to any application that accepts pictures.

bargain

Tom Taylor, the program's author, asks only that if you find Artisto useful, you send him a donation in any amount you like. His address is 3707 Poincianna Dr., #137, Santa Clara CA 95051.

♦ *SkipFinder*

very good feature

SkipFinder is a desk accessory that does just what the name implies: it lets you skip the Finder (and thus not wait for the Mac to reconstruct all the open windows on the DeskTop) when you quit an application. Instead of the Desktop, you're presented with a list box that displays just applications. If you decide you need to go back to the Finder after all, there's also a button that lets you do that.

SkipFinder is particularly handy if you're using a hard disk and frequently change applications. After using it just a few times, you won't want to be without it.

bargain

The program's author, Darin Adler, asks that you try it, then send him what you think it's worth. His address is 2765 Marl Oak Dr., Highland Park IL 60035.

♦ *TopDesk*

very good feature

Our favorite in this collection of powerful DAs is MenuKey, which lets you install and remove Command key equivalents for the commands on almost any menu. And if you don't like the Command key already assigned by the application, you can remove it and change it to something else.

Applications like MacWrite are much easier to use when you add keyboard commands to do repetitive things like Save and Print. (Now if they would just expand MenuKey to work on Word's keyboard cursor movement keys...)

Another TopDesk DA is called Launch. Like SkipFinder, it allows you to quit an application and move directly to another, completely bypassing the Finder. You can either launch the next application immediately or tell the program to take you there when you quit the current application. This can be a great timesaver.

Shorthand is another program in the package; it gives MacWrite a Glossary function like the one in Word.

View also makes a great enhancement for MacWrite, (although it works with many other applications as well), because it lets you open as many as eight documents simultaneously. Although you can't edit them, you can Copy text from them into the main document you're working on. Since all text attributes survive the transfer, View gives MacWrite almost the same multiple-window feature that Word has.

very good
feature

Another program in the TopDesk collection is a screen saver called Blank (for info on why screen savers are useful, see the entry titled 'protecting the phosphor on your screen' at the beginning of chapter 12). You can tell Blank how long to wait after the last activity on the keyboard or mouse before it blacks the screen.

What makes this particular screen saver stand out is that it doesn't suspend whatever activity the Mac happens to be engaged in when it blacks the screen. So if you're in the midst of a file transfer, it won't interrupt it.

very good
feature

TopDesk also contains a print spooler called BackPrint which isn't of much use, since it won't let you queue more than one document at a time.

Although the Top Desk DAs are not copy-protected, you have to use its own installer program to put them into your system file. Priced at $60, TopDesk is an excellent value.

bargain

♦ BatteryPak

BatteryPak (from a company called Batteries Included) is another useful collection of DAs. Probably the best of these is a NotePad that holds up to 250 pages and lets you dial any phone number directly from the NotePad.

very good feature

A DA called Disk Tools lets you do things from within applications that you normally have to be on the Desktop to do: create folders, copy and delete files, and Get Info on a file or a disk.

bargain

BatteryPak also includes two Hewlett-Packard-like (Reverse Polish Notation) scientific calculators, one a scaled down version of the other. The package is not copy-protected. At $50, BatteryPak is well worth the money.

♦ Acta

Because this desk accessory is such an excellent, full-featured outliner, it's discussed in the 'Writing tools' section of chapter 15, rather than here.

♦ ClickOn Worksheet

This handy desk accessory is all the spreadsheet most people need (it even creates graphs). It's also useful when you want to Paste a table into a word processing document (see pp. 94–95 for more details).

gossip/ trivia

The program was sold by T/Maker to Borland and it's not clear exactly what form it will be marketed in, or what it will cost.

♦ Word Count

Word Count is a simple desk accessory that does one thing very well: it counts, with lightning speed, the number of characters, words, and lines in any Word 1.05 document, or any other document saved as 'text only'. If you write for a living, you'll find this DA very handy.

Word Count is another free offering from Léo Laporte, author of QDial.

bargain

⚫ *Talking Moose*

Talking Moose is the only desk accessory we've seen that makes almost everyone laugh out loud the first time they encounter it. When you activate it by choosing it from the ⚫ menu, Talking Moose monitors your keyboard and mouse activity. When a certain amount of time (which you specify) has elapsed without any activity, a small moose pops up in the upper left corner of the screen and says things like *What's holding things up?*, *Don't fall asleep!* and *Why don't we ever go out anymore?*

gossip/
trivia

The program's author points out that all this isn't quite as trivial as it seems. A more sophisticated program of the same type could monitor keyboard and mouse activity for content, and comment accordingly. The possibilities for self-regulating, context-sensitive, on-line tutorials are mind-boggling.

very good
feature

Talking Moose was written by Steve Halls of Edmonton, Canada. It's available from the usual sources and, in addition, was also published on a Cauzin SoftStrip in the September, 1986 issue of *MacUser*. There's no charge for this public-domain delight.

bargain

A great companion to Talking Moose is Moose Frazer, written by Jan Eugenides. This program lets you add phrases to the Talking Moose's vocabulary, and is also free.

very good
feature

Miscellaneous utilities

❤ a word of warning

important
warning

Some of the utilities described below have caused problems at one time or another, especially with unstable versions of the System prior to 3.2 and the Finder prior to 5.3—although they all seem to be stable now. If you begin to experience any problems with your system after using one of these utilities, remove the utility. It's not likely that it's the cause of your problem, but it's worth checking it out.

❤ Quick & Dirty Utilities volume 1

bargain

Quick & Dirty Utilities Volume 1, from Dreams of the Phoenix, is an incredible value at $40, and should be one of the first software purchases you make after you learn your way around the Mac. So many useful utilities are included in the mix that it's hard to know where to begin in describing them.

very good
feature

The desk accessory called Q&D Filer is worth the purchase price all by itself, and it's just one of fifteen. When you open Q&D Filer, a new menu is added to the menu bar; it gives you the ability to print, copy, rename and delete any file on any disk from within an application. You also can Get Info about any file, and find out how much memory you have free, and how much space is available on any disk.

Another powerful desk accessory included in the package is File Info, which allows you to change the type, creator and other attributes of files from within almost any application.

very good
feature

There's also a screen blanker, an excellent disk cataloging program and Super NotePad, which has a "top view" that shows you the first line of twenty different pages. (Even people who never bothered with Apple's regular Note Pad love Super Note Pad.) And then there are several communications desk accessories, including one that emulates VT52 (which is important to people who know what that means.)

One of the more intriguing items on the Q&D disk is DA Installer+, which lets you install up to 35 desk accessories. (That's the theoretical limit; the practical limit is more like 25. But still....) Here's how it works:

very good
feature

The Mac has something called software "slots," some of which are reserved for desk accessories, some for use by the serial ports, some for the SCSI port, and some that are "undefined." DA Installer + lets you use the undefined slots—and even the SCSI slots if you're not using a SCSI hard disk or other SCSI device—for more desk accessories.

How many desk accessories do you really need? If you're using a floppy-based system, you're limited more by available disk space than by Apple's imposed limit of sixteen. But if you're using a hard disk, the size of your system file becomes more or less irrelevant, and having all the DAs you need gains in importance, because you're using just one system file almost all the time.

For example, you'll probably want some DA's to help keep track of the hundreds—or, more likely, thousands—of files on your hard disk. It's easy to want more than sixteen desk accessories on the menu, even if you're not particularly a DA freak.

Quick & Dirty Utilities Volume 1 is one of the best Macintosh bargains you'll ever find. Dreams of the Phoenix seems to always deliver exceptional value in their products, all of which retail for $40. And their upgrade policy is without peer. The most recent upgrade cost registered users exactly $2! This is a great company that offers great software at great prices.

very good
feature

Calculator Construction Set

If Apple's regular calculator DA is a bit too primitive for you, Calculator Construction Set is what you want. Published by Dubl-Click Software, it lets you assemble the ultimate monster calculator of your dreams (you can stretch it to any size you want and keep loading in the keys). Then when you're done, you can install it as a desk accessory.

very good feature

Rather than go into endless detail about all the functions Calculator Construction Set makes available, we'll just say that if you want it, they've almost certainly got it. And the user interface is good, so you won't have any trouble creating what you want.

Here's a calculator Paul Hoffman put together that should give you some idea of what's possible:

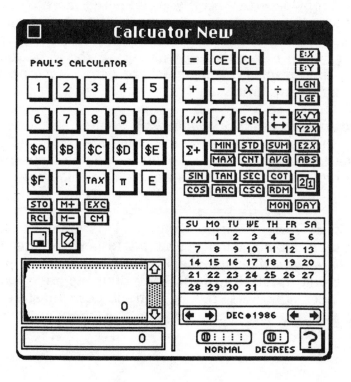

● *continuing to work while printing*

If you use the ImageWriter often, you know that print time is break time. Time to stretch your legs, get a cup of coffee or—if the document's long enough—even go to the store. The problem is, of course, that you may not want to take a break then. You may want to go on working and take a break some other time. But there's no way to do that, because printing takes all the Mac's attention.

What you need is something that:
—lets the Mac generate output as fast as possible, without having to wait for the relatively slow ImageWriter
—stores it somewhere until it's needed, and then
—spoon-feeds it to the ImageWriter on demand,
—thus freeing up the Mac so you can go on to other things.

These requirements can be met by either hardware or software. The hardware solution is called a *print buffer*, and it's basically just a bunch of memory that stores the computer's output before sending it to the printer.

The hardware approach works well on simple computers, but the Mac's lovely fonts and graphics take up a lot of room. To be able to handle a Mac's huge print files, a print buffer needs to have more than a meg of memory, and that can easily cost more than you paid for your ImageWriter. (That's why the optional 32K buffer available for the ImageWriter II is only recommended for the Apple //.)

very
hot
tip

One of the best print buffers available is MacBuffer by Ergotron, the same people who make the MacTilt swivel. There are 256K and 512K models, but for use with the Mac, we recommend the 1MB model. MacBuffer has the added advantage of allowing two Macs to be connected to one ImageWriter.

● *ImageWriter print spoolers*

The software solution to the working-while-printing problem is called a *print spooler* (the name is a leftover from

gossip/
trivia

the archaic world of CP/M and stands for "simultaneous print operations on-line"). Spoolers intercept the print file on its way to the printer and reroute it to the disk, where it's held until the printer is ready for it.

A good print spooler should let you continue to use your Mac while printing, without significantly hampering the performance of either of the printer or the computer. It should also be totally transparent to you, the user—i.e., no special commands or options, just the standard print dialog box.

A third feature to look for is control over the spooling process. Let's say you've spooled several documents for printing, but decide that the second or third document shouldn't be printed after all, or that the last document in the queue needs to be printed right away. A good print spooler should let you change the order of the documents in the queue, and cancel the printing of any document without affecting the others.

very good
feature

Of all the ImageWriter print spoolers on the market so far, only one meets all these requirements—SuperSpool, from the wizards at SuperMac Technology. SuperSpool now comes standard with the DataFrame hard disks, and is also available separately for $50.

Installing SuperSpool is easy: you just place the file in the system folder (if you intend to use it regularly—and you probably will—make it the startup application), then install a desk accessory called Print Queue.

bargain

That's all there is to it. When you print from an application you won't notice anything different—the print dialog box will look the way it always does. But as soon as the printer output is written to the disk (which takes about two minutes for a fifteen-page Microsoft Word document), control of the Mac is returned to you.

We've discovered one disappointing bug in SuperSpool version 2.0. When used with the ImageWriter II with a sheet feeder, it occasionally prevents a sheet of paper from feeding. The ImageWriter then proceeds to print the entire page on the platen. Because this can seriously damage the platen over time, we recommend that you not use SuperSpool with the ImageWriter sheet feeder.

important warning

★ *LaserWriter print spoolers*

Spooling a LaserWriter print file is a much bigger job than spooling an ImageWriter print file, because LaserWriter print files are much, much larger. You can spend several minutes waiting for them to be sent to the disk, and if your job is fairly long, you'll probably run out of disk space.

The only LaserWriter print spooler we've seen so far is MacAmerica's LaserSpool. It works fine, with one major exception: it can't handle automatically downloaded fonts. But this drawback is easy enough to get around—you just manually download the fonts you need. The main problem with this and any other LaserWriter print spooler is finding enough room on disk to store the print files.

★ *Keeper*

Simply put, Keeper remembers what your Desktop looked like before you launched an application—so when you quit the application, it can display the Desktop for you immediately. You have to see it to believe how fast it happens.

shortcut

That's the good news. The bad news is that you can occasionally run into problems with Keeper. For example, if you install or remove a desk accessory, Keeper won't display it on the ★ menu until you restart the system. But this is a small price to pay for having your Desktop reappear virtually instantly, whenever you quit an application.

JClock

JClock is a very simple public-domain utility that displays a twelve-hour digital clock at the far right end of the menu bar. All you have to do to use it is put the file in your system folder; when you boot the Mac, it installs itself automatically.

When you need the extra space on the menu bar (or simply don't want to be reminded of the time), you can turn the clock display off just by pointing to it and holding down the mouse button for about three seconds. The same procedure turns it back on.

JClock is one of those utilities that you either love or hate. Some people really miss it when they're using a system that doesn't have it installed; other people can't stand it.

MacWait

gossip/
trivia

When the Mac is busy doing something, it turns the pointer into a little wristwatch, set at 9 o'clock. (Intense debate rages in the Mac hacker community about whether the watch is indicating 9 am or 9 pm. This seems a little strange to us, since the answer is obvious: no hacker worthy of the name is up at 9 am.) Wouldn't it be nice if the watch displayed a different time depending on which version of the System and Finder you're using?

Anyway, if you make MacWait the startup application, the minute hand on the watch revolves frantically. How's that for an earthshaking product?

As with JClock, you either love it or hate it. Dale found it quite amusing to use for a few weeks. Eric Alderman, on the other hand, though it was pretty stupid. (He did, however, use ResEdit to change the time displayed on the watch from 9:00 to 4:30, so he's hardly one to talk.)

Programming languages

❖ *a little background*

If you already know something about programming, you'll probably want to skip this entry. But for those of you who are thinking about getting into programming, it may provide some useful information.

Programming languages occupy a middle ground between *machine languages* (the actual instructions computers understand) and human speech. Those closer to machine language are called *assembly language* and those closer to human speech are called *high-level languages*.

Assembly languages are specific to one particular microprocessor chip and are named after it. The microprocessor at the heart of all Macs to date is the Motorola 68000, and thus the assembly language used to program them is called *68000 assembly language*.

The first popular high-level language, FORTRAN, was developed for scientific and mathematical applications. While extremely rigid, it's still favored by some people who need its particular capabilities. Another early high-level language was COBOL, developed for business applications.

During the 1960's, two professors at Dartmouth developed a high-level language specifically for educational purposes, and called it BASIC. You might not be reading about BASIC here except for the fact that Bill Gates created a version of it that became the first software to run on a microcomputer; it was called Microsoft BASIC, after the company he founded. By the time the 1980's arrived, BASIC was so popular it was being hardwired into computers like the Apple // and the IBM PC.

As computers have become more sophisticated, so have the languages designed to run on them. Hardly anyone uses

FORTRAN or COBOL on personal computers today. Most Macintosh applications are written in Pascal, C, assembly language, or a combination thereof.

● *compilers vs. interpreters*

There are two ways to implement a programming language—with a compiler or with an interpreter. Interpreters execute each line of a program individually each time the program is run, while compilers translate the whole program at once, before it's run. From that point on, you can run the compiled program whenever you want, without having to use the compiler to translate it again.

Compiling is more time-consuming when you're editing a program for mistakes, because you have to recompile the whole program each time you want to check out the effect of a change you've made (and large programs can take an hour or more to compile). But compilers are less time-consuming when you want to use the finished program over and over again.

Interpreters are better for learning, because there's no compilation time, but they run more slowly each time through.

● *the Toolbox*

One thing that makes the Mac's programming environment stand head and shoulders above that of other computers is a built-in feature called the Toolbox. It's part of the ROMs and works like this:

very good feature

Let's say you want to draw a circle on the screen. With old-fashioned computers, you'd have to write a great deal of code specifying every aspect of circle. On the Mac, you simply have your program call the Toolbox and use the code already written there to draw the circle. Many wonderful things are included in the Toolbox, including all the information the Mac needs to create windows and popdown menus.

If you have any intention of writing programs that look and behave like other Mac programs, make sure the programming language you use supports the Toolbox.

▲ languages for learning programming

This boils down to the great BASIC vs. Pascal debate. Because BASIC doesn't really care if your code is brilliantly written or not, you can develop some sloppy programming habits using it.

Pascal, on the other hand, is what's called a *structured* language. This means that you have to carefully plan out what you want your program to do ahead of time. This makes Pascal harder to program in but the code you end up with is "modular," which means you can move whole chunks of it around and reuse it.

very good
feature

So which should you use? If you already know BASIC from another computer and don't have any great ambitions to write the next great word processor or integrated application, you might feel right at home with Microsoft BASIC—and you can take comfort in the fact that it is one of the most powerful BASICs available for personal computers.

The major disadvantages of Microsoft BASIC (through version 2.1) are that it doesn't have full access to the ToolBox and doesn't work with HFS. (As we go to press, Microsoft has announced BASIC 3.0, which eliminates these last two limitations.)

If you don't know programming but want to learn it, take a long hard look at MacPascal from Apple. It's an interpreted language, so you don't have to sit around waiting for it to compile, and you'll learn better habits from it than BASIC.

⌘ languages for writing applications

Both Pascal and C are highly structured, and in very similar ways. If you learn one of them, you probably won't have too much trouble learning the other. Both are great languages, and we wouldn't presume to recommend one over the other. We can give you some recommendations, however, on which compiler of each to use.

bargain

TML Pascal allows good access to the Toolbox, and will generate assembly code for the Macintosh Development System (MDS). It's the first real Pascal compiler for the Mac and costs just $100.

Lightspeed C has the best interface to the Toolbox of any of the several C compilers on the market. (A Pascal compiler from Lightspeed Software should also be on the market soon, possibly by the time you read this.)

For more detailed and up-to-date information on programming languages, look into CompuServe's Developer's SIG, *Byte* magazine and *MacTutor* magazine.

Chapter 15

Recommended applications & games

Writing tools

🍎 MacWrite and Word 1.05

As this book goes to press (January, 1987), MacWrite 4.5 and Microsoft Word 1.05 are still the standards for word processing on the Mac. By the time you read this, however, other products—much superior to these two—will be on the market and busy gathering followings.

things to come

But MacWrite and Word 1.05 will retain at least one advantage—the fact that many other programs are already able to accept text from them. You may prefer to do your writing in WriteNow, say, but what if the page-layout program you want to use won't accept text from it?

MacWrite ($125) is likely to survive for a long time, because it's cheap, fast, rock-solid, intuitive and easy-to-use. (Many people seem to only think about how many features a program has, but speed, or ease-of-use, is often the most important consideration.)

very hot tip

Anyway, MacWrite isn't really all that limited in terms of what it can do; Arthur used it throughout the writing of this book and for two earlier books as well. But it's true that

MacWrite's headers, footers and search function are very weak, and it only lets you have one document open at a time.

very bad
feature

Up until now, Word 1.05 ($200) has been the only choice for people who needed features like leading control, nonstandard font sizes, footnotes, headers and footers that change within a document, and so on. That's too bad, since it's a slow, clumsy program which Microsoft delayed improving for as long as they could.

Fortunately, by the time you read this, Word 1.05 will have been replaced by Word 3.0, which is faster, less clumsy and more powerful (see the next entry).

✦ *Word 3.0*

After Apple decided not to include a copy of MacWrite with the Mac Plus, the market opened up for new word processors, and by the end of 1986 many new ones were being readied for release. Their target was not MacWrite, but Microsoft Word, which hadn't been updated for almost two years and was beginning to show its age. At a time when most Macs had at least 512K of memory, and many had 1MB or more, Word was still hamstrung by tradeoffs that allowed it to run on a 128K Mac.

One of these new word processors was the next version of Word—3.0. From prerelease versions of the program we've seen, it looks like Microsoft has listened to users and provided most of what they've been looking for—including an index and table of contents generator and a built-in spelling checker with an 80,000-word dictionary. Up to sixteen windows can be open at the same time.

very good
feature

Most importantly, Microsoft has speeded up the program. In fact, if you're used to Word 1.05, the first thing you notice about the Word 3.0 is how much faster scrolling is (thanks to a technique called "off-screen bit-mapping" which was pioneered by an outliner called More).

Overall performance has been improved in other ways as well. For example, you can tell 3.0 to keep your document in RAM, instead of constantly writing it to—and reading it from—disk. This should be particularly appreciated by floppy-disk users who've grown gray listening to Word 1.05 spin the disks. Word 3.0 also has a Fast Save option that appends changes to the end of an existing document rather than taking the time to save the whole file (which it only does periodically).

Word's font and size commands are now listed on menus, instead of just in a separate dialog box. And three new character styles are also available—double underline, strike-through and "hidden" (which might be used for comments in a complicated document worked on by several people).

Even better, the menus can be customized. Word 3.0 starts in Short Menu mode, with stripped-down menus a lot like MacWrite's. You can also choose Full Menu mode and, once there, you can remove commands you don't use, and add new ones from the dialog boxes.

very good
feature

Everyone who has struggled to figure out how Word 1.05 handles headers and footers will be relieved to know that 3.0 has adopted the same sensible interface used in MacWrite. Headers and footers open in windows of their own, and date, time and page number icons are now available.

Like the MS-DOS version, Word 3.0 for the Mac includes a very nice outlining feature. You can have the outline open in one window and the associated document open in another. And they're linked, so when you scroll through the outline, the document scrolls too.

Microsoft has also extended their practice of making as many functions available from the keyboard as possible—a feature much beloved by some people. Not only do the arrow keys on the Mac Plus keyboard give you full PC-style cursor control, but you can pop down menus with a COMMAND key combination, move down (and between) them with the arrow keys, and choose commands with the RETURN key. In other words, you can use the Mac without ever touching the mouse (just what you've always dreamed of, right?).

The Save and Save As... commands have been significantly expanded and now include seven formats: normal, Text Only, Text Only with line breaks, Word 1.05, DOS Word 3.0, MacWrite and something called RTF (which stands for "rich text format"). RTF is a new standard—developed by Microsoft and said to be supported by other vendors—that allows you to retain font, style and graphic information when transferring text between applications.

3.0 also allows some interesting new graphic options. For example, you can specify vertical rules (lines) within a paragraph at specific tab stops and you can specify a box around a paragraph that gets bigger as you add text to the paragraph.

Word 3.0 also offers easy column manipulation. You simply hold down the OPTION key while selecting text to activate the column mode. In addition, Word 3.0 lets you do simple math on numbers in your documents.

very good
feature

3.0's "style sheet" feature is very powerful. (A *style sheet* lets you assign formatting settings to a particular kind of text—all subheads, say, or all regular text paragraphs. Then when you change the style sheet, all such pieces of text throughout the document change automatically.) Word 3.0 goes one step beyond normal style sheets—it lets you incorporate one style sheet within another. For example, you can define headlines as *normal style + centered + 24 point*.

This nesting of style sheets makes it very easy to change the formatting of your document in major ways. For example, let's say almost all of a document is in Times (in other words, that's the normal style and several other style sheets are based on it), except for one other font that's scattered throughout. You decide you want to change Times to Bodoni.

In virtually any other program, you'd have to select the whole document, change it all to Bodoni, then go back and manually insert the second font where needed. But in Word 3.0, you just change the normal font, and all the other changes ripple through.

You can even specify which style you want to immediately follow another style. Let's say you want your headlines to always be followed by a paragraph in normal style. Word will let you automatically switch back to normal style as soon as you hit the RETURN key at the end of the headline.

very good
feature

All in all, it looks as if Microsoft will continue to be the leader in full-featured word processing software for the Mac. Nothing else we've seen comes close to matching the elegance of Word 3.0 or its richness of features, and people are probably going to be willing to pay its hefty price ($400).

There's one other program that may give Word 3.0 a run for its money: WordPerfect for the Mac. It's expected in the first quarter of 1987, and we personally hope it's as good as it is on the PC (where it's the most popular word processing program, and deserves to be), because WordPerfect Corporation has been much more responsive to—and responsible toward—their users than Microsoft has.

things
to come

The versions we've seen of WordPerfect for the Mac were far too preliminary to evaluate, but based on the company's track record, and their excellent PC and Apple // products, we expect WordPerfect for the Mac to give Word 3.0 some strong competition.

WriteNow

This is a fast, easy-to-use word processor with a slew of useful features, including nonstandard type sizes and leading control. Its built-in spelling checker contains a dictionary of 50,000 words and is particularly good at suggesting alternate spellings.

Most spelling checkers use a rather simple algorithm that begins by looking at the first letter of the suspect word to determine the range of possibilities. If you type the first letter wrong, all their suggestions will be useless. Write Now uses a much more sophisticated method for finding alternate spellings.

Despite its many good points, WriteNow has a major drawback that prevents us from recommending it: you can't read MacWrite or Word files into it from within the program (you have to go out to the Desktop and use a separate file-conversion utility). What's worse, you can't save documents as Text Only, so you have no way to export them to any program that doesn't recognize the WriteNow format (so far—needless to say—none do). Among other things, that means you're stuck with the formatting WriteNow gives you, because you can't use a page-makeup program to improve it.

It's too bad WriteNow has this fatal flaw, because the program has a lot of advantages, and would appeal to people who like programs that resemble sports cars, rather than 12-cylinder Bulgemobiles with electric rear-view mirrors.

Acta

Outlining programs have been available on the Mac for some time; in fact, one of the first Mac programs available was an outliner called ThinkTank.

Although there are people who use ThinkTank as their primary Mac application, we have some problems with it. For one thing, it doesn't follow the standard Mac interface, and for another, it's a stand-alone application. An outliner should be available from within your word processing application so you can switch between it and the text you're organizing with minimal effort.

Acta, from Symmetry Corporation, is the answer to many of ThinkTank's shortcomings. It's a desk accessory you can install either in your system file or right within a word processing program. Even better, it follows the Mac interface to such an extent that you don't really need its brief but excellent manual (except possibly to look up some basic outlining terminology). That's very rare in a powerful program, and very praiseworthy.

very good feature

Acta also allows you to Paste MacPaint pictures into your outline. (We can't think of any compelling reason to Paste pictures into an outline, but it's the kind of thing you want to be able to do on a Mac.)

The real power of any outlining program is the ability it gives you to organize your thoughts. You just enter ideas as they occur to you, then go back and shuffle them around until they're in a logical order (or at least the order you want them to be in). In Acta, doing this shuffling is as simple as clicking on an entry (called a "topic") and dragging it where you want it.

The terminology Acta uses is quite sensible. Topics on the same level are called "sisters." Topics on the next level down are called "daughters" of the ones they're under. And topics on the level above—but not directly over—a topic are called its "aunts."

Another feature that's useful in organizing your thoughts is the ability to see both the forest and the trees, the big picture and all the details. Acta accommodates this need by letting you "collapse" a topic—that is, show only the main topic, but none of the topics below it.

A triangle that precedes each topic tells you whether any subtopics are hidden under it. If the triangle is solid, there are none; if it's hollow, there are. If you want to see the hidden subtopics, you simply click on the hollow triangle and they're displayed instantly.

Acta files can be saved in Text, Acta or MacWrite format. Saving in MacWrite format allows you to transfer the outline to most word processing programs with all formatting intact (including any pictures you may have Pasted in).

very good feature

Acta's publisher, Symmetry Corporation, distributes a public-domain program that reads the names of all the files and folders on a disk and makes an Acta outline of them. Each folder becomes a topic, and each file or folder in it becomes a daughter topic. When combined with Acta's ability to store outlines in MacWrite format, you have a handy tool for creating floppy disk labels. But it's probably most useful for keeping track of what's on a hard disk.

bargain

Although it's a bargain at $75, and is all most people need, Acta isn't the ultimate outliner. For one thing, it only lets you use eight of the fonts installed in your system file. While this isn't a devastating deficiency for an outliner, it's certainly annoying. And it's strange, too, because Acta was written by David Dunham, the author of miniWRITER, a MockWrite-like desk accessory that looks and feels a lot like Acta but gives you access to all the installed fonts. (On the other hand, miniWriter doesn't have tabs.) Hopefully this shortcoming will be fixed in a later version.

Another drawback of Acta's is that you have to save an outline as text or a MacWrite document before you can print it. And here's a more minor complaint: When you close an Acta file, and you're asked if you want to save the changes, your only options are Yes and No; the standard Cancel option is missing.

Acta won't do organizational charts. It won't do cloning, hoisting, or a lot of other esoteric stuff. And it won't do mathematical calculations. If you need an outliner with more power than Acta, check out the next entry.

⬤ More

More, from Living Videotext, goes far beyond basic outliners like Acta or ThinkTank. Not only does it offer a very rich collection of features, it also adheres the Mac interface better than virtually any other program we've seen (which is particularly refreshing in view of the fact that the company's earlier product, ThinkTank, did just the opposite).

More is also one of the fastest Mac programs you've ever use. This is mostly due to the fact that it uses a sophisticated technique called "off screen bit mapping." After you've scrolled through a large More document, MacWrite will seem positively lethargic (and Word 1.05 glacial).

very good feature

More retains ThinkTank's powerful features, like hoisting and cloning. Hoisting is useful when you're working on a particularly long or complex outline. You select a topic, hoist it, and all the rest of the outline disappears; just that topic, along with its subtopics, remains. (You can, of course, get the rest of the outline back when you want it, but it's out-of-the-way until then.) When you clone a topic, any changes you make in it are immediately reflected in the clone as well.

With a simple menu selection, More lets you create a chart of almost any kind, including bullet charts, organizational charts and tree charts, and then gives you powerful but easy-to-use tools for modifying them. You can save More outlines and charts in several formats—Word, MacWrite, MacDraw and Text Only (with or without tabs)—and they can be read directly by PageMaker and Ready,Set,Go!.

You can even use More to do simple animation. Steve Michel used the Phoenix 3D program to create a globe, rotated it incrementally (saving the image with each rotation), then read the saved files into More to create an animated spinning globe.

More does math and can even be used as a simple spreadsheet. It also lets you dial phone numbers from within an outline.

For all its virtues, More does have some defects; for example, you can only work in one font at a time. Much more seriously, there's no Undo command—which is not only a treacherous omission but a real departure from the Mac interface.

A final drawback is the program's $400 price. That's a lot of money to pay for even the sexiest outliner imaginable—but then, More is a lot more than just an outliner.

● *spelling checker checklist*

What makes a good spelling checker? Well, it should have an adequate dictionary, somewhere in the neighborhood of 80,000 words. It should be able to recognize common prefixes and suffixes, and not stumble on capitalization and punctuation. You should be able to add words to the dictionary, and delete them as well.

A good spelling checker should be capable of suggesting reasonable alternatives to what you typed. Finally, it should be integrated into the word processor—that is, you should be able to run it without having to exit to the Desktop. To do that, it has to either be part of the program or a desk accessory. The first two programs described below have taken the desk-accessory approach, with radically different results.

● *MacLightning*

MacLightning ($100), by Target Software, is a desk accessory that stays active in the background, watching your every keystroke. When a word is typed that's not in its dictionary, the machine beeps at you. While some may prefer this interactive technique, we personally find it hard enough to keep our thoughts in order without having the Mac jabbering at us continually.

Fortunately, MacLightning also lets you turn off this

interactive feature and check the entire document—or a selected portion of it—all at once. But that doesn't help the program's user interface, which is one of the clumsiest we've seen outside a PC.

Flagged words aren't shown in context. And instead of offering suggestions about the correct spelling, MacLightning opens up the dictionary at the first entry that comes close to the suspect word. You then have to scroll through many, many words to get to the correct spelling. After you find it, and tell MacLightning to insert it, the program uses your word processor's Find function to replace it, which usually takes a while.

very bad feature

🍎 *MacSpell+* (Dale)

MacSpell+ ($100), from Creighton Development, is also a desk accessory, and it has most of the features you'd expect in a good spelling checker. Its dictionary is adequate (75,000 words), it understands prefixes and suffixes, it lets you add to the dictionary, it's reasonably fast, and it shows your errors in context. I used it extensively in preparing the manuscript for this book.

very good feature

MacSpell+ does have some drawbacks. It won't let you delete words from the dictionary unless you purchase a special utility that costs extra. It rarely makes suggestions for correcting flagged words. And it would be a lot faster if it didn't display every word as it's being checked. In spite of these shortcomings, I found MacSpell+ to be the most useful of the many Macintosh spelling checkers I've tried.

🍎 *Spelling Champion* (Arthur)

I like to work with programs that are lean and fast, even if that means sacrificing a few features, and that's why I like this stand-alone spelling checker, published at the bargain price of $40 by a small company in Wisconsin called Champion Software.

bargain

I've found that how long a spelling program takes to check a file matters a lot less than how many correctly spelled words it presents to you as suspected misspellings. One Mac spelling checker I used didn't recognize *affords, buzzer, magnify, modesty, shouldn't, sticker* and *tab* . You can, of course, add all these words to its dictionary, but that can take forever, and besides—why are you doing the work the people who wrote the program should have done?

very good feature

Spelling Champion queries me about fewer correct words than any other spelling checker I've used, and it's fast, intuitive and easy-to-use. When you correct a spelling, it automatically corrects the word in the document you're checking and saves the corrected document when you're done (if you want it to). I don't like the fact that it won't check hyphenated words or add them to the dictionary (it treats them as two separate words) and I wish it were a desk accessory so I wouldn't have to keep going out to the Desktop. But basically I love it.

The version I have only corrects MacWrite files (it can check Word 1.05 files but not enter the corrections in them) but that's probably already been fixed; I've just been too busy to get a new version.

Champion Software offers *no* telephone support (although you can write them with questions). This sounds like a major drawback, but since the program is so simple to learn and use, and so inexpensive, I really don't think it makes much of a difference. Besides, the phone lines of some companies that supposedly offer support are so understaffed that they might as well not offer phone support; the effect is the same (I'm thinking, for example, of Microsoft at certain periods in its history).

♠ *Spellswell* (Arthur)

Is it Spells Well or Spell Swell? Only Greene, Johnson Inc. know for sure. Either way, their spelling checker is one of the better ones on the market (although its dictionary isn't as good as Spelling Champion's).

I used Spellswell for a while but fell afoul of its inability to ignore special characters like dashes—which, as you can see, I use all the time—and foreign accents (I was writing a book on Central America and got tired of adding words like Jos to the dictionary because Spellswell couldn't deal with the é in José).

But aside from that, this is an efficient, well-written program and a bargain at $40. If for some reason you can't use—or don't like—Spelling Champion, you definitely should take a look at it.

bargain

Spreadsheets

Excel

When it comes to selecting a spreadsheet on the Mac, the choice is simple. You can pay $400 and get the state-of-the-art, or you can pay less and get less (which may be all you need).

The state-of-the-art is Microsoft Excel. Its graphing capabilities are the best of any spreadsheet in the world and include about 90% of what Microsoft Chart can do. (Actually, just about anything it does is the best of any spreadsheet in the world.) Its ready-made functions are virtually limitless, and its macro feature lets you automate just about any procedure.

very good
feature

Excel gives you a theoretical worksheet of 256 columns by 16,384 rows (that's 4,685,824 cells, which should be adequate for your personal budget)—although you won't be able to even approach that limit unless you upgrade your Mac to 4MB of RAM and beyond.

Although Excel's manual is terrible and some of its dialog boxes confusing, the program is relatively easy to learn and use—especially considering everything it can do. If you're serious about spreadsheets, you shouldn't even consider another product. In fact, if you're *really* serious about spreadsheets, you should buy a Mac just so you can use Excel.

⬥ *other spreadsheets*

If you're not a spreadsheet junkie but do need to use them occasionally for light work, you might be interested in MacCalc from Bravo Technologies. This small (999 rows by 124 columns) and inexpensive ($100) product provides all the power you'll need for simple tasks like balancing checking accounts and doing simple projections.

But don't expect the sophistication you find in Excel. For example, if text in a cell is wider that the width of the cell, the text won't display in the next cell to the right, even if that cell is empty—the way it does in Excel.

Another possibility for the occasional spreadsheet user is Microsoft Works. (For a description of Works, see the 'Miscellaneous applications' section below). While not as powerful as Excel, Work's spreadsheet offers most of the important features of Multiplan, and for the extra money you spend, you also get a word processor, a filing manager, and a communications program—plus the added flexibility of having all of these applications available from within one program.

Databases *(Steve Michel)*

⬥ *a note on terminology*

Technically, *databases* are mailing lists and other large accumulations of data maintained on computers, and *database managers* are the programs that manage them. But in common usage the programs themselves have come to be called databases, and that's the way the term is used in this section and throughout the book.

🍎 *databases for the Mac*

The Macintosh has always suffered from an embarrassment of riches when it comes to databases. Databases were some of the first third-party products to appear. Why was that?

gossip/ trivia

The way I heard the story was that in the early days of the Macintosh—late 1983 and early 1984—when Apple was looking for companies to develop software for the machines, they told them, "Don't develop word processors—there'll be plenty of those; do databases." If that's true, Apple's reasons for giving the advice are open to debate. One theory is that they wanted to keep the market for themselves...and for a certain software developer in the Pacific Northwest (no, I don't mean Bigfoot Software).

Be that as it may, three years after the Mac was introduced, fewer than a dozen Mac word processors have been announced and of those, only four are actually available. But Mac users can choose from an uncountable number of databases. (Oh, I suppose you could count them, but what's the point?)

Before I go on to discuss them, there are a few general matters that should be taken care of.

🍎 *some useful database terms*

Since I'll be using some database terminology you may not be familiar with, here are a few definitions:

record — One item in a database file. For example, in a mailing list, each name and address is a record. If your mailing list has 500 names and addresses in it, it contains 500 records.

field — One item in a record. In a mailing list, Name is a field. So is Zip Code.

calculation or *calculated field* — A field whose values are determined by the contents of other fields. For instance, a field called "total purchases" might contain a formula that defines it as equal to previous purchases + current purchases.

relational — Databases are called "relational" because they relate two or more files together. For example, let's say an inventory application contains two files—one that contains the customer information and another that contains the information about the inventory itself.

When a customer buys something, you type in some basic identifying information (her name, say, or her customer number) and the program looks up other data (shipping address, payment terms, etc.) in the customer information file. You can then enter some data about her purchases, like the item number. For each item number, the program looks up a description (including, say, quantity on hand, pricing, weight, etc.) in the inventory file .

very hot tip

"Relational" is one of the hottest hype-words in computerdom, and it's a rare database that doesn't have that label slapped on it. You probably don't need a relational database (most people don't), but if you do, make sure the product you buy deserves the label.

multiuser database — A multiuser database is one that operates over a network and allows more than one person to access a file at the same time. For example, in a sales and inventory application, one person could enter sales data while another person on a different machine could simultaneously enter inventory data.

Typically, multiuser databases include *record-locking*, which means that only one person at a time can edit a particular record. Other users are prohibited from doing anything more than looking at that record until the first person is done.

Multiuser databases are really a new concept, and right now there are few products. But as AppleTalk networks grow in number and users grow in sophistication, these products will become more and more important.

things to come

✎ *tips on selecting a database*

1. Don't worry about the statistics

If you're looking for a chart in this section that gives you various statistics on these programs—number of records allowed, characters per field, etc.—forget it. I've looked at dozens of those charts over the last couple of years, and none of them has ever given me any help in choosing a database. Who cares if program A will only let you enter 65,536 records, but program B will let you enter two or three billion?

very hot tip

Few people ever use even a fraction of the theoretical capabilities of a program. And the charts never really tell you what those numbers mean, or how large amounts of data affect things like the speed of the program. Program B might let you enter ten times as much data, but program A may let you work more quickly and easily.

2. Look for flexibility

In choosing a database, try to find one that is as flexible as possible. Don't buy one that won't let you add a field to a file after creating it. You also should be able to change the type of a field after creating the file. For example, you might find that you've inadvertently made the "date" field a text item and therefore won't be able to sort on it. You should be able to change the data type of that field.

very hot tip

3. Little things mean a lot

Look to see what kind of thoughtful small touches the program offers you. For example, it's nice to be able to assign default values to selected fields—so if you're creating a mailing list of people 90% of whom live in—say—Kansas, you can tell the program to make KS the default for the state field, instead of having to type KS thousands of times. (Then you just tab past the field and KS is entered automatically).

Other nice little touches might include being able to:
—choose what fields to index
—make the current date the default in any date field
—customize reports
—print to the LaserWriter.

4. So does the ability to transfer information

One of the nice things about the Mac world is the existence of some fairly standard ways of moving data from one program to another. This can be very useful. For example, there's one database file I use quite often that I first created in Microsoft File. Later I wanted to try it out in Filemaker, and had a pretty easy time moving the data in. Currently it's in Double Helix, but I've also worked with it in Excel, OverVUE, Word (as Text Only, to check spelling and make some global changes) and several applications on the PC.

There are many reasons why you might want to move a file around like this. You may need to do some calculations on the data in it, or print it out in a certain form, or access it from another database file set up by a different program. Or you may simply have discovered a new program and decide you want to do all your work in it.

Most programs store information in their own specialized formats. This lets them get at it quicker, or offer certain unique special features. Fortunately, certain standard data-transfer formats allow information to pass from application to application. Make sure any database you buy supports at least one of these four: Clipboard, DIF, SYLK or delimited (meaning that a standard character—usually a tab—is placed between fields).

In addition to the data itself, DIF and SYLK also pass information on things like how many fields and records there are, and what their names are.

The "delimited" format is less sophisticated—it just transfers the data itself (usually with each record on a line of its own). Different delimiters are used. The Mac standard is tab between fields, RETURN between records, but sometimes commas separate the fields—in which case Word can use the file for mail merging. (Word also expects that the first line in the file to contain the field names.)

The last file-transfer method is the Clipboard, and every Mac program should support it. Although it's handy for moving small amounts of data from one program to another, especially within the Switcher, the Clipboard does limit you to transferring one file at a time, and it holds the data being transferred in RAM, rather than on disk, which makes it much riskier.

5. Buy from a committed manufacturer

This rule applies to software of any kind. Buy from a manufacturer who has a good track record of supporting their products and their customers. Typically, companies that offer good support also offer fairly frequent updates. If they consist of modest improvements, they should be free or very inexpensive; if they consist of complex enhancements to the product, they should obviously cost more, but still shouldn't penalize you (in effect) for buying the earlier version.

very
hot
tip

6. Don't be (too) afraid to spend money

Powerful software costs a lot to create and support. If you can get by with Record Holder, great—you only need to spend $70. But if you really need Helix or Omnis and buy Record Holder instead, that $70 is wasted.

very
hot
tip

Of course, it's important to take price into consideration, but first evaluate your needs as well as you can and try to make sure you're buying enough power. It's almost impossible to buy too much power, but it's very easy to buy too little.

7. Look for file templates

very
hot
tip

If you know somebody who's using a database for the same purposes you want one for, see if you can get a copy of their database file—emptied of records, of course. You can save a great deal of time by not having to reinvent the wheel. Don't be reluctant to pay them something for the template, but if you have to pay a lot, make sure they'll explain it to you and support it.

This works the other way around as well—if you take the time to develop a good application, be sure to let other people know about it.

♦ *eight programs compared*

That's enough about databases in general. Now let's talk about some specific products.

To my mind, there are eight databases for the Mac that are worth considering. Each has its own particular strengths and weaknesses—so much so that a well-stocked software library could include two or even three of them and not be overburdened. A job that's too complex for Microsoft File may be just right for Helix; a job that takes too long to develop in Helix may work well in Filemaker; and a job where speed is of the utmost importance may demand OverVUE.

The eight databases (in the order in which I'll discuss them) are:

Helix (Double Helix and various other incarnations)
Microsoft File
Filemaker (and Filemaker+)

Record Holder
OverVUE
Filevision (and Business Filevision)
Omnis 3 (and 3+)
dBASE MAC

Doubtless there are other Mac databases I'm not familiar with, but these seem to be the most popular, and they cover the broad range of capabilities available.

🍎 *Helix, Double Helix, etc.*

Odesta's Helix was one of the most eagerly awaited products during the first year and a half of the Macintosh's life. Big ads in Macworld promised a new way of working with files—using icons to represent data and calculations.

When the product finally appeared, a lot of us were disappointed. Helix took longer to learn than we were used to with Mac programs, and what had seemed to be great promise instead looked like a case of icons gone wild. Many people are still down on Helix, but I've changed my mind.

Working with Helix is a unique experience, but after you get the hang of it, it's a lot of fun. It uses icons to represent fields, forms, indexes, queries, and calculations. And it encourages you to play with your data—that is, to work with it and find new ways of looking at it to get different kinds of information from it.

In addition to being fun, Helix is powerful, and makes it easy to do hard things. Odesta has been very good about supporting the product, with very regular (and usually free) product updates, and a vision of a growing line of software that will support almost anybody's database needs in the future. They also offer excellent, free technical support. I've never come away from a phone call with them frustrated.

very good
feature

What's the downside? Helix is not one of the fastest database programs on the Mac, nor is it one of the easiest to learn. But the most serious problem is its lack of a procedural programming language—which means there is no way to structure what the program does. You can't tell it to "first do A, and then if the user says H, do N." Although this is a fairly serious hindrance to building serious applications, it's one you can work around.

Helix is most useful for:
• screen forms that resemble paper forms· complex analysis of data, particularly for business applications like inventory and billing
    • files that incorporate graphics
    • multiuser applications.

⚫ *Microsoft File*

very bad feature

Microsoft brought this program out fairly early in the life of the Macintosh, and as with Word, they've shamefully neglected to provide significant updates to it. (That's what happens when you're successful, I guess. You don't feel the heat of competition and you work less on your products.)

File doesn't necessarily need a major "features" update—though, as with Word, it wouldn't hurt. What File needs, at this late date, is a "performance" update, one that brings its speed up to par with other programs on the Mac.

In fact, the reason I'm talking about File here is not because it's such a great program, but because it still seems to be selling fairly well, even in the face of much superior competition.

That's not to say that File is a bad program. I've used it a lot, and I know many people who use it every day. It's very easy to learn—I've even shown people the basics in an hour or so, and some of them have gone right to work on it without reading the manual. (But, then again, the manual isn't much help).

File was the first Mac database that allowed you to Paste pictures into the file. That was one of the big selling points of the program—though I, for one, have never done it, and I don't know anybody who has needed to do it.

File lets you create many different forms in which to view your data. The forms are very easy to create, but managing them is another story. Each file can have two forms stored with it on the disk. Other forms can be stored separately (by choosing Save Form As... from the File menu).

When you're closing a program, File always asks, "Save this Form with the Datafile?" whether or not you've already saved it. Most users are afraid to say No, thinking the form will be lost altogether. But if you say Yes, you lose one of the original files that was stored with the file.

If this is sounds confusing, that's because it is. It takes a lot of work to figure this out, and you still get confused. My advice is: if File seems to be the program that's right for you, try working with its Forms for a while, and see if you can make any sense out of them.

File is most useful for:
• screen forms that resemble paper forms
• mailing lists or other simple files
• files that incorporate graphics.

🍎 *Filemaker and Filemaker +*

Filemaker (from Forethought) is somewhat similar to Microsoft File. It's a simple filing program that's easy-to-use, provides adequate performance and is very flexible at designing screen forms. However, where File is hard-to-use (managing Forms) and slow, Filemaker is facile and (fairly) fast.

The way Filemaker indexes its file is unique. With most databases, you choose the fields to be indexed; Filemaker

very good feature

indexes not only every field in the database, but every word. This makes it *very* easy to search for specific entries—you just type in a word to be searched for and the program finds it virtually instantly.

Filemaker's screen-form function includes helpful tools like "whiskers" (dotted lines that point to a ruler location and make it easy to place things precisely) and has great versatility with text fields (if your field isn't long enough for the text you want to type, Filemaker allows it to expand to accommodate the entry).

Filemaker + adds some nice features to what was already an impressive program. The program now has relational capabilities: one file can find information in another file and import it. Filemaker +'s relational capabilities are not nearly as powerful as those of Helix or Omnis, but they're quite adequate for most people.

Forethought is aiming Filemaker + at people for whom File, Record Holder or standard Filemaker don't have enough power, yet who don't have the time or inclination to learn Helix or Omnis. From the quick looks I've had at it, it seems that they've done a good job. But this can be a tricky niche for a publisher to stake out, and before I'd buy this program, I'd consider carefully whether it will meet my growing needs.

very good feature

[Note from Dale: I used Filemaker to compile the notes for this book and I loved it. It's fast and easy-to-use and it never let me down.]

Filemaker is most useful for:
- *long text files*
- *applications that require relatively limited relational capabilities*
  - *screen forms that resemble paper forms*
  - *files that incorporate graphics*
  - *small applications that have to run fast.*

◆ *Record Holder*

Software Discoveries' Record Holder ($70) is a relatively new entry in the arena, and my comments are based on just a couple days' use of the program. The program is aimed at the same users as File or Filemaker and has about the same capabilities. But where those programs are easy-to-use, Record Holder is positively a breeze.

bargain

One of the unique things Software Discoveries has done is to add a "Table of Contents" window that's kept on the screen along with the main form window. This window shows the key field (the one the file is sorted on) and one other field. Using a standard scroll bar, you can scroll through the file until you find the record you want. Click on it and the full record appears instantly in the form window.

This is really a good approach for applications like short mailing lists, and is far easier than using a Find function—though it is slower for larger files. Unfortunately, you can't search the file in other ways, or to create alternate screen forms for the same file.

One of Record Holder's best features is the way it lets you work with long text fields. When you format the screen form, you can size any text field to be as large or as small as you like. However, when you make the text field more than one line long, Record Holder includes a standard text scroll bar on the right of the field. This lets you type in text that is longer than the screen form has room for, and scroll through it to see more.

very good feature

I can't believe how useful I've found this feature. Compared to the way File works (you can type in as much text as you want—you just can't see it!), this is a blessing. It's also unique in my experience among Mac databases, and something I wish everyone would add.

Record Holder is most useful for:
• short, simple files, like address books
• inventorying home possessions
• people who know something about the Mac and don't want to spend a lot of time learning a new program.

❖ *OverVUE*

very good
feature

In many ways OverVUE resembles a spreadsheet more than a filing program. For one thing, you normally enter data on a spreadsheet-like grid. For another, the program packs impressive power for working on subsets of your data, and for doing calculations on the data. Finally, like a spreadsheet, OverVUE holds your whole file in memory while you're working on it (this limits the document size to some extent, but also allows searches and sorts to happen with blinding speed).

There are some drawbacks to this approach. One is that it's cumbersome to work with forms in OverVUE, both because you have little control over how the form will be designed on the screen, and because you can't choose different fonts for the reports: everything is in Monaco.

very bad
feature

But the main problem with OverVue is that it doesn't follow the Mac interface. For example, COMMAND-Z, which is the command for Undo in virtually every other Mac program, shifts a column of data up one row in OverVUE. If you make this mistake and don't catch it instantly, you can completely destroy a whole file. Do that once or twice and you won't care about OverVUE's speed or number-crunching ability.

OverVUE is most useful for:
• amazingly fast sorts and searches
• people who need to do a lot of calculations in their database files
• unimportant files, where the risk of destroying your data is acceptable
• people unfamiliar with the standard Mac interface

• files without a lot of text material (long text entries don't display well where you only have one line per record).

♦ *Filevision and Business Filevision*

Filevision was a very exciting product when it first came out, and Business Filevision is a worthy extension to that product. Both are graphics databases that take advantage of the Macintosh's graphic orientation in a totally unique way.

To begin using them, you create a picture on the screen that includes many different kinds of objects. Each object becomes an individual record in the database. Double-click on one of the objects and a screen is displayed that gives you information about that object (you have to enter the information first, of course). Use the program's sort or selection functions and objects that meet your criteria are highlighted. (It's hard to describe in print; it has to be seen to be appreciated.)

Filevision has several limitations, however. First of all, you need to be able to draw, and that's no small problem for many of us. (If I'm going to use something a lot, it should look nice. But I have trouble drawing anything I'd want to look at very often.)

Secondly, what do you use these programs for? Their ads used to show a wine cellar. Click on a certain bottle, they said, and Filevision will tell you all about it. Ask it to select the Zinfandels and those bottles will be highlighted.

But if you have a wine cellar, you pretty much know what's where; and if you don't know what's where, it's easier just to go and look than to fire up Filevision. Not to mention the fact that you could simply put a Location field into a conventional database, and use something like "Shelf B" to tell you where the wine is.

The products' publisher, Telos Software, publishes a fine newsletter with examples of how to use them. One suggestion they made was home inventory. I've seen at least one person use Filevision for this: little pictures of everything in the house, all matched to serial numbers for valuables, insurance information, etc. But again, that's easy enough to do with a standard program—and what do you do when you move things around?

These are great programs, and if you can think of useful things to do with them, they're probably worth having. The problem is thinking of that useful thing.

Filevision is most useful for:
• maps that locate objects and associate written information with them.

⚫ *Omnis MAC and Omnis III +*

Omnis offers much the same power as Helix. It's relational (meaning you can work and link data contained in separate files) and is well suited for building complex, powerful applications. But Omnis is a much more traditional type of database than Helix—both the vocabulary it uses and the user interface feel more like an MS-DOS database than Helix does.

Omnis is like Helix in many ways, not just in its capabilities. Both products have evolved through many versions, and Blyth Software's commitment to Omnis is obvious from the way they've upgraded it. Omnis started out as a very unMaclike product that used very few of the Mac's features. It grew into the powerful Omnis III and the recent upgrade to Omnis III + that includes multiuser capabilities. (Since they previously published Omnis I and Omnis II, I wish they would have simply called the new one Omnis IV, but perhaps that's too much like the Rocky movies.)

To be honest, I've never really gotten onto the Omnis bandwagon. There are a couple of reasons for this. The first is that I've heard that the company charges customers for support. I've always felt that if you spend several hundred dollars on a product, support should be free. Perhaps the changing nature of the computer industry makes that prohibitive these days, but many other companies still give free support.

Support policies are subject to change, so I recommend you don't take my word for the quality of their support (I haven't used it), but check with the company or another user.

The other reason I haven't used Omnis much is because it still doesn't seem very Maclike to me. I haven't seen Omnis III+, but Omnis III doesn't support standard Mac features like multiple fonts, graphics in files and so on. Fonts aren't very important to some people, and I recognize that it's easy to get carried away with them, but they're one of the things I like about the Macintosh, and I hate to give them up.

Omnis is also not as "free-form" as many other Mac products. For example, virtually all the other programs I've discussed let you change the structure of an already created file. With Omnis, however, you have to specify at creation time the length of every field in the record. If you set up a mailing list with a "city" field twelve characters long, then a certain West Coast city will have to be entered as "San Francisc" forever after.

Unalterable, fixed-length fields also waste space. In the twelve-character "city" field mentioned above, Seattle would waste five spaces and Miami seven, and that begins to take up a lot of room on the disk.

Omnis III does have a lot of power. One of its strongest features is its ability to carry out "sequences" of commands (macros, in other words). You can even install sequences of your own devising in the menus, and that gives you great power to create applications for use by clerical personnel and others who don't know all the ins-and-outs of a complex database like Omnis.

For example, you could set up a sequence that finds all unpaid invoices more than 60 days old, sorts them by customer name, and totals the amount owed by each customer. Then you could install the sequence on a menu with a command name like '60+ by Cust'.

I've heard from friends who use Omnis sequences that once you get used to them, it's hard to imagine a database without them. Even if you're not creating applications for naive users, sequences come in handy: if there's a particular series of commands you use often, you just put them into a sequence, install it on a menu, and save yourself a lot of trouble.

Omnis is most useful for:
• creating sophisticated applications for naive or inexperienced users
• large databases, or those that require relational capability
• multiuser applications.

⌘ *dBASE Mac*

For those of you who don't know about dBASE, here's a little background. The program has been around for some time, and has gone through many incarnations. It started out as "Vulcan" and ran on some of the first microcomputers. A later version, dBASE II, became the most successful of the CP/M databases. There were several reasons for that.

For one thing, the program wasn't copy-protected. For another, it didn't do anything fancy with the system, so you could run it on just about any terminal. (One of the curses of the CP/M world was having to configure software for the particular terminal you were using. You'd buy a program and take it home, and then you'd have to wade through an "installation" program that asked you endless questions about how your system was configured. Even if you knew the answers, you'd find you knew them in, say, Hex, but the program wanted them in Octal. For those of us who suffered through all this, it's something to tell our kids about—like our parents telling us how they had to walk ten miles through the snow to go to school.)

dBASE also became the leading database in the MS-DOS world. Dozens of books have been published about it and multitudes of consultants make their livings creating dBASE applications for customers who then find they had to keep them on retainer, because nobody but the consultants can understand how to use the applications. (Maybe this accounts for why consultants like dBASE so much.)

This program is *hard* to use. To even speak of a "user interface" in the same breath as dBASE is a contradiction in terms. Early versions of the program presented you with a command that looked like this:

very bad feature

That's not a typo. That's dBase's infamous "dot prompt." When you saw it on your screen, you were supposed to give dBASE a command. You don't know what command to give? Well, don't type "help," because there isn't any. And don't look in the dBASE manual, because until recently, it didn't make any sense. Do what everybody else does: Go buy a book on dBASE—and when you can't understand the book, hire a consultant.

In spite of its wretched—virtually nonexistent—user interface, dBASE contained a powerful programming language that could be used to create applications with menu-driven facades that hide the inner workings of the program. Much of dBase's popularity is due to the power of that programming language.

Over the years, Ashton-Tate has improved the program a great deal. Its most recent incarnation on MS-DOS machines, dBASE III Plus, imitates the Macintosh user interface, with popdown menus and extensive help. Even so, I didn't expect much from the Macintosh version, which is called dBASE Mac, but I was pleasantly surprised.

very good feature

Like MacPaint and MacDraw, dBASE Mac gives you a palette of icons on the left side of the screen that represent various commands. Like Helix and File, it lets you include graphics in a file. You can even link files together graphically.

very good feature

dBASE Mac can read files created on PCs (which is very important for the growing number of offices that have both types of machines). Even more impressively, its programming language includes all the power of the PC version, with special enhancements for the Macintosh (alert boxes, customized popdown menus and so on).

As of this writing, I haven't had a chance to test dBASE Mac out. But if it does what they say it does, it's worth checking out.

dBASE Mac is most useful for:
• applications that require accessing multiple files (in other words, relational applications)
• creating complex and powerful applications for inexperienced users.

Graphics programs

❖ *the two basic kinds*

Graphics programs for the Mac fall into two broad categories: bit-mapped "paint" programs and object-oriented "draw" programs. The difference between the two is fairly simple.

Bit-mapped programs treat the entire screen as a collection of dots. For example, if you want to move something you've drawn, you have to use the Marquee, the Lasso or some other special tool to encircle all the dots that make it up and thus select them as a group.

Object-oriented programs treat what you draw as a discrete object. All you normally have to do to select it is click on it. (But you can't go into FatBits and fine-tune it, removing a dot here and adding one there.)

In general, bit-mapped programs are better suited for artistic tasks and object-oriented programs for business applications like drafting and diagramming. If you do a fair amount of graphics work on the Mac, you'll probably want to have at least one program of each kind in your software library.

FullPaint

The first drawing program for the Mac was MacPaint, and when it was introduced it was one of the most innovative programs available on any personal computer. For the first couple years of the Mac's existence, MacPaint and MacWrite were given away with every Mac sold. But Apple stopped doing this in 1986, and you now have to shell out $125 for MacPaint. If you're considering doing that, we suggest you shell out $180 for FullPaint instead.

FullPaint looks and acts a lot like MacPaint, and anyone familiar with MacPaint will feel immediately at home with it. In fact, FullPaint incorporates at least 95% of MacPaint's features, right down to the obscure keyboard shortcuts that expert users are so fond of. At the same time, FullPaint overcomes several of MacPaint's shortcomings.

very good
feature

For example, it lets you open as many as four documents at a time. You can click on the title bar to cause the window to grow to full screen size. You can move the tool and pattern palettes, or hide them altogether (along with the title bar), so your document takes up the whole screen (which is, of course, where the program's name comes from). If you've ever been frustrated by MacPaint's small window, this feature alone is almost worth the price.

FullPaint also comes with the excellent ColorPrint program that lets you to print multiple color pictures on an ImageWriter II equipped with a multicolor ribbon. And Full Paint is not copy-protected.

Back in the days when almost everyone had MacPaint, there was some question as to whether upgrading to FullPaint was worth $180. Now that Apple is no longer including MacPaint with every Mac, we think FullPaint is a better value.

⌘ *SuperPaint*

things
to come

This program was just coming out as we we're going to press, so our review of it will have to wait for the first update. (We've seen prerelease versions, but we don't want to base a review on those.)

bargain

The concept behind SuperPaint is terrific: basically, it lets you combine bit-mapped and object-oriented graphics in the same document. Master Mac artist Gerald Clement says it does the job quite well, really giving you the best of both worlds. If this is true, SuperPaint would definitely be the program to get—and at $100, a terrific bargain as well.

⌘ *MacGrid*

very good
feature

This is the best tool we've seen for learning how to produce really gorgeous bit-mapped pictures on the Mac, whether in MacPaint, FullPaint or whatever. To get an idea of the sort of things you can create with it, take a look at the drawings facing the title pages for Part I and Part II, which were drawn using MacGrid by the program's author, Gerald Clement.

⌘ *MacDraw*

The standard for object-oriented drawing programs is Apple's own MacDraw. Essentially, the program lets you create objects and move them around on the screen to create a drawing. What makes MacDraw so powerful are the rulers, alignment grid, size commands and various other tools that give you precise control over an object's position and size.

One thing MacDraw does well is embellish presentation charts created in Excel or other graphing programs. You can use MacDraw's tools to enhance the title and even change the widths of the bars in a bar graph.

Many people use MacDraw to create professional-looking business forms. MacDraw can also serve as a simple page-makeup program for short documents—as long as you don't need advanced features like kerning and leading.

MacDraw does have some drawbacks. It only lets you use eleven fonts, regardless of how many you have installed, and the program hasn't been updated nearly as often as it should have been. But it's still a relatively useful tool.

very bad feature

Communications software

🍎 *telecommunications on the Mac*

Telecommunications (hooking up your computer to talk to other computers over phone lines) has a reputation for being one of the least friendly areas of personal computing. That's because it *is* one of the least friendly areas of personal computing. It also can be tremendously exciting, useful and fun.

Actually, telecommunications is a little easier on the Mac than on other computers. You still have to deal with bizarre terms like "parity" and "stop bits," but some standards have emerged, and most Mac programs walk you through whatever nonstandardized decisions remain.

There was no communications software on the Mac for months after it was introduced. Then Dennis Brothers wrote MacTep and put it in the public domain, and finally the Mac was smart enough to dial the phone.

Perhaps because of this beginning, many the most popular Mac communications programs are shareware. Or maybe it's because bulletin boards and information services are the primary sources of shareware, and thus the people who use communications programs are already tuned into the shareware concept. Whatever the reason, several of the recommended products below are shareware, and one of the commercial ones was written by shareware pioneer Dennis Brothers.

⬥ *Red Ryder*

Red Ryder is the most powerful and controversial of the four products discussed here. (For more information about it, see Dennis Klatzkin's in-depth discussion on pp. 195–202.)

very good feature

Red Ryder offers just about every feature you could ask for in a communications program. Its macro capabilities, while difficult to learn, are extremely flexible, as are its terminal-emulation features (you'll appreciate them if you need to connect your Mac to a mainframe computer).

If you have a thorough understanding of the ins and outs of telecommunications, Red Ryder may be just what you're looking for. If you don't, Red Ryder may still be just what you're looking for, because its documentation provides an excellent introduction to the basics of computer communications, and even some of the advanced topics. This alone is reason enough to take a look at the program.

bargain

Red Ryder is available from most bulletin boards, user groups and information services. If you like and use it, it costs just $40 to register as an owner.

It's rare to find such a powerful, full-featured application that you can test-drive before paying for. Anyone with a Mac and a modem should at least try Red Ryder.

⚫ *MicroPhone*

MicroPhone is Dennis Brother's first commercial offering. It's received rave reviews and is generally an excellent program.

MicroPhone walks the thin line between maximum power and flexibility on the one hand, and maximum user friendliness on the other. Both strengths are obvious in its "script" feature, which records your every move in a short program you can then install on the menu as a command, in a button at the bottom of the screen, or both.

very good
feature

You could, for example, devise a very complex script that called CompuServe, GEnie and several bulletin boards in the middle of the night (when rates and usage are low) and uploaded and downloaded files based on any number of contingencies. To initiate this flurry of activity, all you'd have to do would be click on a button, or choose a command from a menu. If you then made MicroPhone the startup application on the disk, you'd have a system that almost any novice could use.

As with any good Mac application, you can use MicroPhone's basic features without having to open the manual. But there's one feature of the manual that deserves mention—a special section in the back entitled "I Don't Need to Read the Manual." It provides a concise summary of all of MicroPhone's features and is designed specifically for experienced telecommunications users.

very good
feature

We do have a couple of complaints about MicroPhone. In its first release, when running on Macs with the 128K ROMs, the program would sometimes report that there wasn't enough room on the disk to receive a file—even if several megabytes were available. And it took Software Ventures longer to fix this bug than it should have.

In the interests of user friendliness, you're prevented from permanently altering some of MicroPhone's parameters. For example, if you change the redialing interval from the standard 30 seconds to 15 seconds during a MicroPhone session, it will automatically be reset to 30 seconds when you exit the program.

But in general, this is a fine piece of software. If you need the telephone support that Software Ventures gives you (and Software Ventures does support their customers), or if you need to set up custom system that people with little or no training will use, MicroPhone is an excellent choice.

⌘ *TermWorks*

TermWorks takes a different approach than Red Ryder and MicroPhone. The strengths of this shareware program are simplicity and speed. And because it's smaller, it loads faster and takes up less space on disk. Although there's no script facility, TermWorks does include a dialing directory and macro capability.

The major drawback to TermWorks is that there's no provision for turning off the MacBinary option when doing Xmodem transfers. This isn't a problem if you deal exclusively in Macintosh files (it doesn't matter if you transfer them to another Mac, an MS-DOS machine, a minicomputer or a mainframe, as long as they're eventually used on a Mac). But if you often work with DOS files on your Mac, you'll need to be able to turn off MacBinary, and TermWorks isn't the program to use.

TermWorks is shareware, but with an interesting difference. To quote from its documentation:

TermWorks is being distributed under the Shareware system with a twist. It works like this. You receive a copy of this program from a friend. You try it out and decide that it's a pretty good job and that you want to use it. You fill out the registration form in the distribution notice in the Apple menu and send it in with your check for $20.00.

You receive a disk by return mail with the latest copy of TermWorks, this documentation and a unique serial number registered in your name. The registration form you send in had the serial number on it of the person who registered that copy. He will receive $5.00 as a finder's fee.

You then make copies of your disk with your serial number on it and distribute them to your friends. If any of them registers TermWorks, you will get the $5.00 finder's fee. Get four people to register and your copy is free!

This unorthodox approach to marketing shareware only proves how imaginative Mac users can be. TermWorks was written by James Rhodes and is copyrighted by Horizon Software.

FModem

FModem is another of those small no-frills programs offered under the shareware system. It gives you all the major features, including simple macros and VT52 emulation. Its major advantage over TermWorks is that you can turn off the MacBinary option of Xmodem. This is the program to use if you often transfer files between your Mac and a MS-DOS machine.

The program is simple, easy to use, and quite powerful. FModem is shareware and can be registered for $40 from the author, Christian Doucet.

♦ local networks

The two best LAN products we've seen are MacServe and TOPS, both of which are described in detail in chapter 9. For communicating with Tandem minicomputers, you want MacMenlo, which is also described in chapter 9.

Miscellaneous applications

♦ PageMaker vs. Ready,Set,Go!

PageMaker has set the standard for page-makeup software on the Mac (and the Mac has set the standard for other machines). Version 1.2 fixed most of the bugs in earlier versions and has become far and away the most popular product in the field. But the program is still fairly clumsy and slow, and it still crashes if you try to do more than minimal editing in poured text.

We used version 3.0 of Ready,Set,Go! to lay out this book and found it to be a lifesaver. Although it has many defects— no Undo command (there's one shown on the Edit menu but it's always dimmed), a nonstandard scroll bar, no style sheets, not enough keyboard commands and a thoroughly deranged method of dealing with tabs—it's still head-and-shoulders above anything else available.

very good feature

Ready,Set,Go! 3.0 lets you view your work in six different sizes, from facing pages to 200%. You can edit in every view except facing pages. The program is very intuitive and easy-to-use; in fact, we were able to design virtually this whole book with it before we received the manual. Ready,Set,Go! is also amazingly rock-solid for an early release; we really put it through its paces, and did a *lot* of editing in it, and it never crashed once.

The program's publisher, Manhattan Graphics, couldn't have offered better support. When we called them with questions and problems, we didn't identify ourselves as reviewers, but we still received the promptest, friendliest, most helpful support we've ever gotten.

By the time you read this, PageMaker may have come out with its new version, 2.0, which we'll review in a future update; it should be a marked improvement over version1.2. Even 1.2 is a useful tool for newsletters, ads and other complex designs. But for books and other relatively simple designs—at this point in time—Ready,Set,Go! has no peer.

¢ integrated software

The three kinds of applications most commonly used on personal computers are word processors, databases, and spreadsheets. Programs that combine two or more of them (along with graphing programs, communications software or whatever) are called integrated software.

The most popular software product of all time, Lotus 1-2-3, is an integrated program, combining spreadsheet, database and graphing. But its success is mainly due to its powerful spreadsheet, and only peripherally—if at all—to its rather weak chart program and its even weaker filer.

The only integrated package whose success is due mainly to its integration, rather than to the strength of one of the programs integrated into it, is AppleWorks, which runs on the lowly Apple II.

¢ integrated software on the Mac

Of the three basic programs—word processor, spreadsheet, database—the word processor is by far the most often used. So when Apple introduced the Mac, they made sure to bundle a word processor (MacWrite) with the system. Soon after Microsoft introduced a spreadsheet (Multiplan) and a graphing program (Chart), and many other third parties then jumped in with databases, communications software and so on.

Because of the de facto integration between programs that the Mac's standard interface provides—which was greatly enhanced by Andy Hertzfeld's Switcher—it isn't clear that integrated software is needed on the Mac (other than spreadsheets that graph your data and other mini-integrations like that). But publishers keep trying, hoping for that big 1-2-3 jackpot.

⚫ *Jazz*

The first major attempt to market a full-scale integrated program for the Mac, Lotus' Jazz, was a complete failure. There are several possible reasons for that. Jazz was expensive (originally $600, now $400) and heavily copy-protected, and it required both 400K drives to just run the program (which left little room for data without extensive disk-swapping).

But perhaps the most important reason for Jazz's failure was that the individual modules were weak. The word processor was actually less powerful than MacWrite, and there were no macros (and this from a company made rich and famous by macros). Mac owners stayed away in droves, preferring to integrate more powerful individual programs through the Clipboard and Switcher.

⚫ *Microsoft Works*

This is Microsoft's attempt to emulate the success of AppleWorks. For $300 you get a word processor, a spreadsheet, a graphing program, a database and a communications program. These individual applications are not as powerful as the most powerful individual applications available, but neither are they crippled, and they work well together.

The spreadsheet is in many respects more powerful than Multiplan. For example, you can sort on up to three levels (Multiplan only lets you sort on one) and it gives you a graphing capability that's adequate for many purposes. But it does lack the powerful macros found in Excel, and you can't link worksheets.

The database is very much like Microsoft File, and also more powerful than it in many ways. It's certainly faster, since all of your data is kept in RAM. Report generation is significantly less flexible than in File, but it's easy to transfer a report to the word processing module for further modification. This isn't a powerful relational database, so if you need to create a multiuser inventory system for a chain of auto parts stores (say), forget about trying to do it with Works.

Although the word processor is graceful, flexible and more powerful than MacWrite, it lacks many of the features of Word 1.05. One area where it really shines is in mixing graphics and text. You can run text on either side of a picture, on both sides of it, or even right on top of it.

The communications module lacks many of the bells and whistles found in Red Ryder or MicroPhone (for example, you can't write scripts), but the critical parts are all there, including the ability to do Xmodem file transfers. And it can do something even those powerful programs can't:

You can begin a long file transfer, then change to another window and continue working while the transfer goes on in the background. The transfer is slowed when you're working in the other window, but being able to continue using your Mac at all while it's doing a file transfer is a great bonus.

Even if you need a more powerful application than the Works module in one particular area, the program may still be adequate for your other needs. For example, if you're a writer, you'll probably want to use Word 3.0 or some other powerful word processor. But your database, spreadsheet and communications needs may be quite moderate, and Works may do fine in these areas. If so, it will probably be cheaper than buying three separate programs (although not necessarily so).

very
hot
tip

Works' spreadsheet data can be shared with Excel and Multiplan, and Word 3.0 and PageMaker 2.0 will accept formatted documents from Works' writing module.

Works is a good program for beginning Mac users and for any user who doesn't need a lot of power. With the money you save buying Works instead of a bunch of stand-alone applications, you can start saving up for a good SCSI hard disk.

Games

⁕ *Flight Simulator*

very good feature

For years Flight Simulator has been the most successful simulation program on MS-DOS machines, and the Mac version was eagerly awaited. It was worth the wait. The graphics are much superior to the MS-DOS version and the sound effects are startlingly realistic. You have the choice of a Lear jet or a light propeller plane, and there's a large selection of airports to take off from.

Flying around an area you're familiar with can really be a kick. We know people who've crashed hundreds of times before successfully flying under the Golden Gate Bridge, which the manual says is impossible.

Our only complaint about Flight Simulator is the way Microsoft chose to implement the menus. It's the only Mac product we've seen that doesn't use the standard menu routines that are built into the Mac ROMs. Instead, they programmed them from scratch. In addition to appearing in a different font, they aren't as responsive as normal Mac menus. Why did they do this? Probably to make it easier to convert the program to run on the Amiga and the Atari ST.

The nonstandard menus are annoying, but they don't really interfere with your enjoyment of the game unless your aesthetic sense—or your loyalty to the standard Mac interface—is stronger than average.

♥ *Fokker Triplane*

Fokker Triplane (Bullseye Software) is another flight-simulation game, but in this case you're flying a classic World War I fighter. This game requires much more aeronautical skill than Flight Simulator, but we've heard people with real airplane licenses say that this is the closest you can come to flying without leaving home. The sound and graphics are excellent.

very good feature

♥ *One-on-One*

Like Flight Simulator, Electronic Arts' One-on-One has been available for some time on other computers, but the graphics and sound capabilities of the Mac are really used to good advantage in this version. You play a basketball one-on-one against either Julius Erving or Larry Bird in front of a cheering crowd.

very good feature

If you're sure that only your height stopped you from being another Dr. J, you won't want to miss this classic.

♥ *MacGolf*

MacGolf, from Practical Computer Applications, is another sports simulation game that makes good use of the Mac's graphics and sound capabilities. (The splash as the ball hits the water will bring back memories to more than a few players.)

very good feature

To win at MacGolf you need to figure out which club to use, keep an eye on the weather conditions and remember the peculiarities of each hole. Like golf itself, MacGolf can be slow at times (in this case because it's redrawing the elaborate scenery) but you can use the time to plot your next move. We've seen people who never play golf spend hours on MacGolf's fairways and greens.

⬢ *Smash Hit Racquetball*

bargain

Some action-game connoisseurs really like Primera Software's Smash Hit Racquetball. It provides 273 frames of animation and some very realistic digitized sounds. Even better, it costs only $15 and comes with a ten-day unconditional money-back guarantee.

⬢ *Deja Vu*

Playing Mindscape's Deja Vu is one of the most intriguing and entertaining things we've ever done on a computer, and that's partially because the user interface is so great. With most adventure games you're limited to using simple commands like "pick up rock" (which half the time the program doesn't even understand), and its remarks to you are usually equally exciting ("you can't go that way").

very good
feature

Deja Vu puts you in a much more real world. The graphics are stunning, and the Mac interface is faithfully followed. If you want to examine an object, you just double-click on it; if you want to take something with you, you simply drag it into your personal inventory. In fact, you can play the entire game without using the keyboard, except when you want to speak to another character.

The premise of the game is also quite interesting. You awake, drugged, in a dingy toilet stall in a seedy bar, sometime in the 1940's. Your memory is gone, but you gradually surmise that you've being framed for a murder. You have to discover who actually committed the crime before you're killed or the police find you.

One of the things we like best about the game is how logical and believable it is. Characters and events seem to take on a life of their own. When several friends of ours were playing Deja Vu at the same time we were, we could often be overheard saying things in public like: *John was just standing around in the bar last night when the police came in and arrested him.*, or *Of course! I never thought of tipping the cab driver!* or *The only way you can keep the hooker from shooting you is to hit her.* This is how reputations are ruined.

very good
feature

Here's a Deja Vu tip for you: if you find yourself with some object that you want to dispose of permanently, look below street level for a place to put it.

Uninvited

This is the second adventure game from MindScape, the creators of Deja Vu, and it's set in the present day rather than the 1940's. You awaken to find yourself in your crashed car, with your younger brother missing. You have to find him in a seemingly deserted house.

MindScape somehow managed to make Uninvited even more realistic than Deja Vu. The interface is the same, but this time they've added limited animation and some truly eerie sound effects.

very good
feature

As with Deja Vu, things make sense. Sometimes you might have to set the game aside for a day or two to let your subconscious mull things over, but the solution to every dilemma can be deduced. You never have to do something illogical, the way you do with some other adventure games.

very good
feature

Uninvited is a lot more difficult to solve than Deja Vu, so here's a tip for you: when you run into the deadly ghost in the hallway, go upstairs immediately and look around for something you might be able to use the next time the two of you meet.

● *Balance of Power*

very good
feature

Balance of Power is one of the most thought-provoking games on any computer. The subject is geopolitics and the object is to prevent a thermonuclear war (while gaining as much prestige as possible).

Like Chess, there are just two sides, and like chess, games tend to last for hours and require extraordinary skill and concentration. You play either as the President of the United States or as Premier of the Soviet Union. Just as in real geopolitics, things quickly become very complicated. No action you might take is all good or all bad, totally productive or totally counterproductive.

Balance of Power requires a lot of preparation before the playing actually begins. This is one game where reading the manual is an absolute requirement. After you understand the economic, diplomatic, and military tools available, you have to examine the current status of each country and determine how best to draw it into your sphere of influence without provoking your opponent to war.

● *Klondike*

very good
feature

Klondike is an excellent Mac adaptation of the popular card game by the same name. If you know how to play it, you can start immediately, but the Mac version adds some new twists. In addition to keeping score for you, it times you, and the faster you play, the more points you accumulate. Another twist is that there's no way to cheat, except for the option of peeking to see where the aces are hidden.

bargain

Klondike is a shareware product published by Computer Capabilities Corp. A donation of $10 is requested, and it's available on many bulletin boards. But we have to warn you: If you value your productivity, do *not* acquire this game.

If you do buy it, don't keep its icon out on the Desktop of your hard disk (the way Dale does), where it beckons you for just one quick game every time you're between applications. The truth is, there's no such thing as "one quick game" of Klondike. Either the luck of the draw is so bad that you have to try just one more hand, or you do so well that you choose the New Game option just to see if you can repeat your last success.

important warning

There are few things you can do to rehabilitate yourself if you wake up one morning and realize that you've developed a serious Klondike dependency. Some major cities have chapters of KAA, Klondike Addicts Anonymous, but this is no trivial addiction like heroin, tobacco or alcohol. The only real cure for it is to destroy all copies of the game. Don't even dream of keeping one last copy in the attic or the trunk of your car.

The cold-turkey approach is rough, but it works. Whenever you're overcome with the urge to call up a bulletin board and get a copy for a quick fix, pull out a picture of your family—or maybe a copy of your mortgage—to help you overcome temptation. Just say no.

Drawing copyright © 1986 by Esther Travis.

Appendixes

Appendix A

Glossary of basic Mac terms

active window

The currently selected window, where the next action will take place (unless the next action is to select another window). The active window is always on top of all other windows, and its title bar is highlighted (that is, there are six parallel horizontal lines on either side of the title).

Alarm Clock

A desk accessory that lets you set the time and date on your Mac, and will also sound an alarm at a given time (if the Mac is on at that time).

algorithm

The precise sequence of steps required to do something. The first step in programming is figuring out the algorithm. *Both programs do the same thing, but because they use different algorithms, the second one is much faster.*

Apple (⌘) menu

A menu available both on the Desktop and from within virtually all applications; its title is an ⌘ at the far left end of the menu bar. The ⌘ menu gives you access to the installed desk accessories, information about the current application, and sometimes help screens.

application program (or application)

The software you use to create and modify documents. Some common types of applications are word processors, spreadsheets, databases, graphics programs, page-makeup software and communications programs.

arrow pointer

The basic shape the pointer takes—a left-leaning arrow.

BBS

An abbreviation for *bulletin board system*.

bomb

A message box with a picture of a bomb in its upper left corner. It appears unbidden on the screen to let you know that a serious problem has occurred with the system software. Bombs usually force you to restart the system. Compare *crash* and *hang*.

box

An enclosed area on the Mac's screen which resembles a window but lacks a title bar. Because it has no title bar, you can't move it. A dialog box and a message box are two examples.

bulletin board (or **bulletin board system**)

A computer dedicated to maintaining a list of messages and making them available over phone lines at no charge. People upload (contribute) and download (gather) messages by calling the bulletin board with their own computer.

button

On the Mac's screen, an outlined area in a dialog box that you click on to choose, confirm or cancel a command. For example, when you quit from most applications, you get a dialog box that asks if you want to save the current document, and it gives you three buttons to choose from: Yes, No and Cancel. *Button* is also used to refer to the switch on top of the mouse you use for clicking. When there's a danger of confusion, it's called the *mouse button*.

Calculator

A desk accessory that simulates a simple calculator. You can Cut, Copy and Paste to and from it.

Cancel button

A button that sometimes appears in a dialog box, giving you the choice of cancelling the command that generated the dialog box.

check box

A small box or circle in a dialog box used for turning options on and off. When you click on an empty check box, an X appears inside it, turning the option on. When you click on a check box with an X in it, the X disappears and the option is turned off.

Chooser

A desk accessory used to tell the Mac which printer you want to use, and what port it's connected to.

clicking

Pressing and immediately releasing the mouse button. To *click on* something is to position the pointer on it and then click. *A* click is the action of clicking.

Clipboard

The area of the Mac's memory that holds what you last Cut or Copied. Pasting inserts the contents of the Clipboard into a document.

closing

On the Desktop, closing a window means collapsing it back into an icon. Within an application, closing a document means terminating your work on it without exiting the application.

close box

A small box at the left end of the active window's title bar. Clicking on it closes the window.

command

The generic name for anything you tell a computer program to do. On the Mac, commands are usually listed on menus, or are generated by holding down the COMMAND key while hitting one or more other keys. To choose a command from a menu, you drag down the menu until the command you want is highlighted, then release the mouse button.

COMMAND key

The key on the Mac's keyboard that bears the ⌘ symbol. When held down while other keys are struck, the COMMAND key generates commands. For example, COMMAND-1 ejects the disk in the internal drive.

commercial

Said of computer products which are sold for profit through normal distribution channels, with the purchaser paying before taking possession of the product. Compare *shareware* and *public-domain*.

Control Panel

A desk accessory that allows you to set things like how loud the beeps (and other sounds the Mac makes) are, how fast the insertion point blinks, how fast you have to click in succession for the Mac to recognize it as a double-click, and so on.

Copying

Duplicating something from a document and placing the duplicate in the Clipboard. To do that, you select what you want to copy and then choose Copy from the Edit menu (or hit COMMAND-C).

crash

A noun and verb which mean that your system has suddenly stopped working, or is working wrong. You normally have to restart. (A crash is like a bomb, except you don't get a message. Also see *hang*.))

Cutting

Removing something from a document by selecting it and then choosing Cut from the Edit menu (or hitting COMMAND-X). What you Cut is placed in the Clipboard.

DA

An abbreviation for *desk accessory*.

default

What you get if you don't specify something different. Often used to refer to default settings (for example, margins in a word processing program, or Speaker Volume on the Control Panel).

desk accessories

Programs that are always available from the menu, regardless of the application you're using.

Desktop

Apple's official definition for this term is: "Macintosh's working environment—the menu bar and the gray area on the screen." But in common usage, it refers only to the Finder's desktop—that is, what the Mac's screen displays when no applications are open. One sure way to tell if you're on the Desktop (in this second, popular sense of the word) is to look for the Trash in the lower right corner.

dialog box

A box on the screen requesting information, or a decision, from you. In some boxes, the only possible response is to click on the OK button. Since this hardly constitutes a dialog, we call these messages, or message boxes, even though Apple calls them dialog boxes.

dimmed objects

Objects are dimmed (gray) on the Mac's screen to show that they aren't currently accessible. For example, commands you can't choose (in a given context) appear dimmed on the menu. When you eject a disk, its icon is dimmed, as are all windows and icons associated with it.

directory

The contents of a disk or folder, arranged by icon, size, date, type, etc.

disk

A round platter with a coating similar to that on recording tape, on which computer information is stored in the form of magnetic impulses. Although the disk itself is always circular, the case it comes in is usually rectangular. The two main types are floppy disks and hard disks.

disk drive

A device that reads information from, and writes information onto, disks. The Mac has one internal drive for floppy disks and can be hooked up to a second (optional) external floppy drive. Many hard disk drives are available for it.

document

What you create and modify with an application—a collection of information on a disk or in memory, grouped together and called by one name. Some examples are a letter, a drawing and a mailing list.

dots per inch

A measure of screen and printer resolution; the number of dots in a line one inch long. Abbreviated *dpi*.

dots per square inch

A measure of screen and printer resolution; the number of dots in a solid square one inch on a side. Abbreviated *dpsi* or dpi^2.

double-clicking

Positioning the pointer and then quickly pressing and releasing the mouse button twice without moving the mouse. Double-clicking is used to open applications and documents (when the pointer is an arrow) and to select whole words (when the pointer is an I-beam).

downloading

Retrieving information from a distant computer and storing it on your own. Opposite of *uploading*.

dpi

An abbreviation for *dots per inch*.

dpsi, dpi²

Abbreviations for *dots per square inch*.

dragging

Placing the pointer, holding down the mouse button, moving the mouse and then releasing the button. If you place the pointer on an object, dragging moves the object. If you place the pointer where there is no object, dragging generates the *selection rectangle*. If you place the pointer on a menu title, dragging moves you down the menu (and if you release the button when a command is highlighted, chooses the command).

Edit menu

On the Desktop and in most applications, the third menu from the left. It typically contains commands for Cutting, Copying, Pasting, Undoing.

ENTER key

A key on the Mac's keyboard that doesn't generate a character and is used for different purposes by various applications. In dialog boxes and on the Desktop, the RETURN key usually has the same effect as the ENTER key.

FatBits

In MacPaint and several other applications, a feature that lets you edit graphics in a magnified view, dot by dot.

file

A collection of information on a disk, usually either a document or an application. (Although the information is almost always related, it doesn't actually have to be; what makes it a file is simply that it's lumped together and called by one name.)

File menu

On the Desktop and in virtually all applications, the

second menu from the left. Within applications it contains commands for opening, saving, printing and closing documents, quitting the application and so on. On the Desktop it contains commands for opening and closing windows, duplicating icons, ejecting disks and so on.

Finder

The basic program that generates the Desktop and within which all applications run. Together with the System file, it comprises what—on other computers—is called the operating system.

floppy disk

A removable disk that's flexible (although the case in which the actual magnetic medium is housed may be hard, as it is on the 3–1/2" floppies used by the Mac). See *disk* for more details.

folder

A grouping of documents, applications and other folders that's represented by a folder-shaped icon on the Desktop. Equivalent to a subdirectory on MS-DOS machines.

font

A collection of letters, numbers, punctuation marks and symbols with an identifiable and consistent look; a Macintosh typeface in all its sizes and styles.

Font/DA Mover

A utility program used for installing, removing and moving fonts and desk accessories.

footer

A piece of text automatically printed at the bottom of several pages (although the text may vary from page to page—as it would if it contained page numbers, for example).

Get Info window

The window that appears when you choose Get Info from the File menu (or hit COMMAND-I). It tells you the size of the file, folder or disk, where it resides, and when it was created and last modified. There's also a space for entering comments and, in the case of a file or a disk, a box for locking and unlocking it.

hang

A condition where the Mac ignores input from the mouse and the keyboard, usually requiring you to restart the system. Compare *bomb* and *crash*.

hard disk

A fixed, rigid, usually nonremovable disk and the disk drive that houses it. Hard disks stores a lot of data (generally 20MB or more) and access it very quickly. See *disk* for more details.

hardware

The physical components of a computer system.

header

A piece of text automatically printed at the top of several pages (although the text may vary from page to page—as it would if it contained page numbers, for example).

HFS

A multilevel method of organizing applications, documents and folders on a Mac disk in which folders can be nested (contained) in other folders. Now standard on the Mac. Shorthand for *hierarchical file system*. Compare *MFS*.

hierarchical file system

See *HFS*.

highlighting

Making something stand out from its background in order to show that it's selected, chosen or active. On the Mac, highlighting is usually achieved by reversing—that is, by substituting black for white and vice versa.

I-beam

The shape the pointer normally takes when it's dealing with text.

icon

A graphic representation, usually of a file, a folder or a disk.

ImageWriter

A dot-matrix printer manufactured by Apple that's the standard one used with the Mac. There have been two models: the original Imagewriter (that's not a typo; the *w* wasn't capped) and the ImageWriter II.

ImageWriter font

A bit-mapped font used on the Mac's screen and for printing on the ImageWriter. Compare *laser font* and *screen font*.

information service

A large commercial timesharing computer that gives users access to a wide variety of information. CompuServe, GEnie and The Source are three examples.

initialize

To prepare a disk for use on the Macintosh. If it contains information, initializing will remove it. Disks can be initialized again and again.

insertion point

The place in a document where the next keystroke will add or delete text. The insertion point is represented by a blinking vertical line and is placed by clicking with the I-beam.

K

A measure of computer memory, disk space and the like that's equal to 1024 characters, or about 170 words. Short for *kilobyte*. Compare *meg*.

LAN

Abbreviation for *local area network*.

laser font

A font composed of instructions in the PostScript programming language, used for printing on the LaserWriter and other PostScript-compatible printers and typesetters. Compare *ImageWriter font* and *screen font*.

LaserWriter

A laser printer manufactured by Apple that optimizes many of the Mac's capabilities.

launching

Opening an application.

leading (LEHD-ing)

The amount of space from one line of type to the next. Usually measured in points.

list box

A box with scroll bars that appears within a dialog box or a window and lists things—files, fonts or whatever. The Open... and Save As... dialog boxes contain list boxes, as does the Font/DA Mover window.

local area network

A network of computer equipment confined to a relatively small area—like one office or one building—and usually connected by dedicated lines, rather than by regular telephone lines. Abbreviated *LAN*.

locking

Preventing a file or disk from being changed (until you unlock it). To lock a file, you use the Get Info window. To lock a floppy disk, you move the plastic tab so that you can see through the small hole. On a disk, another name for "locked" is "write-protected."

Macintosh File System
See *MFS*.

macro
A command that incorporates two or more other commands.

MB
Abbreviation for *megabyte*.

meg, megabyte
A measure of computer memory, disk space and the like that's equal to 1024K (1,048,576 characters), or about 175,000 words. Sometimes people try to make a meg equal to an even million characters, usually for sleazeball marketing purposes.

memory
Integrated circuits (chips) that store information electronically. There are two main types: RAM and ROM. RAM is used for the short-term retention of information (that is, until the power is turned off), and ROM is used to store programs that are seldom if ever changed. The original Macintosh had 128K of RAM and 64K 'of ROM; the Mac Plus has 1024K of RAM and 128K of ROM; and the LaserWriter has 1536K of RAM and 512K of ROM.

menu
A list of commands that pops down when you point to a menu title and then hold down the mouse button. Dragging down the menu highlights each command in turn (except the dimmed ones).

menu bar
The horizontal area across the top of the screen that contains the menu titles.

menu title

Both the name by which a menu is called and the way you access it. Menu titles are arranged across the top of the screen in the menu bar; when you point to one and hold down the mouse button, the menu pops down.

message box

A box that appears unbidden on the screen to give you some information, and which doesn't require any information back from you. A *bomb* is one example.

MFS

A single-level method of organizing files and folders on a Mac disk in which folders can't be nested (contained) in other folders. Originally standard on the Mac, it's been superseded by *HFS*. The name is shorthand for *Macintosh file system*.

modem (MOE-dum)

A device that lets computers talk to each other over phone lines (you also need a communications program). The name is short for *mo*dulator-*demo*dulator.

monospaced

Said of fonts where all the characters occupy the same amount of horizontal space. One such font on the Mac is Monaco. Compare *proportionally spaced*.

128K ROMs

A set of ROMs introduced in early 1986 that contain updated system information for the Mac (for example, HFS is built into them). The 128K ROMs are standard on the Mac Plus and the Enhanced 512K Mac, and are available as an upgrade for earlier machines. Compare *64K ROMs*.

opening

Expanding an icon, or a name in a list box, to a window. With disk icons and folders, this happens on the Desktop. With document icons, the application that created the icon is launched first, then the document is opened within it.

parameter RAM

A small portion of the Mac's RAM that's used to store Control Panel settings and other basic, ongoing information. It's powered by a battery so the settings aren't lost when the computer is turned off (but they are lost if you pull the battery).

Pasting

Inserting something into a document from the Clipboard by choosing Paste from the Edit menu (or hitting COMMAND-V).

pica

A typesetting measure equal (for all practical purposes) to 1/6 of an inch.

point

A typesetting measure equal (for all practical purposes) to 1/72 of an inch. The size of fonts is typically measured in points.

pointer

What moves on the screen when you move the mouse. Its most common shapes are the arrow, the I-beam and the wristwatch.

pop down

What the Mac's menus actually do. Compare *pull down*.

port

Computerese for a jack where you connect the cables that connect computers and other devices together. The Mac has two serial ports on the back (printer and modem), a floppy disk port, etc.

PostScript

A page-description programming language developed by Adobe, specifically designed to handle text and graphics and their placement on a page. Used in the LaserWriter and other printers and typesetters.

print buffer

A hardware device that intercepts a print file on its way to the printer and reroutes it to the buffer's own memory, where it's held until the printer is ready for it. This allows you to continue working on other things while the printing takes place.

printer driver

A file that tells the Mac how to send information to a particular kind of printer.

print spooler

A piece of software that intercepts a print file on its way to the printer and reroutes it to the disk, where it's held until the printer is ready for it. This allows you to continue working on other things while the printing takes place.

program

A group of instructions that tells a computer what to do. Also called *software*.

programmer's switch

A small piece of plastic that, when inserted in the vents on the left side of the Mac, allows you to restart the system (using its reset button) or access debugging software (using its interrupt button).

proportionally spaced

Said of fonts whose characters occupy different amounts of horizontal space, depending on their size. Proportional spacing makes fonts much easier to read. Virtually all Macintosh fonts are proportionally spaced. Compare *monospaced*.

public-domain

Said of products you have the right to copy, use, give away and sell, without having to pay any money for the right. Things come into the public domain either because the copyright on them has expired or—as is the case with computer programs—because the copyright holder (usually the author) puts them there. Compare *shareware* and *commercial*.

pull down

What most people—including Apple—say the Mac's menus do (but it's not true). Compare *pop down*.

quitting

Leaving an application and returning to the Finder (or substitute for it, like the MiniFinder).

RAM

The part of a computer's memory used for the short-term retention of information (in other words, until the power is turned off); programs and documents are stored in RAM while you're using them. The name is short for "random-access memory"—although, actually, just about all kinds of memory are accessed randomly these days. Also see *memory* and *parameter RAM*.

RAM cache

An area of memory set aside to hold information recently read in from disk—so that if the information is needed again, it can be gotten from memory, which is much faster than getting it from disk. The size of the Mac's RAM cache, and whether it's even turned on, is set on the Control Panel.

RETURN key

In text, it causes the insertion point to move to the beginning of the next line. Elsewhere it's often used to confirm an entry or a command.

ROM

The part of a computer's memory used to store programs which are seldom or never changed. The name is short for "read-only memory," because you can read information from it but can't write information to it the way you can with RAM. A ROM chip is often called simply a ROM. Also see *memory*.

sans serif

Said of a font that has no serifs.

saving

Transferring information—usually a document—from memory to a disk.

screen font

The bit-mapped representation of a laser font on the Mac's screen. Compare *laser font* and *screen font*.

Scrapbook

A desk accessory that stores frequently used material so you have easy access to it.

scrolling

Moving through the contents of a window or a list box in order to see things not currently displayed (normally done with the scroll bar). Scrolling is usually vertical, but horizontal scrolling is also possible.

scroll arrow

The arrow at either end of the scroll bar. Clicking on a scroll arrow moves the window's view up or down one line. Pointing to a scroll arrow and holding the mouse button down results in relatively smooth and continuous scrolling.

scroll bar

A rectangular bar that appears on the right and/or bottom edges of a window when there's more in it than what's displayed. Clicking in the gray area of the scroll bar moves the window's view up or down one screenful. Also see *scroll arrow* and *scroll box*.

scroll box

The white box in the scroll bar that indicates how what's displayed in a window relates to its total contents. Dragging the scroll box allows you to scroll large distances.

SCSI

An industry-standard interface for hard disks and other devices that allows for very fast transfer of information. It's short for "small computer system interface" and is pronounced 'scuzzy'. A SCSI port is standard on the Mac Plus.

selecting

Telling the Mac what you want to be affected by the next command or action. If what you're selecting is in the form of discrete objects, you normally select them by clicking on them. If it's in the form of a continuum, you normally select part of it by dragging across it.The single most important concept for understanding the Mac is: *You always have to select something before you can do anything to it.*

selection

Whatever is selected (and thus will be affected by the next command or action). The insertion point is also a kind of selection, because it indicates where the next event will take place (unless you move it).

selection rectangle

On the Desktop and in many applications, a dotted box that appears when you click on an empty spot and drag. When you release the mouse button, the box disappears and everything that fell within it is selected.

serif

A little hook, line or blob added, as decoration, onto the basic form of a character. Also used as an adjective to describe a font that has serifs. Compare *sans serif*.

shareware

Software that's distributed on the honor system, usually through bulletin boards, user groups, information services, etc. You're allowed to try it out and give copies to others, and you only pay the (usually nominal) registration fee if you decide you want to continue using it. Compare *commercial* and *public-domain*.

SHIFT key

Either of two keys on the Mac's keyboard that are used to make letters uppercase and for many other purposes (for example, see *shift-clicking*).

shift-clicking

Holding down the SHIFT key while clicking the mouse button. Shift-clicking allows you to select multiple objects or large amounts of text, depending on the application.

64K ROMs

The original set of ROMs used in the Mac. They were superseded by the 128K ROMs in early 1986.

size box

An icon consisting of two overlapping boxes, found in the bottom right corner of most windows, that allows you to change the window's size and shape.

software

The instructions that tell a computer what to do. Also called *programs*.

spooler

See *print spooler*.

startup disk

A disk containing the systems software the Mac needs to begin operation (i.e. the System file and the Finder).

style

A variation on a font, like **bold**, *italic*, outline, shadow and so on.

system bomb

See *bomb*.

system crash

See *crash*.

System file (or simply *the System*)

The basic program the Mac uses to start itself and to provide certain information—like what fonts are available—to all applications. The System file can't be launched like a regular application; instead, it launches itself when you start up the Mac and insert a disk that contains it. Together with the Finder, the System file comprises what—on other computers—is called the operating system.

System Folder

A standard folder on Mac disks that normally contains the System file, the Finder and other systems software.

system hang

See *hang*.

systems software

A catchall term for the basic programs that help computers work; it includes operating systems, programming languages, certain utilities and so on. Some examples of systems software on the Mac are the Finder, the System, the Clipboard, the Chooser, the Control Panel, the Font/DA Mover, and printer drivers like the ImageWriter, LaserWriter and Laser Prep files.

tab key

In text, the tab key moves the insertion point to the next tab stop. In dialog boxes, database files, spreadsheets and the like, it often moves the insertion point to the next area where information can be inserted (in other words, the next field, cell or whatever).

telecommunications

Transferring information between computers over telephone lines.

template

A document with a special format you use repeatedly. You modify it to the present use and save it with a different name.

title bar

The horizontal strip at the top of a window that includes the name and the close box, and tells you whether or not the window is active. To move a window, you grab it by the title bar.

uploading

Sending information to a distant computer from your own. Opposite of *downloading*.

user group (or users group)

A club made up of people who are interested in a particular kind of computer hardware or software. User groups are typically nonprofit and independent of any computer manufacturer or publisher.

utility

A program that performs a relatively simple task—like searching for a specific file on a disk, or counting all the words in a document. Unlike applications, utilities normally don't generate documents.

window

An enclosed area on the Mac's screen that has a title bar (which lets you move it around, and open and close it). Disks and folder icons open into windows, and documents appear in windows when you're working on them.

wristwatch

The shape the pointer takes when you have to wait for the Mac to do something (although some poorly written applications don't always implement this feature, or do so less than they should).

zoom box

On systems using the 128K ROMs, a small box on the right side of the title bar of most windows. Clicking on the zoom box expands the window to fill the screen; clicking again returns it to its original size and shape. (In many Microsoft products, you can do the same thing by simply double-clicking on the title bar.)

Appendix B

Where to find good information & cheap software

❤ magazines

Magazines devoted to the Mac come in many flavors, from slick productions published on the coasts to pulp periodicals from America's heartland. We've found the ones described below to be useful.

Macworld is the slickest of the lot; in fact, it's one of the prettiest magazines you're ever likely to see (unless you're a fan of European design magazines). *Macworld* is particularly strong on articles about broad trends in the market, and also has good product reviews. Since it boasts the largest circulation of any publication listed here, it's a good place to look for ads about new products.

Always a pleasure to read, *Macworld* has been getting even better, mostly by improving the amount of useful, nitty-gritty information it provides.

The other main Mac magazine is *MacUser*; its strengths are its irreverence, the great attention it pays to tips, and its lists. Two of the lists we find most useful are the one that tells you the most current version number of virtually every piece of Mac software that exists, and the cumulative list in the back of the magazine that capsulizes *MacUser*'s reviews of hundreds of products and rates them for you. Whenever we want to see what products are available in a particular area, we pull out the most recent issue and look on that list.

Each *MacUser* also contains a section of tips submitted by users, and usually at least one article full of useful tips on some aspect of an important product. Finally there's the Rumor Manager, which strikes us as being quite well-informed about future developments. The people at *MacUser* are excited about the Mac, and their enthusiasm shows.

very good
feature

The Macintosh Journal is sort of like Consumer Reports for the Mac. Each issue concentrates on a particular kind of product—databases, SCSI hard disks, spelling checkers or whatever—and tries to cover the field with a thoroughness that's absolutely breathtaking. When *The Macintosh Journal* covers an area, it's *covered*—at least until their conclusions get to be out-of-date.

The magazine doesn't accept advertising, and thus it doesn't hesitate to state flatly not only which products are better than the others but also which ones are simply no good at all. It provides extensive tables that show exactly how various products compare, and you can even send away for the templates they used for their benchmark tests, so you can run the tests yourself! We highly recommend *The Macintosh Journal*.

MACazine is an independent publication whose specialty is in-depth articles about products that often get passed over by the big guys. It's aimed at readers who are somewhat more sophisticated about the Mac than the average reader of *Macworld* or *MacUser*. After a rocky start, the design of *MACazine* has improved greatly over the past few months.

MacTutor is a journal for Macintosh programmers and hackers. These guys are so serious about content that (like *The Macintosh Journal*) they print their table of contents on the cover. If you want to keep up with the latest developments in the world of Mac programming, this is the place to look.

✦ *users groups*

Users groups are an excellent source of good information—which isn't surprising, since sharing information is their main purpose. Nowhere else are you likely to find so many dedicated people anxious to help you solve your problems, none of whom would dream of charging you a nickel for it.

Users groups meetings are usually open to the public and free. Joining the group normally costs somewhere between $25 and $40 a year and gives you access to the group's library of public domain and shareware software.

bargain

Large groups often feature guest speakers from the computer industry who describe new products at their meetings, and also have subgroups for members with particular interests or needs: beginners, developers, musicians, graphic artists, desktop publishers, and so on. The country's largest users group, the Boston Computer Society, has more than 40 of these special interest groups, each of which publishes a newsletter (in addition to BCS's own slick magazine).

Unless you live in a very remote area, finding a local users group shouldn't be hard—especially if there's a college or university nearby. One fast way to find one is to check with an Apple dealer. Any good dealer will know all the local users groups. If you can't find a group in your community, get together with some other Mac users and start one of your own.

The group we belong to and depend on as a source of information is the Berkeley Macintosh Users Group (BMUG), which has more than 3000 members. Membership is open to anyone and costs $40 a year; their "newsletter," published twice a year and running into the hundreds of 8-1/2 x 11 pages, is worth the price alone.

BMUG also maintains one of the most extensive public domain and shareware libraries anywhere; as of this writing, their disks contain more than *1500* separate files! While that's exceptional, virtually any users group will astound you with the quantity of stuff it has available.

To give you an idea of what a large users group meeting is like, we'll describe BMUG's, which is held on the University of California campus every Thursday evening. About 300–400 people come to a typical meeting, and their knowledge of the Mac varies from extensive to very limited (although there are many more of the former).

Before the meeting starts, people line up to buy disks and other items like modems that the group sells to members at fantastically low prices. The meetings begin with an open session where people can ask any question they have about any aspect of the Mac, and usually get a definitive answer from someone in the room. When the question-and-answer session is over, one or two guest speakers describe their products (using a Mac that projects onto a giant screen).

Because BMUG is so large, and so close to Silicon Valley, it's able to attract representatives of just about every major software publisher and hardware manufacturer, as well as local freelance talent like the ebullient Andy Hertzfeld (who wrote Switcher, Servant and the software that runs on ThunderScan and the Radius FPD). We vividly remember the night Hertzfeld debuted Switcher at BMUG. When the display on the big screen shot from the application in the first partition to the one in the second, the entire audience leapt to its feet and cheered.

🍎 *bulletin boards*

An electronic bulletin board (commonly abbreviated BBS for "bulletin board system") is another good place to tap into the latest rumor mill or get a problem solved. All you need is a modem, communications software, access to a phone line and a little bit of experience.

Bulletin boards are a lot like electronic users groups: you'll find plenty of people there who are willing and able to answer your questions. Most good bulletin boards also have the latest versions of public-domain and shareware software available for downloading. And for all they provide, they don't charge a penny.

bargain

A complete list of every active Mac BBS in the country would take up many pages of this book and would probably be out of date by the time you read it. So we've just listed a few that we have personal experience with. They're among the best in the country and they've all been around for a long time, so they should still be active when you read this. All of them maintain extensive lists of other bulletin boards which they update frequently.

<u>name</u> <u>sponsor, location</u>	<u>phone</u>
BMUG BMUG, Berkeley CA	415/849-2684
Mac Boston Steve Garfield, Boston MA	617/262-9167
Mac Circles Pat O'Connor, Pleasanton CA	415/484-4412
MacQueue #1 Léo LaPorte, San Francisco CA	415/661-7374
MacQueue #2 Léo LaPorte, San Francisco CA	415/753-3002
RR Red Scott Watson, St. Louis MO	314/428-8057

very
hot
tip

🍎 *Information services*

A final source for good information and cheap software are commercial information services like CompuServe, GEnie and The Source. There are two drawbacks to using them; they charge you for each minute you're connected to them, and they present you with a bewildering series of menus that can be frustrating for first-time users (and for many experienced users as well).

Most large information services have Mac special interest groups, which amount to bulletin boards with an area for messages (and for conferences on various subjects) and another area that contains public-domain and shareware software you can download.

The major benefit of using a commercial information service rather than a bulletin board system is that you'll never get a busy signal. If you need some information or a new utility right away, you'll appreciate not having to dial repeatedly just to log on. There are many commercial information services available, but we've found CompuServe and GEnie to be particularly good sources for Mac-related information and software.

CompuServe is an extremely popular service, though its rates are higher than some others. To register, you need to purchase a CompuServe Starter Kit (available at most computer and software dealers for $40). The kit includes a list of available phone numbers, a login code, and instructions for signing up. You'll also need a major credit card for billing. The hourly connect charge during nonprime time (prime time being 8 am to 6 pm Monday through Friday) is $6.25 at 300 baud and $12 at 1200 baud.

bargain

GEnie is the new kid on the block, but you'll find most of the same Mac information on it that you find on CompuServe. And its charges are substantially lower—$5 per hour for both 300 and 1200 baud during nonprime time, plus a one-time registration fee of just $18.

To register, set your modem to "half duplex" (sometimes called "local echo") and dial 800/638-8369 with your credit card in hand. After the connection is made, type **HHH**. You'll get a prompt that reads: **U#**. Type in **5JM11985,Genie** and RETURN. They'll take it from there.

List of products & companies

Abaton Technology Corp.
Suite 500, 7901 Stoneridge Dr.
Pleasanton CA 94566
415/463-8822
   Abaton Scan 300 ($2500)

Acta
$60; Symmetry

Adobe Systems, Inc.
Suite 100, 1870 Embarcadero Rd.
Palo Alto CA 94303
415/852-0271
   laser fonts (Benguiat, Optima, Zapf
     Chancery, etc.)
   PostScript

Affinity Micro Systems
1050 Walnut St.
Boulder CO 80302
800/255-5550, x425
   Tempo

Alderman, Eric (computer consultant)
4798 Geranium Pl.
Oakland CA 94619
415/530-8533

Aldus Corp.
411 First Ave. South
Seattle WA 98104
   PageMaker

Allgood, Edith (graphic designer)
801 Miramar Ave
Berkeley CA 94707
415/527-1731

Ann Arbor Softworks
Suite 106, 2393 Teller Rd.
Newbury Park CA 91320
818/769-8615
   FullPaint

Apple Computer, Inc.
20424 Mariani Ave.
Cupertino CA 95014
408/996-1010
   ImageWriter
   laser fonts (Times, Helvetica, Courier,
     Symbol)
   LaserWriter
   MacDraw
   Macintosh, Macintosh Plus, Macintosh XL
   Macintosh 68000 Development System
   MacPaint
   MacTerminal
   MacWrite
   Switcher

Ashton-Tate
20101 Hamilton Ave.
Torrence CA 90502
213/204-5570
   dBASE MAC

Aztec C
$200; Manx Software Systems

Balance of Power
$55; Mindscape

Batteries Included
30 Mural Street
Richmond Hill, Ontario
L4B 1B5 Canada
800/387-6707
 BatteryPak

BatteryPak
$50; Batteries Included

BCS
see Boston Computer Society

Becker, Loftus E., Jr
41 Whitney St.
Hartford CT 06105
 Other...

Belec, Chris (computer consultant)
#102, 138 Monte Cresta Ave.
Oakland CA 94611
415/658-7540

Benguiat (font)
 $185; Adobe

Berkeley Macintosh Users Group
Suite 62, 1442A Walnut St.
Berkeley CA 94709

Blyth Software Corp.
2655 Campus Dr.
San Mateo CA 94403
415/571-0222
 Omnis 3

BMUG
see Berkeley Macintosh Users Group

Bonsu Corp.
1360 Bordeaux Dr.
Sunnyvale CA 94089
408/747-4400
 MacGrid

Borderline (font)
(included on Fluent Fonts disks); Casady Co.

Borland International
4585 Scotts Valley Dr.
Scotts Valley CA 95066
408/438-8400
 Reflex for the Mac

SideKick
ClickOn Worksheet (new name?)

Boston Computer Society
One Center Plaza
Boston MA 02108

Bravo Technologies
c/o DPAS, Box T
Gilroy CA 95021
800/345-2888
 MacCalc

Bullseye Software
P.O. Drawer 7900
Incline Village NV 89450
 Fokker Triplane

Business Filevision
$400; Telos Software

Cairo (font)
(comes with the Mac); Apple Computer

Calculator Construction Set
$80; Dubl-Click Software

Calligraphy (font)
$70; Casady Co.

Casady Co.
Box 223779
Carmel CA 93922
 Fluent Fonts

Centram Systems West
2560 Ninth St.
Berkeley CA 94710
800/222-8677 (CA: 800/445-8677)
 TOPS

Century Software
2306 Cotner Ave.
Los Angeles CA 90064
213/829-4436
 LaserFonts

Challenger Software
18350 Kedzie Ave.
Homewood IL 40430
 Mac3D 2.0

Champion Software
4201 South Hill Dr.
Madison WI 53705
  Spelling Champion

Chart
$125; Microsoft

Chesley, Harry R.
1850 Union St.
San Francisco CA 94123
  Packit III

Chicago (font)
(comes with the Mac); Apple Computer

Chubby Shadow (font)
(included on Fluent Fonts disks); Casady Co.

Clement, Gerald (Macintosh artist)
Diablo Valley Design
7138 Shelter Creek Lane
San Bruno CA 94066
415/589-8806

ClickOn Worksheet
$80; T/Maker Company (*new owner:*
Borland)

Coleman, Dale (computer consultant)
#4, 35 Alpine Terrace
San Francisco CA 94117
415/863-4620

Color Print
$50; Esoft Enterprise

CompuServe
5000 Arlington Centre Blvd.
Columbus OH 43220
800/848-8199 (OH: 614/457-0802)
  ($40 + hourly rates)

Computer Capabilities Corp.
465-A Fairchild Dr.
Mountain View CA 94043
415/968-7511
  Klondike

Computer Cover Co.
Box 3080
Laguna Hills CA 92654

800/235-5330 (CA: 714/380-0885)
  computer covers

Cortland Computer
Box 9916
Berkeley CA 94709
  Top Desk

Courier (font)
(comes with the LaserWriter); Apple
Computer

Creighton Development
16 Huges
Irvine CA 92718
  Macspell+

DataFrame
$1100—$2000; SuperMac

DataPak
14011 Ventura Blvd.
Sherman Oaks CA 91423
  Liberty Spell Checker

dBASE MAC
Ashton-Tate

Deja Vu
$50; Mindscape

Dell'Aquila, Mei-Ying (Macintosh artist)
3450 Princeton Way
Santa Clara CA 95051
408/246-8875

DiskInfo
$10; Maitreya Design

dMac III
$500; Format Software

Double Helix
$500; Odesta

Dream (font)
(included on Fluent Fonts disks); Casady Co.

Dreams of the Phoenix
Box 10273
Jacksonville FL 32247
  Phoenix 3D
  Quick & Dirty Utilities, Vol. 1

Dubl-Click Software, Inc.
18201 Gresham St.
Horthridge CA 91325
818/349-2758
   World-Class Fonts, vols. 1 & 2
   Calculator Construction Set

Easy3D
Enabling Technologies

Enabling Technologies
600 South Dearborn
Chicago IL 60605
   Easy3D

Ergotron
5637 Woodlawn Blvd.
Minneapolis MN 55417
612/724-4952
   Mac Buffer
   MacTilt

Esoft Enterprises
Box 179
Owasso OK 74055
   ColorPrint

Excel
$400; Microsoft

Farallon Computing
#64, 1442A Walnut St.
Berkeley CA 94709
   PhoneNet

Fedit Plus
$40; MacMaster Systems

File
$200; Microsoft

FileMaker, Filemaker Plus
$200, $300; Forethought Software

Filevision
$200; Telos Software

Flight Simulator
$50; Microsoft

Fluent Fonts, Fluent Laser Fonts
$50, $70; Casady

Fokker Triplane
$60; Bullseye Software

Forethought Software
250 Sobrante Way
Sunnyvale CA 94086
800/622-9273
   FileMaker
   FileMaker Plus

Format Software
11770 Bernado Plaza Ct.
San Diego CA 92128
   dMac III

The FreeSoft Corp.
10828 Lacklink
St. Louis MO 63114
   Red Ryder

FullPaint
$100; Ann Arbor Softworks

General Computer Corp.
215 First St.
Cambridge MA 02142
617/492-5500
   HyperDrive

General Electric
voice: 800/638-9636
data: 800/638-8369
   GEnie Information Services

Geneva (font)
(comes with the Mac); Apple Computer

GEnie Information Services
$15 + hourly rates; General Electric

Glazer, Allen (printing consultant & broker)
846 Hillside Ave.
Albany CA 94706
415/549-2700

Greene, Johnson, Inc.
15 Via Chualar
Monterey CA 93940
408/375-2828
   Spellswell

Helix
$400; Odesta

Helvetica (font)
(comes with the LaserWriter); Apple
Computer

Hoffman, Paul (computer consultant)
#2024, 2140 Shattuck
Berkeley CA 94704
415/644-0433

HyperDrive
$1400—$1700; General Computer

Infosphere
4730 SW Macadam
Portland OR 97201
   MacServe

Innovative Data Design, Inc.
1975 Willow Pass Road
Concord CA 94520
415/680-6818
   MacDraft

International Typeface Corporation
2 Hammarskjold Plaza
New York NY 10017

ITC
see International Typeface Corporation
and/or name of particular font

Jazz
$400; Lotus

Just Text
$200; Knowledge Engineering

keyboard cables
12'–$10, 25'–$13; Your Affordable Software
Co.

Klatzkin, Dennis (computer consultant)
2263 Market St.
San Francisco CA 94114
415/552-0599

Klondike
$10; Computer Capabilities

Knowledge Engineering
G.P.O. 2139
New York NY 10116
   Just Text

LaPorte, Léo
MacQueue #1 (415/661-7374)
MacQueue #2 (415/753-3002)
   QDial
   Word Count

LaserFonts
$35–$45; Century Software

LaserSpool
MacAmerica

Liberty Spell Checker
$60; DataPak

Living Videotext
2432 Charleston Rd.
Mountain View CA 94043
415/964-5300
   More
   ThinkTank

Lotus Development Corp.
55 Cambridge Parkway
Cambridge MA 02142
   Jazz
   1-2-3

MacAmerica
18032-C Lemon Drive
Yorba Linda CA 92686
714/779-2922
   LaserSpool

MacBuffer
1 meg—$700; Ergotron

MacCalc
$140; Bravo Technologies

MacChimney
$15; Swain, Tom

MacDraft
$240; Innovative Data Design

MacDraw
$200; Apple Computer

MacGolf
$60; Practical Computer Applications

MacGrid
$40; Bonsu

Macintosh 68000 Development System
$200; Apple Computer

MacLightning
$100; Target Software

MacMaster Systems
939 East EL Camino Real
Sunnyvale CA 94087
408/773-9834
    Fedit Plus

MacMemory
473 Macara
Sunnyvale CA 94086
800/862-2636 (CA: 408/773-9922)
    MaxChill

MacPaint
$125; Apple Computer

Mac Pascal
$125; Apple Computer

MacServe
$250; Infosphere

Macspell+
$100; Creighton Development

MacTerminal
$100; Apple Computer

Mac3D 2.0
$250; Challenger Software

MacTilt
$100; Ergotron

MacWrite
$125; Apple Computer

Maitreya Design
Box 1480
Goleta CA 93116
    DiskInfo

Manhattan Graphics
401 Columbus Ave,
Valhalla NY 10595
800/634-3463
    Ready,Set,Go! 3.0

Manx Software Systems
One Industrial Way
Eatontown NJ 07724
800/221-0440 (NJ: 201/542-2121)
    Aztec C

MaxChill
$50; MacMemory

MDIdeas, Inc.
Suite 205; 1111 Triton Dr.
Foster City CA 94404
415/573-0580
    HD-20 ($1100)
    HD-30 ($1600)

MDIdeas HD-20 & HD-30
$1100, $1600; MDIdeas

Micah, Inc.
Suite 111; 2330 Marinship Way
Sausalito CA 94965
415/487-8300
    Micah AT SCSI drive

Michel, Steve (computer consultant)
1027 Pomona
Albany CA 94706
415/528-2418

MicroPhone
$75; Software Ventures

Microsoft Corp.
16011 NE 36th Way
Redmond WA 98052
800/882-8088 (WA & AK: 206/882-8088;
Canada: 416/673-7638)
    Chart
    Excel
    Microsoft BASIC ($150)

Microsoft Works $300)
MS-DOS
Multiplan
Word

Mindscape
3444 Dundee Rd.
Northbrook IL 60022
800/443-7982 (IL: 800/654-3767)
Balance of Power
Deja Vu
Uninvited

Monterey (font)
$70; Casady Co.

More
$300; Living Videotext

Multiplan
$200; Microsoft

Nordic (font)
(included on Fluent Fonts disks); Casady Co.

Oblique (font)
(included on Fluent Fonts disks); Casady Co.

Odesta Corp.
4084 Commercial Blvd.
Northbrook IL 60062
800/323-5423 (IL: 312/498-5615)
Double Helix
Helix
Multiuser Helix

Omnis 3
$500; Blyth Software

Optima (font)
$185; Adobe

Orcutt, Guy (photographer)
2504 NE Skidmore
Portland OR 97211
503/280-0413

Other...
$5 (send him $10); Becker, Loftus E.

OverVUE
$300; ProVUE

Packit III
$10; Chesley, Harry R.

PageMaker
$500; Aldus

Peripheral Land
3677 Enochs St.
Santa Clara CA 95051
408/733-7600
SCSI hard disks

Personics Corp
Building # 2, 2352 Main St.
Concord MA 01742
617/897-1575
VCS

Phoenix 3D
$40; Dreams of the Phoenix

PhoneNet
$50 (per node); Farallon Computing

PostScript
Adobe

Practical Computer Applications
1305 Jefferson Highway
Champlin MN 55316
612/427-4789
MacGolf

Primera Software
33 Norwood Ave.
Kensington CA 94707
Smash Hit Raquetball

ProVUE
222 22nd St.
Huntington Beach CA 92648
OverVUE

Q&D
see Quick & Dirty

QDial
free; LaPorte, Léo

Quick & Dirty Utilities, Vol. 1
$40; Dreams of the Phoenix

Radius, Inc.
Suite F, 1050 East Duane Ave.
Sunnyvale CA 94086

408/732-1010
Radius Full Page Display ($2000)

Ready, Set, Go! 3.0
$200; Manhattan Graphics

Record Holder
$50; Software Discoveries

Red Ryder
$40; FreeSoft Corp.

Reflex for the Mac
$100; Borland International

SetFile
(included in Q&D Utilities, Vol. 1);
Dreams of the Phoenix

SideKick for the Mac
$85; Borland International

Silicon Beach Software
Box 261430
San Diego CA 92126
619/695-6956
    SuperPaint

Slim (font)
(included on Fluent Fonts disks); Casady Co.

Smash Hit Raquetball
$15; Primera Software

Software Discoveries
99 Crestwood Rd.
Tolland CT 06084
    Record Holder

Software Ventures
2907 Claremont Ave.
Berkeley CA 94705
    MicroPhone

Special Effects (font variations)
$35; Century Software

Spelling Champion
$40; Champion Software

Spellswell
$40; Greene, Johnson

SuperPaint
$100; Silicon Beach Software

SuperMac Technology
950 North Rengstorff Ave.
Mountain View CA 94043
415/964-8884
    DataFrame hard disks
    memory upgrades

Swain, Tom
Suite 117, 2560 Bancroft Way
Berkeley CA 94704
    MacChimney

Switcher
$20; Apple Computer

Symbol (font)
(comes with the LaserWriter); Apple
Computer

Symmetry Corp.
761 E. University Dr.
Mesa AZ 85203
800/624-2485 (AZ: 602/884-2485)
    Acta

Target Software
14206 Southwest 136th St.
Miami FL 33186
800/622-5483 (FL: 305/252-0892)
    MacLightning

Thames (font)
$35; Century Software

Telos Software
3420 Ocean Park Blvd.
Santa Monica CA 90405
    Business FileVision
    FileVision

Tempo
$100; Affinity Micro Systems

ThinkTank
$200; Living Videotext

ThunderScan
$230; Thunderware

Thunderware
21 Orinda Way
Orinda CA 94563
415/254-6581
    ThunderScan

Times (font)
(comes with the LaserWriter); Apple
Computer

T/Maker Company
2115 Landings Dr.
Mountain View CA 94043
415/692-0195
    ClickOn Worksheet (*new owner*: Borland)
    ClickArt Special Effects
    WriteNow

TML Systems
Box 361626
Melbourne FL 32936
904/636-8592
    TML Pascal ($100)

Tomafsky, Lou (printing consultant &
broker)
DD Associates: 408/988-5150
pager: 408/995-2563; home: 408/257-6478

Top Desk
$60; Cortland Computer

TOPS
Mac node: $150, PC node: $390; Centram

Travis, Esther (Macintosh artist)
2778 Yale St.
Vancouver, British Columbia
V5K IC3 Canada
604/255-4109

VCS
$200; Personics

Vines (font)
(included on Fluent Fonts disks); Casady Co.

Word Count
free; LaPorte, Léo

Word 1.05, Word 3.0
$200, $400; Microsoft

Works
$300; Microsoft

World-Class Fonts, vols. 1 & 2
$40, $60 for both; Dubl-Click

WriteNow
$175; T/Maker Company

Your Affordable Software Company
1525 North Elston Ave.
Chicago IL 60622
312/235-9412
    12' and 25' keyboard cables

Zapf Chancery (font)
$185; Adobe

Index

Disk offer

We describe a lot of good public-domain programs and shareware in this book. They're all available on good bulletin boards and information services, or from user groups (see Appendix B for more details), but if you don't normally have dealings with any of those admirable institutions, you may prefer just to send us $15 for The Macintosh Bible Disk.

In addition to some of our favorite software, this 800K disk includes our template for viewing fonts (described on pp. 49-53), our chart for locating the standard special characters (described on pp. 64-65) and other goodies. (You'll need MacWrite—or some program that reads MacWrite files—to use the font template and MacDraw to use the special characters chart.)

The disk comes with an unconditional 30-day money-back guarantee, so you can return it if you don't think it's worth the money. Just to keep things simple, we include postage, handling and sales tax (if any) in the price.

To order, send $15, your name and address, and the word "disk" (you can be more elaborate than that if you want) to:

Goldstein & Blair
Box 7635
Berkeley, California 94707

Notes

Notes

Notes

Notes

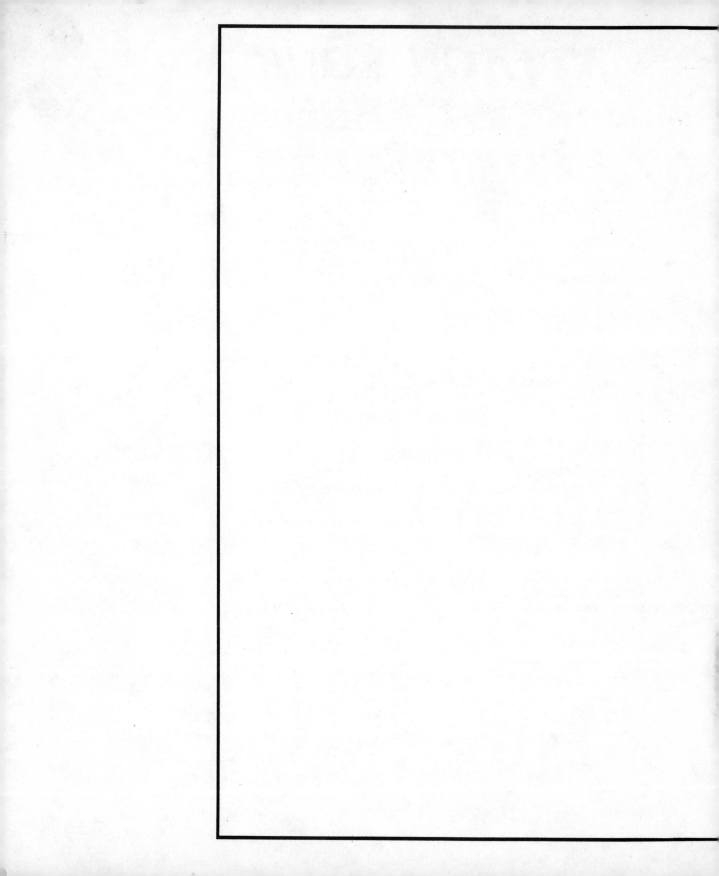